POCKET GUIDE TO

# The Care and Maintenance of Aquarium Fish

POCKET GUIDE TO

# The Care and Maintenance of Aquarium Fish

ALICE BURKHART, RICHARD CROW,
AND DAVE KEELEY

PRC

First published 2002 by
PRC Publishing Ltd,
64 Brewery Road, London N7 9NT

A member of **Chrysalis** Books plc

This edition published 2002
Distributed in the U.S. and Canada by:
Sterling Publishing Co., Inc.
387 Park Avenue South
New York, NY 10016

ISBN 1 85648 632 X

Printed and bound in China

PHOTO CREDITS

The publisher wishes to thank © Photomax for supplying the images on the following pages:
Front cover photograph and pages 2, 7, 8-9, 23, 26-27, 28, 30, 31, 32, 35, 36-37, 39, 40, 42, 53, 54, 57,
58, 60, 61, 62, 63, 64, 76, 77, 78, 82, 85, 88, 89, 90, 91, 92, 94, 95, 100, 104, 107, 109, 110, 111, 114,
115, 116, 118, 120, 123, 126, 127, 129, 130, 133, 134, 135, 136, 138, 144, 145, 146, 147, 148, 150, 152,
153, 156, 160, 161, 165, 167, 168, 169, 170, 171, 172, 173, 174, 175, 177, 178, 179, 180, 184, 185, 186,
188, 189, 190, 191, 192, 193, 195, 198, 199, 200, 201, 203, 204, 206, 207, 208, 209, 211, 212, 213, 214,
215, 217, 218, 219, 220, 221, 222, 223, 224, 225, 226, 227, 229, 230, 231, 233, 234, 235, 236, 237, 239,
240, 241, 242, 244, 245, 246, 247, 248, 249, 250, 252, 253, 254 and back cover photograph.

All other photography and artwork was supplied by Chrysalis Images.

Front cover: The mandarin goby
Back cover: A mixed aquarium of rainbowfish, congo salmon, ancistrus, and corydoras.

# CONTENTS

# INTRODUCTION

Keeping colorful fish from tropical waters in a home aquarium has become a widespread hobby around the world. Each year, thousands of beginners discover the wonders of nature through the aquarium glass. If you are thinking of joining this ever-growing band of fishkeepers, *Pocket Guide to The Care and Maintenance of Aquarium Fish* is designed to be your guide.

The book is arranged in four sections, the first two dealing with creating and maintaining an aquarium for freshwater or marine fish. In the freshwater practical section, photographs illustrate how to convert a glass tank into a miniature underwater scene, complete with lights, rocks, and plants. This is followed by more adventurous ideas for tank decoration as well as tips on buying fish, feeding, regular maintenance, basic anatomy, and health care, plus a brief look at how to encourage fish to breed.

The marine practical section parallels the advice given in the freshwater one, but highlights the differences in setting up and maintaining this type of aquarium.

The next two sections provide detailed information on 150 species of tropical fish, freshwater in section three, and marine in section four. This information includes what temperatures they like, how to feed them, mating habits, and how they interact with other species.

Throughout, the emphasis is on lucid text, helpful graphics, and summary panels, plus a store of fine color photographs, all indispensable for those new to the hobby and experienced fish-keepers alike.

*Right: Queen angel fish (Holocanthus ciliaris)*

# CREATING AND MAINTAINING A FRESHWATER AQUARIUM

"We had a fish tank but all the fish died." "Our tank kept going green." These comments are all too commonly heard among disillusioned, would-be fishkeepers, which is a shame, because fish need not die and tanks need not go green if they are set up and maintained correctly. In this opening section of the book, we look at the practical aspects of setting up a basic freshwater tropical aquarium and answer many of the questions that arise in the process. Start by planning ahead, think about the type and size of aquarium you would prefer, enquire about the availability of equipment, and investigate local aquarium dealers. Some time spent on these vital early stages will undoubtedly save you heartbreak and, indeed, money later on.

In the first section you will find practical advice on selecting a freshwater aquarium and installing the necessary filtration, lighting, and heating equipment. Once these early stages are complete, you can begin to furnish and decorate the tank, before buying and introducing the fish. Later sections deal with feeding and maintaining your stock, as well as coping with health problems and encouraging your fish to breed.

One word of caution: success is never instant, least of all in fishkeeping. Be sure to give your tank time to settle down before putting in the plants, and allow the filtration system to begin to function effectively before introducing the first few fish. Soon you will enjoy the fascination of keeping a healthy, well-maintained, tropical freshwater aquarium.

*Left: A freshwater tropical community aquarium with natural growing plants among sandstone and pebbles.*

# SETTING UP A FRESHWATER AQUARIUM

Before considering the size of aquarium and where to put it in your room, you should first step outside the home and locate your nearest aquarium dealer. Once you have found your local aquarium shop, have a general browse around inside before buying equipment or deciding on anything for certain. Is the shop going to be able to supply the goods you need? Are the staff helpful? Most important of all, are all the tanks nicely presented and kept clean and tidy? Do the fish look healthy? If you peer into a tank and there are several dead fish in it, or if several tanks have the odd dead fish, leave and take your business elsewhere. Are there plenty of customers going in and out of the store? If so, this is usually a sign of a reputable shop. In most cases, it is better to go to a specialist aquarium dealer rather than a general pet shop. Although there are many pet shops that have good stocks of tropical fish and keep them in excellent condition, they are usually dealing in a wide range of animals and may not be able to give you the specialist help you need. Once you have located a dealer near-by and you've seen all those lovely exotic fish, you'll want to get started.

*Above: If you do buy an all-glass tank, make sure that you place a layer of expanded polystyrene about 1.25cm (0.5in) thick under the base. The polystyrene will not collapse under the weight of the tank, but if there are any uneven places between the tank and the stand the polystyrene will absorb them and prevent the bottom glass from cracking, which can be expensive.*

## HOW MUCH WILL AQUARIUMS WEIGH?

60x30x30cm (24x12x12in) 55 liters (12 gallons) 55kg (121lb)

90x30x38cm (36x12x15in) 104 liters (23 gallons) 104kg (230lb)

90x38x45cm (36x15x18in) 156 liters (34 gallons) 156kg (340lb)

120x38x45cm (48x15x18in) 209 liters (46 gallons) 209kg (460lb)

## Where to put the aquarium?

The first thing to do is to decide where you want to put the tank. This decision requires some thought for several reasons. Firstly, the floor must be strong enough to stand the weight of the finished aquarium. Water weighs about a kilogram per liter (10lb per gallon), and as even a small aquarium suitable for a beginner holds about 55 liters (12 gallons), this will weigh 55kg (over 120lb) as a minimum. Fortunately, the load of this weight will be spread over quite an area, so unless the floor is rotten or of dubious quality, you should have no problem, but it is wise to inspect it first. Bear in mind that ground floors are usually stronger than upper floors, so pay particular attention if the tank is going upstairs. Wooden floors can be strengthened by nailing a layer of 12mm (0.5in) plywood over the area the tank will occupy.

Be sure to check if any sunlight falls where your tank will be situated. Excessive light will cause the growth of algae in your aquarium. Algae are primitive plant forms, and although not harmful—in fact, a useful food source for many species of fish—they can be unsightly if they get out of hand, so pick a spot where direct sunlight will not hit the tank.

Next, decide what your aquarium is going to stand on. As mentioned earlier, water is heavy and with the added weight of gravel and rocks, a decorated aquarium will need a strong stand. Aquarium stands are available in many forms. Most aquarium shops sell very basic stands made of square steel framework, which are very safe and strong but quite basic in appearance, while some dealers can supply beautiful cabinets in virtually any wood finish and to any size. The choice of aquarium stand is unlimited. Some superb looking stands can be made from stone with built-in sections for books, video recorder, stereo units, etc. An aquarium can also make an excellent room divider where a room is so large that it needs something to break it in two. If at all possible, place the tank in a warm (but not sunny) position. Nobody wants to spend more money on the invisible commodity—electricity—than is necessary. The tank should also be placed where it can be seen and "got at" without too much trouble. Try to pick a place where you can see it while you are sitting down in an easy chair in the evening. Looking at the tank will become addictive and compulsive, and the last thing you want to do is contort yourself to see it. Try to make it a feature of the room rather than an afterthought.

## HOW TO CALCULATE THE WEIGHT OF YOUR AQUARIUM

*To calculate the weight of your aquarium full of water, multiply the length, width, and height in centimeters and divide the result by 1,000 to obtain the volume in liters.*

*Since water weighs a kilogram per liter, the weight of the full aquarium in kilograms is the same as the capacity in liters. To convert liters into gallons divide by 4.55.*

### Choosing your aquarium

Modern silicone sealants can bond glass together with amazing strength. The basic aquarium is referred to as the "all-glass" aquarium and that is virtually what it is; pieces of glass bonded together with sealant to form a container. All-glass aquariums are relatively inexpensive and perfect for keeping all sorts of fish. There are many shapes that can be made in this all-glass style: long and slim, tall and wide, multisided tanks in hexagons and octagons, or any shape you like. One type that is particularly popular is the large cube, which can be viewed from any of its four sides. You may prefer to have an aquarium with a frame so that the front of the tank looks like a picture.

Framed tanks are available in many materials and colors but the frame is usually decorative rather than structural. Another design is the bowfront aquarium; this is made with a curved piece of toughened glass at the front to give a feeling of real depth. These tanks are attractive, but expensive.

The size of the aquarium is no problem at all. If you go to your local aquarium dealer they will be able to supply a tank made exactly to the size you require. Aquarium silicone sealants are so good that it is not a problem to get them to cope with the water pressure, but finding a glass thick enough can be more difficult. Plastic tanks are available and quite inexpensive but their useful life is not as long as that of a glass tank due to the fact that plastic scratches easily and starts to look shoddy rather quickly. If possible, use a glass aquarium for strength and appearance.

*Left: Aquarium gravel is the best overall choice as a substrate. Sand is not ideal as the grains will clog together and stop water flowing through the undergravel filter plate. Before putting the gravel into the tank, wash it very thoroughly (without using soap) until the water running away from it is clear.*

*Right: Cover the filter plate with a layer of aquarium gravel about 5–7.5cm (2–3in) deep. Avoid gravel used for building purposes as this may have stones which are not suitable for tank use. Pick gravel with a particle size relevant to your fish, i.e. small gravel for small fish and larger gravel for larger fish.*

## Installing filters in your aquarium

All aquariums should have some form of filtration system to keep the water clean and healthy for the fish. There are several types of filters and something to fit every need and every pocket.

Filters work in three ways: mechanical, chemical, and biological. Basically speaking, a mechanical filter removes large particles suspended in the water, a chemical filter changes the chemical balance of the water, and a biological filter harnesses the cleansing power of colonies of beneficial bacteria to purify the water that flows through it. In practical terms, a simple biological filter performs all three types of filtration at the same time.

*Above: Simply place the undergravel filter plate in the bottom of the bare tank as shown. For larger tanks you can fit more than one filter plate as necessary, but do make sure that you insert an uplift tube into each plate. The best arrangement is to position the uplift tube in one of the rear corners, where it can be concealed by rockwork or plants. You can seal the sides of the plate to the tank glass with aquarium silicone sealant to stop the water taking a short circuit around the edge of the plate.*

By far the best all-round biological filter is an undergravel filter. This usually consists of a corrugated piece of plastic with small holes or slots in it. In one corner there is a large round hole in which a plastic uplift tube fits. The whole thing is placed on the bottom of the tank and covered with a layer of gravel substrate to a depth of about 5–7.5cm (2–3in). When the tank is filled with water and an airline is placed down the uplift tube and connected to an air pump, the air bubbles rising to the surface in the tube draw water up with them and set up a flow of water down through the gravel layer over the entire base of the tank. In effect, the gravel acts like a tank-wide filter bed. Not only does this strain out suspended particles, but after a few hours, colonies of useful aerobic bacteria start to develop in the oxygen-rich conditions in

*Below: This is how water circulates through an undergravel filtration system. The 'driving force' for the movement in this basic set-up is provided by air from an electric pump. The rising air bubbles in the uplift tube cause an upward flow of water that 'pulls' water from underneath the filter plate across the whole base of the tank. As long as the pump is working the circulation continues. If you position the air pump as shown here it is advisable to fit a non-return valve in the airline to prevent water siphoning out of the tank if the air pump stops.*

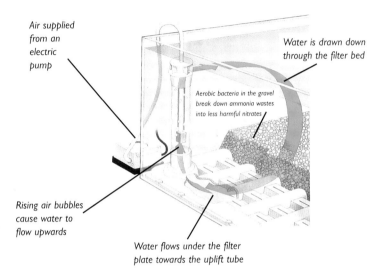

Air supplied
from an
electric
pump

Water is drawn down
through the filter bed

Aerobic bacteria in the gravel
break down ammonia wastes
into less harmful nitrates

Rising air bubbles
cause water to
flow upwards

Water flows under the filter
plate towards the uplift tube

the gravel, and over a period of weeks these will multiply and do battle with any harmful bacteria and chemical waste products. Instead of using rising air to power this type of filter system, a water pump can be fitted on the top of the uplift tube. This so-called "power head" increases the flow rate through the filter bed and up to a point improves the efficiency of its filtration action. (This arrangement is featured in an illustration on page 68 in the section on Creating and Maintaining a Marine Aquarium.)

Another type of filter is the external power filter. External power filters are usually canisters with an electrically driven water pump on top that draws water out of the tank, through the filter body, and back into the tank. If the power filter is filled with coarse gravel, it will work in exactly the same way as the undergravel filter. Various alternative biological filter media are available; these are usually little ceramic rings or complicated plastic shapes with a large surface area for bacteria to grow on. External power filters are very versatile and when filled with a suitable medium, such as sponge or aquarium floss, they can also be used as mechanical filters. In fact, a good combination is to use an external power filter to mechanically clean up the water that flows through an undergravel filter in the tank. (This type of arrangement is particularly recommended for tropical marine aquariums and is illustrated on page 69.)

Other types of mechanical filter include simple power filters that fit inside the tank and air-powered box filters filled with aquarium floss that also go inside the tank. There are also sponge filters; these have their own air uplift and draw water through a cylinder of sponge, giving good mechanical filtration with quite a bit of biological action as bacteria grow within the sponge.

The air supply for filters comes from an air pump. These are obtainable from aquarium shops in a range of types and prices. Some make more noise than others and this may be an important consideration for a tank set up in the living room. Do not be tempted to use air pumps intended for anything other than aquariums; these pumps can have oils in them and if fish come in contact with oils of any type, they will die. Your aquarium dealer will be able to supply you with clear plastic tubing—universally called airline—which attaches to the pump and runs to the aquarium. The dealer will also supply valves, T pieces, and clamps so that you can run several airlines from one pump and adjust the air flow to various pieces of equipment as required. Make sure that your pump is placed above the water level so that if for any reason the pump should stop, water will not siphon back through it and onto the floor. If you cannot place the pump above the water level then fit a non-return valve in the airline near your pump. This will allow air to pass toward the tank but stops water flowing back.

An air supply is also needed in the tank in order to help the fish breathe. This is usually accomplished by passing air from the pump through an airstone that splits the air into masses of tiny bubbles. The rising column of bubbles moves the water around and, in doing so, helps it to absorb oxygen from the surface. There are many types and sizes of airstones; some are pieces of wood, others consist of sand particles glued together.

## Heating the aquarium

The usual way of heating aquarium water is with one or more heater/thermostats. These are glass tubes with an electric element and thermostat inside them. On the top there is a small adjuster that usually turns by hand and controls the thermostat inside. When you buy a heater/thermostat they are usually set at 24°C (75°F), which is about the ideal all-round temperature. In fully submersible models the whole of the heater/thermostat goes in the tank and the wire comes out through the lid to be attached to an electricity supply. Heater/thermostats are available in various wattages, so you need to choose the right size for your aquarium. As a basic guide, allow five watts of heating for every 4.5 litres (one gallon) of water in the aquarium. Of course, during the summer months or if the tank is in a particularly warm spot you may not need as much heating capacity. You can install a higher wattage heater/thermostat to be on the safe side. These usually cost very little more to buy and indeed no more to run, as they will burn more electricity while on but will be working for a shorter period. One disadvantage of using a larger wattage heater/thermostat is that they are usually slightly larger than the next size down.

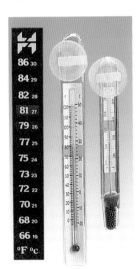

There are heater/thermostats available that have the adjuster built into the external lead, enabling you to adjust the temperature without getting your hands wet. Some models are fitted with microchips, and these types are highly accurate and hold the temperature steady within fine tolerances. There are heater elements that go underneath the gravel, but these are relatively expensive and have to be wired to a thermostat on the outside of the tank; nevertheless, they do mean that you have no problems trying to hide heater/thermostats behind rocks or plants. Under no circumstances should you ever put an ordinary glass tube heater/thermostat under the gravel as it will burn out, with disastrous effects. And no

*Left: There are several types of tank thermometers. The flat stick-on type at the extreme left is a good choice. Next to it are two spirit-filled models (the right hand one also floats).*

*Right: Attach the heater/thermostat to the inside back panel of the tank. The unit should come ready supplied with a rubber or plastic sucker for this purpose. Fix it at an angle so that the thermostat is above the heater element, which occupies the lower part of the glass tube. Make sure it is a fully submersible model before positioning it where it will be covered completely with water. This photograph also shows the air pump in place, with a length of plastic airline running into the uplift tube.*

## WHAT TOTAL HEATER RATING WILL MY AQUARIUM NEED?

*60x30x30cm (24x12x12in) 55 liters (12 gallons) 75 watts*

*90x30x38cm (36x12x15in) 104 liters (23 gallons) 100 watts*

*90x38x45cm (36x15x18in) 156 liters (34 gallons) 150 watts*

*120x38x45cm (48x15x18in) 209 liters (46 gallons) 200 watts*

*These recommendations are based on allowing five watts of heating per 4.5 liters (1 gallon) of water to maintain a temperature of 24°C (75°F) in a normally heated room. Aquarium heaters are usually rated in multiples of 50 watts. Of course, you can fit two or more heaters of lower ratings to make up the figure.*

matter what type of heater/thermostat you use, always disconnect the electricity before adjusting the temperature control.

You need to install some method of keeping a check on the temperature of the water. There are various types of aquarium thermometers. Some float in the tank, others stick on the inside or outside of the glass. The most convenient type are the stick-on strip thermometers that change color according to the temperature of the water in the tank. These stick on the outside of the glass. The best configuration is to have the under-gravel filter uplift and heater/ther-mostat in one of the rear corners and the thermometer stuck on the outside of the glass at the opposite front corner. In this way, the water flow from the filter will carry the warm water from the heater/thermostat around the tank and the thermometer will be in what is most likely to be the coolest spot.

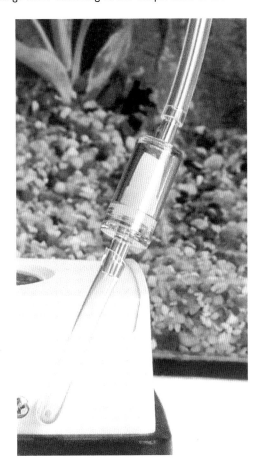

*Right: This is a close up of the airline running from the air pump into the uplift tube of the undergravel filter. There is a non-return valve fitted in the airline that will allow air to pass into the tank but will prevent water passing back into the pump should it fail. Since the end of the airline is submerged below water, there is a natural tendency for a siphonic flow to start up that would eventually drain the tank down to the level of the tube opening. Another way of guarding against this happening is to position the air pump above the level of the water in the aquarium.*

# BASIC AQUARIUM KIT

*For a basic freshwater aquarium, you will need the following items:*

- *Stand* • *All-glass aquarium* • *Layer of expanded polystyrene* • *Aquarium grade gravel* • *Undergravel filter (or other biological filter)* • *Air pump* • *Airstone* • *Airline, T- pieces, clamps* • *Heater/thermostat* • *Thermometer* • *Cable tidy* • *Cover glass* • *Light fitting* • *Rocks and plants*

## Lighting the aquarium

Assuming the aquarium is going to be covered with a hood, the most suitable method of lighting is with fluorescent tubes. Tubes suitable for aquariums are very much the same as household ones and are available in various sizes. Do not buy a fluorescent tube exactly the same length as the tank; always buy the next size down so that it will fit inside the hood. You can alter the appearance of the aquarium with various types of tubes, including ones that enhance the red colors in fish and plants, as well as "cooler" daylight balanced tubes that give a more neutral light.

You can mix tubes of different sorts to get the best of both worlds. Keep lighting well away from the water and always use waterproof endcaps on the tubes; water and electricity do not mix!

If the aquarium is not going to be covered with a hood then there are other possibilities. Spotlights mounted on the wall above the aquarium and allowed to play down on the tank at varying angles can make dramatic effects. Shadows cast by intense spotlights, such as those fitted with metal halide bulbs, make superb places for timid fish to hide in and also give the tank a dramatic appearance. The movement of the water surface also creates very effective rippling patterns on the gravel. Mercury vapor lamps are ideal for lighting an aquarium. These very powerful bulbs burn incredibly white and use very little electricity compared to their light output. They can be mounted from the

*Below: This metal hood has space for one fluorescent tube, here wisely fitted with waterproof endcaps. The silvery finish inside the hood will help to reflect light down into the aquarium. The black bulge on the left hand side is a cable tidy, a plastic block that literally tidies up the wiring to the air pump, lights, and filters.*

wall or direct from the ceiling above the tank. Avoid using ultraviolet tubes for safety reasons; looking directly at them can cause eye damage.

There are no fixed limits to lighting levels, all you need is enough light to be able to see the fish, so if the tank is in a bright spot, there is no need to have a light. However, if you plan to grow plants in your aquarium you will need at least four watts of light per 4.5 liters (1 gallon) for healthy growth. Leave the lights on for 12 hours a day to simulate tropical day length. Use a time switch to turn them on and off; remember that both fish and plants need a dark rest period.

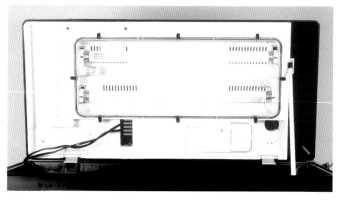

*Above: Aquariums come with integrated lighting systems such as this one with two fluorescent tubes.*

## GOOD AQUARIUM SENSE

- *A new aquarium should be tested and guaranteed, but it is wise to test it outdoors for your peace of mind. Simply fill it with water and check it carefully for leaks.*

- *If you buy a secondhand tank and discover it has a leak, do not panic. You can use aquarium silicone sealant to repair it. Find the spot that is leaking, clean and dry it thoroughly, and apply a bead of sealant. This smells of vinegar, so carry out the job in a well-ventilated room. After the repair has set for 48 hours, your leaky tank will be good as new.*

- *Do not use silicone sealants sold for bathroom and kitchen use. Although they look suitable they may contain fungicides, which are poisonous to fish.*

- *Whatever type of tank you buy, never move it with water inside it as the varying pressures created by this can make it crack or spring a leak.*

- *Before you position the tank in your room, give it a good rinse with warm salty water. Do not use domestic soaps or detergents, as they are poisonous to fish.*

# GUIDELINES FOR SAFE FISHKEEPING

- *Water and electricity are dangerous if they come into contact. Disconnect electricity before placing your hand in the tank and before adjusting or fitting electrical items.*
- *Always use the correctly rated fuse following the maker's instructions and double insulate all electrical joints using proper electrical connectors.*
- *Make sure that any electrical equipment such as heater/thermostats are submersible before placing them in the water. Check your wiring regularly.*
- *Fit a cover glass over the water surface and make sure that any lighting cannot fall into the tank.*
- *Never set your tank up on an unsteady stand. If children are about, supervise them and never leave them alone with the tank.*
- *Aquarium remedies and medicines are a necessary part of the hobby. Do not put your hands in a tank that has any of these in it. Do not drink them and keep them out of the reach of children.*
- *Always read the instructions on any remedies and medicines and carry them out meticulously.*
- *Keep all fish foods out of the reach of children.*
- *A few fish are poisonous or electrically charged and these should be clearly labeled at the aquarium shop. Never place your hand in a tank with these fish. Avoid handling fish in general and never place your hand in an aquarium with piranhas or similar fish. Large catfish, cichlids, and some other fish can bite, and may give you a nasty nip, especially if they mistake your finger for food.*

*Above: (Step One) You can add rocks and other basic decorations before adding the water. Make sure they are stable.*

## Completing the installation

The initial setting up is nearing completion now but there are a few loose ends to tie up. Firstly, there needs to be a cover glass; this glass or plastic cover goes over the top of the tank and stops any splashes coming into contact with the electricity and also stops fish jumping out—yes, they jump as well as swim! Whether you have a tank with a hood or not you still need a cover glass just to be safe. You can either buy a plastic cover glass from your dealer or get a piece of glass cut to size at a glass shop, but remember, if you do use glass, ask for each corner to be cut off to allow space for your wiring and airline to run through. Also have the edges smoothed to avoid damaging your hands on the glass as you maintain the aquarium.

The next thing to do is to wire everything into the electricity. The heater/thermostat and air pump need electricity all the time, whereas the light needs a switch in the circuit so that you can turn it off during the night. The best thing is to buy a switched connecting block called a cable tidy from your dealer. This will accommodate all the wires from your tank and allow you to use just one plug. A cable tidy has a switch for your light plus another spare switch and makes a good investment.

*Left: (Step Two) Using ordinary tap water to fill the tank is fine, but treat it with chlorine neutralizing drops from the fish shop. Add enough hot and cold water until it feels just cool but not cold. Trickle the water in slowly so that you do not disturb the gravel and any decorations. Directing the water onto a rock will reduce the impact of the flow. Continue adding water until the level is 2.5cm (1in) from the top.*

Having wired everything correctly and checked it all to make sure there are no water splashes on the electrics, plug in and switch on. With water and electricity so close together, it is vital to make sure that they do not come into contact with each other. Should this happen while you have your hands in the tank, you could suffer a nasty shock.

A wise buy is a circuit breaker. This plugs into the mains and your plugs fit into it. Should a short circuit occur, the power to the tank is cut off in a fraction of a second before any ill-effect becomes apparent. Circuit breakers are not cheap pieces of equipment, but what price life?

*Above: (Step Three) With the tank partly filled you can begin to put in the plants. Start with the back corners and progress forwards, leaving a central space for the fish to swim in. This plant has been grown in a plastic basket of rock wool to simplify planting and reduce the negative impact of the undergravel filter.*

*Right: (Step Four) Fit a transparent cover on top of the tank, whether it is a custom-sized plastic one as here or a piece of glass cut to fit. If you are going to fit a hood with lights, then a cover will stop water splashing onto the electrical connections. A cover also prevents fish jumping out. Keep the cover clean so that the maximum light reaches the aquarium.*

## DECORATING YOUR AQUARIUM

Display aquariums are made or ruined by their decoration, so having looked briefly at a simple set-up now it's time to be at your most artistic and let your talents flow! You can create a background from anything you choose or you can buy ready-made backgrounds from your dealer. These are usually long panoramic photographs of planted underwater scenes, which you can cut to length and apply to the outside back glass of your aquarium. Some dealers can supply three-dimensional backgrounds that make the tank look as if it has more depth of field. Plain-colored backgrounds are probably the most effective options. Blue and black are the most commonly used colors, but it is totally up to you—the fish will not mind what color the background is!

You can create a wide variety of background ideas. Crinkled up aluminium foil makes a good background applied to the outside, as do unvarnished cork tiles applied to the inside of the tank before adding the water. Why stick to one background? If you make a few for the outside of the back glass, you can have a swap around when the mood takes you. If you are successful with plants and the stand you have chosen has room, you can fill the background with lots of real plants and greenery. Set out carefully, they can blend in with aquatic plants inside the tank and create a superb effect.

*Below: How you decorate the aquarium is as important as deciding which fish to introduce to the tank. Make sure you use rocks that don't effect the water chemistry. Here a spotted cachorro barracuda is at home among rocks and plants that decorate the tank.*

## Rocks in the aquarium

Most aquariums have rocks in them. Do take care, however, because not all rocks are suitable. The wisest option is to buy your rocks from an aquarium shop, but this can be expensive if you need a fair amount to create the right sort of underwater scene. Finding your own rock for the aquarium is more fun, plus the fact that it's nice to get something for nothing. As a general guide, if you come across rocks that have thin lines or veins of metal in them, leave them alone. Test any other rocks that you collect with a

*Above: You can create some dramatic effects by using various rocks to form a background that is balanced by complementary plants. You can build up a miniature scene within the aquarium, but make sure that rocks and other tank decorations will not affect the water chemistry and endanger your fish. Anchor them securely so that boisterous fish cannot rearrange your carefully worked-out scheme.*

**Suitable rocks:** The best rocks for most tanks are inert ones that do not affect the water chemistry, such as granite, basalt, gneiss, slate, or quartz.

**Unsuitable rocks:** Avoid rocks with calcium and magnesium compounds that turn water hard and alkaline, such as limestone, marble, dolomite, calcareous sandstones, or any soft, chalky rocks.

few drops of vinegar. If the vinegar fizzes vigorously then these rocks contain calcium compounds that will make the water harder and more alkaline and are suitable only for certain fish. Do not worry too much if a few lines of little bubbles come up, as most rocks have some small calcium deposits. Soak rocks that have passed the acid test for a week in a bucket of water to remove the acid and leach out any other impurities. In fact, it is a good idea to thoroughly rinse rocks that you buy from your aquarium dealer.

Before placing rocks in the aquarium, slope the gravel from front to the back so that it is twice as deep at the back than at the front. This not only allows any debris to accumulate at the front, where it is easy to remove, but also provides a firmer foundation for embedding rocks and other tank decorations. When installing rocks, make sure that they cannot fall or subside. Place the largest, most stable rocks near the back corners to act as a base and then build on or around these. Try to create an overall view like a small stage in a theater, with an appropriate background, some props around the edges to give a three-dimensional feel, and an open area in the middle for your "cast" to act upon. Where possible, you can build the gravel up behind rocks and so vary the levels within the tank.

Remember that the rocks do not have to be laid horizontally. Arranging several narrow pieces of slate vertically or even towering out of the tank can make great effects. Using one type of rock has a superb effect or you can keep to one type in each part of the aquarium. Do not be afraid to use large pieces of rock; two large pieces always have a greater visual impact than four small pieces. If only small pieces are available, glue them together with aquarium sealant to make larger structures and even build up little walls by sticking tiny chips together.

## The artistic possibilities of bogwood

Petrified wood, or bogwood, as it is called, makes a superb tank decoration. It usually comes from peat bogs and consists of tree roots that have been compressed over long periods of time. Bogwood is available in various twisted shapes and sizes. To prepare it for the aquarium, soak it for a week in a bucket of water. Over this time, a dark residue will leach out and the water will begin to look like tea. After the week is up, remove the wood and let it dry. Once dried out completely, give it several coats of polyurethane varnish to stop further weeping of dyes. Wait another few days to make sure that the varnish is fully dry and then install it in the aquarium. As this wood is petrified, it usually sinks, but on occasions it may float. If this is the case, drill a couple of holes in a small piece of slate and screw it to the bottom of the bogwood to weigh it down. Use brass screws to avoid corrosion.

*Above: Used in an aquarium bogwood creates a natural looking background and provides an excellent focal point in the aquarium. You can also use vine roots, which are thinner and more textured than bog-wood, to create interesting shapes and welcome crannies for the fish to swim in and out of. There are also artificial versions that you can use.*

*Below: Petrified wood pieces such as these make stable decorative items for the aquarium.*

## OTHER DECORATIVE MATERIALS

**Cork:** The only problem with cork is that it floats, so you need to devise some way of sinking it. The best method is to screw it to a piece of slate, as described for bogwood, or glue it to the glass with sealant before you begin to fill the tank.

**Bamboo:** Canes placed vertically in the aquarium make a very decorative display. To anchor the canes fit them into holes drilled into a piece of slate placed on the bottom of the tank. Do not worry if the canes do not fit tightly at first, as they will swell when they have been in the tank for an hour.

**Coal:** It is totally safe and makes an inexpensive alternative to rockwork.

## Flowerpots

Clay flowerpots—left whole or split in half—form excellent caves for fish. Other builders' materials made from a similar red terracotta clay can be used to form caves or tunnels. You can cover a clay pot with a thin layer of sealant and roll it in loose gravel to give it a coating that blends in with the aquarium substrate.

## Decorating with aquatic plants

Once you have installed the solid decorations, leave the aquarium undisturbed for a few days with the undergravel filtration system running. This period will allow the useful

*Above: Java ferns can be planted directly into fissures in the sandstone where they will root and grow.*

aerobic bacteria to develop in the gravel and the water to become clear. Keep an eye on the temperature and see that it does not fluctuate by more than a degree or two. Check that the light and pump are working well and that bubbles are flowing out of the uplift tube and from the airstone. After this period, you can start to introduce aquatic plants.

Plants can form a very attractive part of an aquarium but they are not essential for the health of fish. The main reasons for having plants in the aquarium are that they will give the fish somewhere to hide and also supply the tank with oxygen. They will also compete for dissolved nutrients and hopefully get more than their fair share, thus leaving no food for unwelcome excess algae to live on. Reasons for not having plants in the tank are when the particular fish you aim to keep are plant-eaters or gravel-diggers, or when your lighting levels are insufficient to support plant life.

Plants within the aquarium work in much the same way as those in pots around the house. Part of their daily process is to take in carbon dioxide and give off oxygen in return. As oxygen is used by the fish when they breathe and carbon dioxide is given off in return, it is easy to see that a sort of exchange process can be set up. There will never be an aquarium where the plants and fish give off enough gases for each other, but it is nice to think they are living in a harmonious relationship. The fish will also feed partly on the plant life, and their droppings will become a fertilizer for the plants, the plants returning the favor by breaking it down. Again, neither of these actions will be sufficient for the others' requirements but they are better than not being done at all. If plants are not present, the fish will not suffer; they will find other cover among the rocks and they will get oxygen from the work of the airstone and surface movement. So it's your choice, plants or no plants? If you choose to have plants in the aquarium, there are other things to bear in mind. Firstly, plants will need fertilizers to keep them growing well, just as garden plants do. They will also need strong lighting if they are to flourish. You will need to remove any dying leaves in order to keep the tank looking at its best and prune any plants that outgrow their welcome.

## Choosing and using real plants

The choice of real plants is enormous. Not only green, but also colored plants and flowering ones are available. Some only grow 2.5cm (one inch) high, others to 60cm (24in). Some float on the surface, some nestle into little crevices. When you buy aquarium plants at your dealers, take a good look at them to see if they look healthy, and avoid plants that have brown or yellowed leaves. The plants should be supplied to you in a plastic bag or polystyrene freezer-type pack. Try to keep them warm on their journey home, and when you remove the plants from their package try to avoid touching them as much as possible. If you do have to handle the plants, be as gentle as you can. Rinse them under cool tap water to remove snails and snail egg "jelly." Remove any dead or damaged leaves with a pair of scissors and then, holding the plant just above the roots, insert it into the gravel so that it just covers the lighter base of the plant, or crown. Do not push the plant in too far.

It is a good idea to add an aquarium fertilizer to the tank at this stage. Add this weekly or as the instructions recommend. You can also place fertilizer pellets in the gravel around the plants and these are excellent aids to their growth. Some plants are supplied in little perforated flowerpots. If this is the case, plant the whole pot under the gravel and cover the top of the pot with just a little gravel.

## Why plants may not succeed

If you have trouble getting your plants to grow, there may be several reasons for this. Firstly, undergravel filters tend to play havoc with certain plants, causing them to die or grow in a strange manner. If you have used the undergravel method of filtration and experience problems with plants dying within days of buying them, it is likely to be the filter. You then have three choices: go for different plants, use a power filter with gravel in it for your biological filter, or revert to plastic plants. Another reason for plants dying is insufficient light. If you find your plants are dying gradually over the course of a few weeks, then this is probably the cause. Insufficient light is often associated with the growth of brown algae, which confirms that light is the problem. You can try fitting another fluorescent tube in the hood or use a bulb especially designed to boost plant growth.

Water conditions can be a further reason for plant failure. Some plants prefer soft water, whereas others like hard water. Most plants prefer alkaline rather than acid conditions, and if the temperature rises above 27°C (80°F), certain plants will start to die. Snails can also be harmful to plants. They will feed on decaying plants, but also on healthy plant material, just as snails do in the garden. And, of course, the fish themselves may attack your plants.

*Below: Anubias nana plants are planted into pockets of a decorative piece of bogwood to provide an interesting background for the fish to dart in and out of.*

## The benefits of plastic plants

If you are undecided, there is a genuine third choice between plants and no plants, and this choice is plastic plants. In the aquarium, they are often indistinguishable from the real thing and some even move in a realistic fashion. Plastic plants have the advantage that they do not die, do not overgrow the tank and last forever, literally. It really is worth considering plastic plants, especially if the only reason you cannot have plants is because your fish are planteaters.

*Below: When you are happy with a background scene created from pieces of wood, make sure they are securely fixed before introducing plants and filling the tank with water.*

# SOME AQUATIC PLANTS

**Fairy moss** *(Azolla caroliniana)*
A hardy floating plant with small rough leaves. There are several types. Many vary in color; some change from green to red or purple.

**Duckweed** *(Lemna gibba)*
Very small floating leaf with a couple of roots. Provides shade and shelter for surface-dwelling fish. May block light to other plants.

**Water lettuce** *(Pistia stratiotes)*
Like a floating lettuce up to 15cm (6in) across. Roots hang down for fish to hide in.

**Hair grass** *(Eleocharis acicularis)*
A hairlike grass that grows to about 13cm (5in) high. Looks best planted around rocks or pieces of bogwood.

**Hornwort** *(Ceratophyllum demersum)*
Similar to cabomba, but with little rubbery leaves. Grows quickly and not bothered by undergravel filtration. Best planted in bunches at back of tank. Cuttings root easily.

**Elodea**
There are several types of this "oxygenating weed." It will grow rapidly in tropical aquariums as well as in coldwater tanks. Can float but best planted in gravel.

## BUYING AND INTRODUCING YOUR FISH

By now your aquarium is set up and running, with its rockwork and decor all laid out and any plants you have introduced establishing themselves. Once the undergravel filter has been running for a couple of weeks, it is time to consider adding the fish. The choice is completely up to you but there are a few broad points to bear in mind before you go to your local aquarium dealer. You may wish to set up a community aquarium. Other than the fact that the tank holds more than one fish, a community can be anything: a community of all one type of fish, a community of fish that all have the same color, or a community of totally different fish. A theme often runs through a community. Fish from the same part of the world or fish that would naturally live together are communities, as are tanks full of fish with no relationship or connection to each other in any way.

It is a good idea to pick a mixture of fish that will share different areas of the tank. Some species are surface-dwellers, others are midwater swimmers, while others stay near the bottom. A mix of fish from each of these groups gives a nice balance to a tank. Fish that normally shoal in the wild are best kept in small shoals and are happier like that, whereas fish that are antisocial are best kept on their own. Obviously, fish that have a taste for vegetable matter are best kept in tanks with plastic plants or no plants at all, whereas carnivorous fish are best kept away from other fish altogether or at least not with smaller, more vulnerable species.

### Setting up a quarantine tank

If possible, set up another tank equipped simply with a heater/thermostat, a box or sponge filter, thermometer, and an airstone and use this as a quarantine aquarium. Place any new purchases into this tank first. Here, you can monitor new fish for a week to ten days before adding them to your already established tank, thus reducing the chances of introducing any diseases.

*Below: It is a good idea to introduce new fish, such as this silver lyretail molly, into a quarantine tank for a week or so. Monitor it for any sign of disease before adding it to your established tank.*

## Buying your fish

When you buy your first fish they will probably be from your local dealer. Always check beforehand that the fish in the shop are healthy. So what does a healthy fish look like? A healthy fish has good fins held erect and with no splits or white edges to them. The skin should be free of any pimples or white spots and there should be no sores or damaged areas. Avoid fish that hold their fins clamped to the body and closed up. Unless they are bottom-dwellers, fish should be swimming actively in midwater, but not with their heads up or down. Healthy fish do not swim with their mouths near the surface the whole time and they most definitely should not be gasping for air. There should be no other dead or sick-looking fish with the ones you intend to buy and there should be no pieces of food or waste lying around in the tank.

Somebody in the shop will catch the fish for you and place them in a plastic bag with a little water in it. There only needs to be enough water to cover the fish completely and there should be a good pocket of air trapped in the top of the bag to keep the water oxygenated. The dealer should wrap this bag in paper to help keep it warm and dark on the journey home. If the fish you have bought are particularly small, then ask him to tie up the corners of the bag with rubber bands so that the fish cannot get trapped in them. You should take your fish home as soon as possible. If you have an

*Above: Setting up a mixed community of fish provides color and variety in the aquarium. This tank has rainbowfish, congo salmon, ancistrus, and corydoras. It is vital to mix compatible species and to create a balanced effect by choosing fish that will occupy all levels within the tank. Many of the catfish, for example, can create interest at the lower levels to counterbalance the more usual midwater subjects.*

insulated bag or a polystyrene box, place them in this for the journey to keep them warm. If you have other shops to visit while you are out, make your call to the aquarium shop the last stop before you start back home.

## Acclimatizing your fish

Once home, you need to acclimatize the fish. The water in your tank is likely to be at a slightly different temperature to that in the bag, so to equalize them, float the bag in the aquarium, unopened, for 10–15 minutes. After this period, open the bag carefully, and with a small cup pour some water from the tank into the bag. Wait another five minutes and then gently release the fish into the tank. If you feed the original fish in the tank at the same time, this will attract their attention and avoid them bothering your newcomers. All this helps to prevent sudden changes and reduce stress on the new fish.

## How many fish can my tank hold?

As many as you can squash into it, but they will not live! The question should be: "How many fish will live healthily in my tank?" This will not depend so much on the size of the tank but on the surface area. Fish breathe oxygen and this is absorbed mainly through the water surface. The greater the water surface, the more oxygen the tank can absorb.

To work out how many fish your tank can hold, multiply the length of the two top edges together and this will give you the surface area. You should aim to have no more than 2.5cm (1in) of fish length for every 64cm$^2$ (10in$^2$) of surface area. For example, a 91cm (36in) x 38cm (15in) tank has a surface area of 3,458cm$^2$ (540in$^2$). Dividing 3,458 by 64 and then multiplying by 2.5 produces a total recommended fish length of 135cm. This is equivalent to dividing 540 by 10 to produce a result of 54in. (Using 91cm as a more accurate conversion for 36in helps the figures to work out neatly here.)

This is only a very rough guide. Tanks with lots of plants and very strong water movement would hold more fish than a tank with no plants and little aeration. Try to keep as near to this guideline as possible to avoid problems with overcrowding. It is always best to understock your tank rather than use up its full capacity.

### New tank syndrome

The following sequence is common among beginners. Once set up, the tank is left running for a week or so. Then the aquarium is stocked with fish, possibly to its maximum capacity. Soon, fish start dying and the owner is at a loss to explain the cause. Eventually all, or nearly all, the fish die. In desperation, the aquarist strips the tank down, cleans the gravel and starts again, believing that it was some sort of disease that wiped out the fish. The same process is repeated and the fish die again.

There is no disease involved here. The problem is that the filtration system is not being given long enough to establish itself and break down waste. The fish then die from a build-up of nitrite. Washing all the gravel out simply destroys any useful aerobic bacteria that have developed in the biological filter. And the situation is usually exacerbated by the beginner's tendency to overfeed. The best course of action would be to carry out a partial water change and then leave the tank for a further two weeks before beginning to introduce new fish gradually.

To avoid new tank syndrome from the outset, allow the tank to mature for at least two weeks, stock it with fish gradually, do not overstock, and do not overfeed. Above all, be patient when setting up your first tank.

*Left: The red devil (Herichthys labiatus) is a really aggressive fish, particularly toward females, and so is not a candidate for a mixed community aquarium. The body is very thick and stocky and on top of the solid bead, especially in males, you often see a nuchal hump—a large deposit of fat that develops in many cichlids with age. The best option is to keep the red devil alone in a "pet" tank. A single specimen can be kept in a 90cm (36in) tank, but if it is to reach its potential size of 38cm (15in), it will need a tank of 150cm (60in) or more. If red devils are kept together, a tank measuring 180cm (72in) is the only viable option.*

Aquarium fish will eat all types of foods; the only conditions are that the fish actually enjoys the food and that the pieces are small enough to be eaten. As with all animals, fish need to receive nutrients and vitamins essential for healthy growth. Fish also need to have a varied diet in order not to become bored with the same old foods and to avoid becoming addicted to one food, which is undesirable. It is important to offer foods of appropriate size. It is no good feeding tiny flakes of food to a great big fish, just as feeding large lumps of food to a tiny fish is useless.

### The feeding routine

Generally you should feed your fish once a day, a small amount at a time until they have all had a bite—unless they are large carnivores, in which case they will need special requirements and these are dealt with individually later on in the book. If you are feeding flake food, then give them only a very small pinch and check that this is all eaten within three to five minutes. Healthy fish are hungry fish. If your fish are always at the surface looking for food, or if they rush to the surface when you approach the tank, then that is a good sign. If you are giving your fish the messier foods, such as blended

meats or raw fish, then this should all be consumed within a minute or it will pollute the tank. A quite common practice is to "fast" the fish for one day a week. This ensures a better appetite and the fish will not be harmed; in their natural state they can go weeks without food.

*Left: The zebra danio (*Brachydanio rerio*) accepts a variety of foods, including freeze-dried and frozen ones, but can only take tiny pieces. Freeze-dried or live mosquito larvae are often available in summer and make a natural diet for this hardy fish.*

## Flakes and pellets

Flake foods are a convenient way of feeding aquarium fish. There are flakes of different colors that contain various ingredients such as fish, roe, wheat, meat, vegetables, trace elements, and vitamins. Feed only a small amount to your fish at any one time. Flake foods are fine for fish up to 10–13cm (4-5in) in length, but you will need something else to supplement them when they grow larger. Pellets have roughly the same ingredients as flake foods but are more substantial. They are available in various sizes and shapes, whether floating or sinking; some promote color, others promote growth.

## Live foods for free

There are plenty of free live foods in the garden. Your fish will eat virtually anything that moves, provided it is of a suitable size. Woodlice are taken greedily by large fish and there can be no better food for tropical fish than garden earthworms.

## Water fleas

Aquarium dealers will supply water fleas (*Daphnia*) and bloodworms (*Chironomus*—pink water) in plastic bags. Strain the water through a piece of muslin or cloth before feeding them to your fish. The bags should last about a week in a cool place.

## Live foods

There are many live foods available and your dealer should stock at least one or two that you will find suitable. Among these are water fleas (*Daphnia*) and small crustaceans. You can also buy brine shrimps (*Artemia salina*), small shrimps that live naturally in saline lakes; simply rinse these and feed them to your fish.

You can raise brine shrimp yourself from eggs, either in a purpose designed "hatchery" or simply by placing some of the eggs in a warm, aerated saline solution for a day or two and then harvesting the tiny shrimps as they hatch out. Also look out for river shrimps; these are too big for small fish, but large carnivorous fish relish them. Aquarium fish also enjoy bloodworms—red aquatic larvae from river mud. These are excellent for bringing fish into breeding condition.

## Freeze-dried and frozen foods

Freeze-dried versions of the above live foods make safe and nutritious supplements to flake foods. Other freeze-dried foods include Mysis shrimp, Pacific shrimp, Tubifex worms, krill, and plankton. These foods are also available in frozen form. Store these foods in the freezer and thaw out as much as you need each day.

## Meaty foods

Beef heart is good for carnivorous fish. To prepare this, trim off the fat, blend the meat to a puree and then freeze it in thin slabs that you can easily break up into pieces as you need them. You can also do this with chicken, turkey, fish, or any other non-fatty meat.

## Vegetable foods

Many fish enjoy some vegetable matter in their diet, including blanched lettuce; garden peas with the skins popped off, and even baked beans. There is no harm in trying various vegetables—but be sure to remove them from the tank swiftly if the fish ignore them.

---

### *HOMEMADE GENERAL PURPOSE DIET*

*Blend the following ingredients together to form a balanced diet that you can feed three times a day, every day if you wish. You can vary the ingredients slightly to suit your fish's taste.*

*100gm (4oz) ox heart, 100gm (4oz) white fish, 50gm (2oz) processed peas, 50gm (2oz) baked beans, 50gm (2oz) spinach, 2 tablespoonfuls of flake food.*

*Chop the ox heart and the fish into small chunks and carefully blend to a puree in a liquidizer or blender. Now comes the messy bit! Scrape the outer skins off the peas and beans and add the insides to the ox heart and fish mixture. Add the spinach and flake and mix all the ingredients together in a bowl. Spoon the mixture into small plastic bags and roll each bag out until it is about 3mm (an eighth of an inch) thick. Place the bags in the freezer overnight. Next day, all the bags will have frozen and will be ready for use. Simply snap off a small piece of the frozen slab and drop it into the aquarium where you normally feed the fish. The food will quickly thaw out in the warm water of the tank, although many fish will try, and may succeed, to eat it frozen. Aquarium fish usually love this type of food.*

---

Aquarium fish need to be looked after, but the amount of care they need is very small indeed. The best idea is to set aside a certain time each week for "doing the tank." One of the most important regular tasks is to check and maintain the water quality in the aquarium. Fish waste products produce ammonia, which eventually breaks down to become nitrite—a very poisonous substance indeed that is dangerous to fish in any quantity. If your filtration system is working properly, hardly any nitrite will form in the aquarium, but in order to make sure it doesn't, and to remove other harmful chemicals that are not eliminated by the action of bacteria in the so-called "nitrogen cycle," it is vital to make regular water changes. A water change should be between 10 and 15 percent of the tank volume. To judge how much water this involves measure the height of your tank, divide it by ten, and make a small mark this far from the top with a marker pen. Then you will know just how much water to remove each time.

The easiest way to remove the water is to siphon it out. To do this, fill a length of tubing with water—the wider the diameter, the faster the flow—cover both ends with your thumbs and carry it to the tank. Place one end below the water surface and remove your thumb. Place the other end in a bucket and remove your other thumb. A siphonic flow will now begin and continue until you remove the tube from the tank. If you hold the end of the tube just above the gravel then the water flow will also carry away debris. You can buy a gravel washer that digs into the gravel and draws any waste out by siphonic action.

Now replenish the tank with new water, which should be as near to the temperature of the aquarium water as you can possibly manage. The best way to do this is to run tap water at the right temperature into a clean bucket, and add drops that remove chlorine and break down chloramines. Allow the water to set for a few minutes while you tidy up the tank. Chlorine and chloramines are added to tap water by the water company as disinfectants and are harmful to fish. Therefore, any water going into the aquarium should be treated with a dechlorinator containing sodium thiosulfate and sodium carbonate. Add the water gently, trying not to disturb the bottom of the tank and thereby upsetting the fish. Properly carried out, fish actually enjoy water changes, they sparkle more, their growth rate is enhanced, they become more active and it really "replenishes their batteries."

Certain fish are fussy about whether the water is hard or soft, and some are more sensitive to the acid/alkaline balance of the water. Fortunately, most popular aquarium fish are undemanding and adapt to whatever conditions they encounter. As a beginner, it is far better and safer to leave well alone, but as you advance you may want to tinker with the water quality to get it nearer to the ideal.

## Acidity and alkalinity

Tests kits are available for measuring the acid/alkaline balance of the water in your aquarium and most work on a color dye principle. The scale used is pH, which runs from pH 0 (very acid) to pH 14 (very alkaline), with pH7 as neutral. Either side of the neutral point the scale is logarithmic. This means that pH6 is ten times more acidic than pH7 and pH5 a hundred times more acidic than pH7.

The pH values of natural fresh water sources vary from about pH6 for the soft acidic

water of an Amazonian river to about pH8.5 for the hard alkaline water of Lake Tanganyika in Africa. Some of the less tolerant fish from these environments only flourish if the pH value of their tank water reflects the conditions in their natural habitat.

The safest way to make your water more acid or alkaline is to use water changes, removing part of the tank water, and adding water of the correct pH to the aquarium. It is best to adjust the pH of water in a bucket, let the water age for a couple of hours, then test pH prior to adding it to your aquarium. When the bucket pH stays at the desired level, do a partial

*Left: Scouring pads on long handles make cleaning the inside glass of the aquarium relatively easy, at least in fairly small tanks.*

*Nitrite test kits work on a dye method. Of all the test kits to buy, this is the most useful and cost effective one. Nitrite is tested in parts per million (ppm), which is equivalent to milligrams per liter (mg/l). Either way, your kit will clearly indicate if your water has a dangerous level of nitrite. If it has, you must make an immediate water change. Check that your biological filtration system is working well and if this is fine then you are either overfeeding or your tank is overstocked. Another possibility is that there is a dead fish somewhere in the tank.*

*Do not confuse nitrite with nitrate. Nitrate is the step after ammonia and nitrite in the "nitrogen cycle" and, although harmful in quantity, it is not nearly as poisonous as nitrite.*

water change and add it to the aquarium. Filtering through peat or using pH adjusters can change pH very rapidly. Sudden pH changes in the aquarium can cause pH shock, and kill your fish.

## Cleaning up and regular checks

Other jobs to do at this point are to trim and replant any plants that have not stayed rooted. Use a sharp pair of scissors for trimming leaves and the blunt end of any long implement, such as a knitting needle, to push plants back into the gravel. Also remove any algae that has grown on the glass using an algae scraper. If you buy one of the magnetic types, make sure you do not trap any particles of gravel between the plates or they will scratch the glass.

You should also check your electrical wiring and see that there are no faults. Check the water temperature every day and watch your fish carefully for five minutes for signs of disease or odd behavior. Feeding time is an excellent time to observe them.

## Essential accessories for maintaining your aquarium

### Algae scraper
Use these to scrape algae from the glass. Some are like little scouring pads, which can be fitted onto long handles. Another type is like a plastic trowel on a stick. You can fit a razor blade to this type but avoid damaging the silicone sealant, as this could cause a

nasty leak! The most ingenious type consists of two magnets that cling together through the glass so that as you pull the outer one the inner one cleans away the algae. Newer models of magnet cleaners can float to the top if they come loose from the outer magnet.

### Tubing
You will need some wide-bore plastic tubing (say 1.25cm/0.5in) to siphon water out of the tank

### Gravel cleaner
This device fits onto the end of your siphon tubing and digs into the gravel while you siphon water out. As the dirt comes out of the gravel, the gravel drops back so that only dirt and not gravel is removed in the flow of water. Some gravel cleaners have a pump action to start the siphon flow. (One of these is shown on page 80 in the marine section, but is equally suitable for use in freshwater tanks.)

### Net for removing fish
It would be wise to buy at least one, if not two nets from the outset. Try to pick a soft net and one that is a little larger than half the tank's width.

*Left: In this air-driven "vacuum cleaner," the rising stream of air bubbles causes water to flow up the tube and through the net bag, where debris is strained off.*

# WHAT MAKES AQUARIUM WATER HARD OR SOFT?

Tap water contains salts of minerals, especially calcium and magnesium, which make the water "hard." There are two types of water hardness: general, or permanent; and carbonate, or temporary, hardness. A popular scale used for hardness is °dH; 3°dH is considered soft and over 25°dH is hard. To measure hardness use the relevant test kit, which usually involves adding drops of a colored liquid to a sample of water until there is a color change.

The only way to remove general hardness is to pass water through a suitable softener. Carbonate hardness can be lowered partially by boiling and also by passing it through a filter with peat in it. Other ways of softening water include adding distilled water or clean rainwater.

To harden water, add sodium bicarbonate or magnesium sulphate in small amounts so that changes occur very gradually! Remember that sudden changes can kill fish. Sodium bicarbonate will also raise pH.

*Above: Magnetic glass cleaners are useful for deeper tanks, where access to the lower areas is generally difficult. Moving the outer magnetic block drags the inside one across the glass and the plastic brushlike surface scrapes off any algae.*

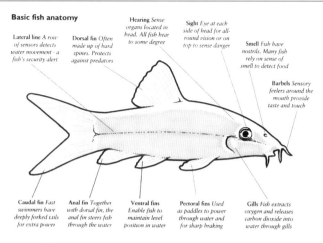

**Basic fish anatomy**

**Lateral line** *A row of sensors detects water movement - a fish's security alert*

**Dorsal fin** *Often made up of hard spines. Protects against predators*

**Hearing** *Sense organs located in head. All fish hear to some degree*

**Sight** *Eye at each side of head for all-round vision or on top to sense danger*

**Smell** *Fish have nostrils. Many fish rely on sense of smell to detect food*

**Barbels** *Sensory feelers around the mouth provide taste and touch*

**Caudal fin** *Fast swimmers have deeply forked tails for extra power*

**Anal fin** *Together with dorsal fin, the anal fin steers fish through the water*

**Ventral fins** *Enable fish to maintain level position in water*

**Pectoral fins** *Used as paddles to power through water and for sharp braking*

**Gills** *Fish extracts oxygen and releases carbon dioxide into water through gills*

*Above: Of course, not all fish conform to this "standard" shape, but if you look carefully you should be able to find most of these features, whatever shape the fish. Some fish have a small additional fin between the dorsal and caudal fin, called the adipose fin and only certain fish have barbels around the mouth. The lateral line along the flanks can be seen more clearly in some fish than in others.*

## FISH PARASITES

**Fish parasites:** These are generally regarded as life forms living on the body of a fish. Parasites are rare in tank fish and usually only occur on imported wild-caught species.

**Gill flukes:** Gill flukes are like tiny worms that anchor themselves to the fish's gills, causing respiratory problems and, eventually, death. Suspect gill flukes if a fish begins to swim at the water surface gasping for air. Treat with a mild parasiticide, but first make sure that the water is being oxygenated properly and that the biological filter is working correctly.

**Skin flukes:** Instead of anchoring themselves to the gills, these flukes attach to the skin. They can be removed with tweezers or a parasiticide.

**Fish lice:** Fish lice such as argulus resemble miniature tortoises on the fish's body. Remove them carefully with tweezers. It is worth getting to know the basic anatomy of a fish in case you need to describe an injury or disease symptom to a veterinarian or dealer; if you know the names of the external parts of the body it will help you to pinpoint the problem more accurately. Another reason is that books often describe the shapes of fish and if you know which particular fins or parts of the body they are referring to, you will have a basic idea of what the fish looks like even without seeing an illustration or photograph.

## Diseases and stress

The majority of fish diseases are caused through stress. So how are fish put under stress? Sad to say, most fish are put under stress by their owners or visitors to the house. People tapping on the front glass, temperatures being allowed to rise and fall, or a poor mixture of fish in which one or two are bullies and the others are bullied all contribute to stress. If fish are not put under these types of stress, then the chances of

*Above: White spot (Ichthyophthirius) appears as tiny white spots, each one a cyst that eventually bursts to send its single-celled, or protozoan parasites into the tank, where they will affect the other fish with potentially fatal results. White spot can be seen on this harlequin fish but the fish will respond to treatment if any stress-causing factors are illiminated.*

them contracting disease are dramatically reduced. Look for signs of stress in the tank on a regular basis. Are the fish nervous? Is one fish chasing all the others about? Does the temperature fluctuate or does it stay too low? If you can remedy these situations diseases will occur much less frequently.

*Above: This female long-finned zebra danio shows severe congenital deformity.*

# COMMON DISEASES

**White spot (Ichthyophthirius):** *White spots that increase in number. Responds to treatment. Eliminate stress-causing factors.*

**Velvet (Oodinium):** *Rusty coloring to skin and clamping up of fins. Effective proprietary remedies are widely available.*

**Bloat Affected:** *fish swells up and does not eat. Investigate water conditions and diet. Treat with antibacterial and remove sick fish from tank.*

**Popeye:** *A condition in which one or both eyes protrude from head. Can be due to injury or bacterial infection. Seek immediate veterinary help.*

**Hole-in-the-head:** *Small holes appear on head and body. This condition often affects cichlids. Cures are slow and expensive. Improve tank conditions with water changes, add vegetable matter to their diet.*

**Fungus:** *Cotton-wool-like growths on the skin and fins. Treat with fungicide. Check water conditions and temperature.*

**Mouth fungus:** *Tuftlike growths around the mouth plus skin ulcers and fin damage. Often seen in cyprinids. Despite name it is caused by bacteria and responds to bactericide. Check stress factors.*

**Fin rot:** *Fins are damaged by bacteria. Use an antibacterial or add salt to the water.*

# WHAT DO I DO IMMEDIATELY IF THESE SYMPTOMS APPEAR?

### Several fish gasping at the surface and breathing fast

- Check to see that the airstone is functioning and that there is good water movement in the tank.

- Check that the undergravel filter is functioning properly.

- See that heater has not stuck on.

- Perform a 30% water change.

- If after a water change these symptoms persist, the fish may be suffering from gill flukes. Isolate the fish if possible and treat them with a suitable remedy.

### Fish holding its fins clamped to the body (i.e. "closed up")

- Check the heater function and that the temperature is correct.

- See that nothing has been added to the aquarium that might be poisonous to the fish, including aerosols possibly sprayed near the tank during routine cleaning of the room.

- If you have checked and cleared the above, make a 30% water change and use a mild bactericide.

### Fish dying and swimming in a "whirling" pattern

- These are classic signs of poisoning. Perform a 50% water change and locate the source of the problem. This may be a poisonous rock or object in the tank, which you must remove. Isolate any affected fish in a separate tank while you clean the original one.

### Fish rubbing themselves against rocks and "flicking"

- Several possible causes, such as white spot, external parasites, or an irritant in the water.

- Inspect the fish closely. If white spots or parasites are present on the skin, treat them appropriately with a suitable remedy.

- If all looks well on the fish' skin, carry out a 30% water change. If the symptoms noticeably decrease after this, suspect the presence of some irritant in the aquarium.

- If symptoms increase after the water change, suspect something wrong with your tap water or conditioner. Is there too much chlorine in the water or are you overdosing with dechlorinator?

## Symptoms of disease

Fish will always show symptoms of disease at an early stage. Signs to look for include fish holding their fins tightly clamped to the body (often referred to as being "closed up"), fish swimming with the head near to the surface all the time, fish swimming with the head up or down, loss of color, ragged fins, scales sticking out or dropping off, and a general loss of appetite and condition.

*Above: Although more commonly encountered on coldwater fish, this fish louse (Argulus) has attached itself to a swordtail, a tropical species. The louse grows to 10mm (0.4in) across and clings on with twin suckers.*

*Below: This speckled molly fish has popeye—a condition in which one or both eyes protrude from head. It can be caused by injury or bacterial infection and immediate veterinary help is required.*

## The hospital tank

If you have a spare tank or one used for quarantining new fish, it will also be useful for isolating sick or injured fish. Set it up with just a heater/thermostat and a thermometer, plus an airstone. It will not need a filter, as sick and injured fish will not be fed for the short time they are in the tank. Transfer any fish found to be injured, sick, or carrying a parasitic infestation to this tank and treat them in isolation from the community tank. Some form of opaque cover is a good idea so that you can reduce the light. This is often helpful during treatment.

## BREEDING YOUR FISH

Breeding fish is highly satisfying, and it is rewarding to raise fish for virtually nothing except a little time and effort. Many freshwater tropical fish will breed in the aquarium, and those most frequently spawned include livebearers, cichlids, catfish, barbs among cyprinids, tetras among characins, and anabantids.

All these fish have different modes of reproduction. Livebearers release live fry, cichlids deposit eggs on a substrate and either guard them or take them up into their mouths, whereas catfish may deposit eggs and abandon them or guard them. Tetras and barbs usually scatter their eggs, and anabantids make bubble-nests and deposit the eggs within these floating rafts of bubbles to hatch. Nevertheless, there are many practical points common to all these fish when it comes to inducing them to spawn.

### Getting the fish to spawn

Simulating the fish's natural environment is the first and most important factor in getting them to breed. If a fish comes from a soft acidic river, it will (in most cases) require soft acidic water in the aquarium if it is to breed. There are exceptions to this rule, and with the constant breeding of fish in the aquarium they are gradually evolving to accept breeding conditions that are further from their natural ones. Generally speaking, however, if you get the water right you are halfway to breeding success.

Next, consider the surroundings. If a fish is used to living in densely planted waters where the sunlight is filtered through overhanging branches, then a heavily planted aquarium with subdued lighting is likely to be just right. These fish may be very timid in other conditions and unless they can settle and feel comfortable they are not going to breed. Too much activity near the tank will also be a deterrent to spawning, so keep things peaceful.

In the wild, fish are usually induced into spawning by some natural stimuli, such as heavy rain. This swells and cools the rivers, increases the oxygen content and washes an abundance of insect and animal life into the water. You can imitate the effect of heavy rain by making slightly larger, more frequent water changes using cooler water. You can make this even more authentic by lowering the water level gradually over a period of a few days. To mimic the high degree of organic matter washed into the water during

*Below: Among the cichlids, angelfish are particularly easy to breed in the aquarium. First signs of a pair developing are two fish snatching brief moments with each other away from the pack, pecking at a rock or leaf together and making strange little flicks of the head. It is best to place this pair in a tank of their own. After anything from a day to a few weeks, the female starts to develop a small tube just in front of her anal fin. The male develops a tube, but this is more pointed and not as broad. The pair select and peck clean a small patch on a vertical rock or leaf (as seen here) and eventually the female will start laying eggs on it.*

heavy rain, add an aquarium tonic, and increased feedings of live foods such as brine shrimp will act as the abundance of insect life that becomes available at this time. After this cooling period of rain, the waters warm up and you can simulate this by turning up the adjustment on the heater/thermostat a degree or two.

Increasing the aeration will give the impression that the water is moving faster and when all these actions are taken together the fish are often "tricked" into believing that their captive environment is entirely natural.

*Above:When the female has laid the eggs the male follows and fertilizes them. The female fans them with her pectoral fins and pecks off any infertile eggs that have turned white with fungus. Fertile eggs hatch after two or three days and the fry are then stuck by little filaments to another leaf or rock until they can swim freely. Feed them on newly hatched brine shrimp four or five times a day until they can eat crumbled flake food. The parents should guard the fry for several more weeks, but due to constant inbreeding they are often bad parents and eat their own young.*

*Below: Angelfish fry are shown here three days after hatching. The fry attach to the leaf by means of mucous secreted from glands on the head.*

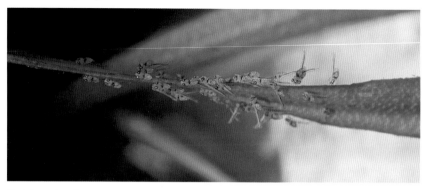

### Raising the fry

Raising the fry can be easy with many species but almost impossible with others. Newly hatched brine shrimp will often be sufficient for their needs, providing the fry are of a reasonable size (pinhead or larger), but smaller fry will need smaller foods. Proprietary liquid fry foods are good, but also consider raising infusoria as a first food. These are single-celled creatures that live on decaying vegetable matter. Start a culture by placing potato peelings in a jar and filling this with hot, nearly boiling water. Leave this in a warm sunlit place. After a couple of days the culture will go cloudy and in another few days it will clear again. Once cleared, you can harvest the tiny creatures by simply pouring small amounts of the liquid into the fry tank. Feed the fry little and often, four to five times a day. As they grow, wean them onto hard-boiled egg yolk and then finely crumbled flake foods.

### Using a breeding trap for livebearers

When breeding livebearers such as guppies you can avoid the young being eaten by floating a breeding trap in the main aquarium. This is usually a net frame or a clear miniature plastic aquarium about 10–13cm (4–5in) square with a small mesh grid in the bottom. When the female is nearly ready to drop her young, place her in the trap above the grid. As she releases the young, they fall through the grid and out of harm's way. As she does not tend the young, the female can be returned to the main aquarium after a little rest. Raise the fry in the breeding trap on finely crushed flake until they are big enough not to be eaten or, better still, place them in another aquarium to grow to a safe size before releasing them into the community tank. Females can store sperm from a male and use it to fertilize up to five or six future batches of eggs, so it is quite possible to have a female and no male and still have several broods of young guppies. Male guppies are very attentive toward females, so buy two or three females for every male or else the female may become worn out.

Young females may produce as few as three or four fry, but older guppies may—and often do—drop more than 100 fry at a go. Be sure to separate males from females as soon as possible to avoid a guppy plague.

*Above: Eventually the angelfish fry detach themselves from the leaf and swim freely in the tank.*

# CREATING AND MAINTAINING A MARINE AQUARIUM

The earth's tropical oceans are the planet's most stable environment. A relatively short distance below the surface, and away from the shoreline, nothing changes from day to night, from winter to summer or from year to year. The parameters of the fish's surroundings are incredibly constant—the temperature, the salinity, the pH level, the oxygen content, the very composition of the water is never-changing. It follows, therefore, that a typical marine fish has no built-in mechanism for change and it is this that makes the hobby of keeping marine fish such a challenge. If the aquarist does not take care to create a similarly unchanging environment for his charges, then disaster looms. Unlike their freshwater counterparts, marine fish do not adapt readily to life in an aquarium and rarely breed in captivity. As a result, the vast majority of all captive marine fish are wild-caught and must be treated with greater respect than even the most temperamental freshwater fish.

All this may make the prospect of keeping marine fish sound rather daunting, but when housed in the right conditions, there is no reason why they should not thrive. This part of the book builds on the foundations laid down in the practical pages of the freshwater section. Many of the same basic principles apply to setting up and maintaining a marine aquarium, but the important exceptions are carefully described and explained. With the wide range of specialist equipment available today, keeping marines is well within the scope of the enthusiastic and dedicated fishkeeper.

*Left: A juvenile French angel (Pomacanthus paru) from the Caribbean, one of the stunning marine fish you can keep in a well set up aquarium. In most cases, the adult coloration outshines that of the juvenile, but with the French angel most aquarists prefer the dramatic yellow and black pattern of the youngsters. Small specimens about 5–7.5cm (2–3in) long are most often seen. The blue ring angel (P. annularis) and the Koran angel (P. semicirculatus) are among the cheapest of the available angels, especially as juveniles, and are often the first angels bought by beginners to the marine fishkeeping hobby.*

The type of tank you choose will depend on the location you have in mind, how you want it to look, and the amount of money you have to spend. As for freshwater tropical fish, virtually every marine tank is made from glass panels sealed with silicone aquarium

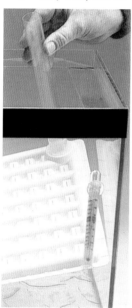

sealant, although there are models that incorporate plastic or wood-grain trimming to improve their final appearance. It is important to avoid metal trims and appendages because these will quickly corrode when exposed to salt water. The tank should have a tight-fitting sliding cover glass, which not only prevents fish escaping, but also reduces evaporation (which upsets the salt balance), prevents water splashing out, and keeps out unwelcome intruders, whether they be cats, children, or simply dust, fumes, and aerosol sprays.

As far as size is concerned, there is no absolute minimum size aquarium in which to keep marine fish, but it is advisable to consider a tank holding 104 liters

*Left: (Step One) Place an undergravel filter plate in the base of the tank, just as you would for a freshwater system. Before you do this, make sure that you place a slab of expanded polystyrene beneath the tank to support it and to cushion any irregularities in the surface of the stand. If you have any doubts about the tank, test it outdoors by filling it with tap water and checking it for leaks.*

*Left: (Step Two) Cover the entire surface of the filter plate with a layer of well-washed coarse medium, such as coral gravel or dolomite chippings from your aquarium dealer. Do not use gravel that is recommended for freshwater systems. Spread the medium about 5cm (2in) deep.*

(about 23 gallons) as the least allowable, and one holding 156 liters (34 gallons) or more as preferable. Transferred into sizes, this means that you should start off with a tank measuring no less than 90x30x38cm (36x12x15in) in length, width, and depth, although one measuring 90x38x45cm (36x15x18in) would be better. The actual dimensions are irrelevant, however, because it is the finished volume of water that is the sole criterion for size considerations.

Marine aquariums can be divided into two sorts: simple boxes, with or without adornment and hood arrangements; and complete systems, with all or much of the equipment included within the fabric of the tank. The step-by-step photographs show how to set up a basic all-glass marine aquarium. In many ways, the sequence follows the same basic steps involved in setting up the freshwater aquarium as described previously. The major differences are that the water will be salty and that the "life-support" systems, such as lighting, heating, and filtration, need to function more efficiently and within stricter tolerances to support the more sensitive marine creatures displayed in the finished aquarium. The captions to the setting up photographs reflect the practical steps involved, while the main text discusses more general points concerned with filtration, lighting, heating, salt balance, and testing equipment.

*Above: (Step Three) Trim a gravel tidy (a sheet of plastic mesh) to fit and place it, curl downward, over the medium. This prevents mixing of the media and stops fish digging down to the plate.*

*Left: (Step Four) Add a 5cm (2in) layer of unwashed coral sand on top of the gravel tidy mesh. You can see the two layers in this photograph. Slope this layer down to the front of the tank.*

## Filtration systems for the marine aquarium

If you were to set up an aquarium without fish, then there would be no need to filter the water. However, as soon as you add animals and food, the resulting waste products pollute the water. The ideal filtration system is for a constant flow of water to pass through the aquarium; with new clean water replacing the old polluted water. This is not exactly practical unless you live next to a tropical shoreline, where the ocean itself is used by the occasional public aquarium.

However, back in the real world of modest-sized tanks in the living room, it is necessary to devise small practical filtration units for home use. Although we have reviewed the basic operation of filtration systems for freshwater tanks, the subject bears repeating here because of the precise control over water quality demanded by marine fish.

Filtration can be divided into three types—physical, biological, and chemical. As the name suggests, physical filtration simply involves physically removing waste matter. This is the ideal method, but it usually only works with large granular matter, and would not work with, for instance, liquid waste. Biological filtration involves bacteria beds that "biologically" consume waste matter, and this method of filtration is the basis of successful marine keeping. Chemical filtration involves chemically removing or absorbing waste matter, usually by means of an agent, such as activated carbon. An ideal marine system usually makes use of these three methods of filtration in combination.

Most marine systems are set up around an undergravel filter bed, the mechanics of which provide the

*A stream of air bubbles creates a beneficial oxygenating effect*

*This tube draws in air and introduces it into the water flow*

*The power head has an electric water pump that pulls water up the uplift tube. It generates a stronger water flow than a simple air-operated system*

*Water is drawn down through the two layers of medium over the whole surface of the filter plate*

### Undergravel filtration using a power head

*Using a power head at the top of the uplift tube creates a strong and consistent flow of water through the undergravel filtration system. It is vital to maintain good water conditions in the marine aquarium and such an arrangement helps to keep the biological filter bed working at top efficiency. Compare the water flow here with the reverse flow system shown opposite.*

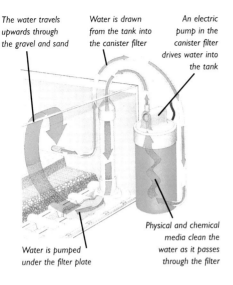

The water travels upwards through the gravel and sand

Water is drawn from the tank into the canister filter

An electric pump in the canister filter drives water into the tank

Water is pumped under the filter plate

Physical and chemical media clean the water as it passes through the filter

**Reverse-flow undergravel filtration**
*This is how an outside canister filter—often called a power filter—can be used to preclean the water before it flows through the undergravel filtration system in the reverse direction, i.e. upward rather than the more usual downward. This arrangement helps to keep the coral gravel and sand clear of clogging detritus so that it can fulfil its biological cleaning role more efficiently.*

necessary biological filtration. The complete system ideally consists of an undergravel filter plate that fits the entire base of the tank, covered by a 5cm (2in) layer of coarse aggregate, such as coral gravel or dolomite chippings, covered by a further layer of coral sand. The two media are separated by a plastic mesh (or "gravel tidy") to prevent intermixing. Water is then drawn down through the media and up the uplift tube, either by means of an external air pump creating a rising column of bubbles, or more efficiently, by a water pump (a so-called "power head") situated on top of the uplift tube. The nitrifying bacteria that flourish in the gravel and sand layers "consume" the fish's waste products and convert them to less harmful substances. In simple terms, nitrifying bacteria have a few basic needs in order to flourish—a surface on which to cling (the gravel and sand particles), plenty of oxygen (drawn from the well-oxygenated water flow), and a food supply (the nitrogenous waste products).

An efficient undergravel filter not only provides biological filtration, but also acts as a physical filter, as solid debris is drawn into and trapped by the coral sand. This can be a disadvantage, as the coral sand can get dirty and clogged. Although it is possible to add an outside canister filter in order to try and remove debris from the water flow before it clogs the sand, an alternative arrangement is to set up a reverse-flow biological system. To do this, direct the water flow from the outlet pipe of a canister filter (containing physical and chemical filter media) into the uplift tube of the undergravel filter. In this way, cleaned water from the outside canister filter is forced underneath the undergravel filter plate and up through the layers of gravel and sand. This is far more

*Left: In this simple air-powered protein skimmer, the rising stream of bubbles creates a froth in the upper part. Molecules of organic waste in the water cling onto the surface of the bubbles and are carried over the lip into a collecting cup at the top. The froth collapses into a yellowish liquid, which can be emptied from the cup. More sophisticated models set up a counter-current flow of water and air so the bubbles stay in contact with the water for longer period. There are also versions fitted with an electric pump.*

efficient than the standard flow biological system, and can be recommended to beginners and more experienced aquarists.

It is worth mentioning trickle filtration here. An undergravel filter is quite "wasteful" of resources, since nitrifying bacteria are naturally "dry" creatures, and when submerged, they drown and have to mutate constantly in order to survive and propagate. Trickle filter systems have the filter medium in small containers above the water and a trickle of water is passed over them. This system is far more effective in the sense that one small container of porous gravel can hold as many nitrifying bacteria as a large submerged filter bed, but its disadvantage is that only so much water can be passed over it before it becomes submerged.

There are several manufactured systems that incorporate trickle filter units, whether as separate components that you attach to your tank or as part of a complete built-in aquarium management system. Some aquarium set-ups combine both trickle filters and undergravel filters. In fact, once you understand the fundamental principles involved, there is no reason why you should not build your own filtration system using both these methods.

The third part of the filtration jigsaw is chemical filtration. In order to supplement biological and physical filtration, many aquarists use activated charcoal and other proprietary filter media, usually placed in a box or canister filter, which absorb waste products. Charcoal is particularly useful in absorbing phenols, which would otherwise tint the water yellow, but has the disadvantage of not being obvious when its useful life is over. Some proprietary filter media not only have much greater absorption capabilities than charcoal, but also indicate when they are spent by changing color.

One disadvantage of absorbent materials, however, is that they also absorb copper compounds, which are a major ingredient in disease treatments, at least in a fish-only aquarium. An alternative method of chemical filtration is a piece of equipment called a protein skimmer, a slightly cumbersome unit that "strips" the seawater of excess protein. Modern aquarists regard this as an essential addition to a system, its presence giving a stability previously unknown, but it is not always easy to find room for one, particularly since the top-collecting cup has to sit just above the water level. For smaller tanks, inexpensive air-driven models are fine, but for larger tanks a more expensive motor driven unit is advisable.

Finally on filtration, we should mention two further items of filtration: ozonizers and ultraviolet sterilizers, both comparatively expensive. Although either or both of these pieces of equipment are beneficial, we advise any potential aquarists that they could spend their money more usefully at this stage, and at least for the time being they should not worry themselves over these expensive acquisitions.

## Lighting a marine tank

Lighting plays an important part in the marine aquarium, for the simple reason that the world's coral reefs are all subject to strong sunlight all the year round, and many of the reef's inhabitants need that sunlight to survive. Also, many of the more colorful show fish, angels and tangs in particular, need algae as an essential part of their diet, and the only way to grow algae is to have sufficient light in the aquarium. Therefore, your tank should incorporate quite strong artificial lighting. There are a number of ways to achieve this. Most simple tanks are supplied with a metal or plastic hood designed to hold a number of fluorescent tubes. Make sure that the hood is easily removable for access, and remember to ensure that the cover glasses are watertight. If the hood is metal, coat it with three layers of polyurethane varnish to ward off corrosion.

There are a huge variety of fluorescent tubes available, many of them especially manufactured for the aquarium fish market. This form of lighting is ideal because fluorescent tubes are not too expensive to buy, are economical to run, last a long time, and do not run hot. They are sufficient for most marine tanks, but you may need something more penetrative for deeper tanks, and for situations where lush growths of algae are required. Do remember that fluorescent tubes only have a limited useful life, even if they continue to give off light. Replace the lights in rotation so that there are always one or two tubes that are less than six months old.

Due to the bulkiness of marine lighting arrangements, many aquarists choose tanks without hoods. You can then either situate the tank in the open and use decorative lighting, or enclose the tank behind a wall or partition and make use of standard, perhaps unattractive, but also less expensive lighting simply suspended over the tank. Ordinary domestic spotlights can be positioned over an aquarium, with the light directed into the water to create some striking effects in moving water.

Mercury vapor lamps are increasingly popular lighting for aquariums. These look like decorative household lights, and are either suspended over the tank or are wall mounted. They are quite expensive but they are a very efficient light source, and can be recommended in those situations where they can be fitted.

Metal halide lamps would be the specialists' choice. Anybody who has seen a large marine tank lit by metal halide lamps would be hard put to go back to "ordinary" lighting without feeling dissatisfied. These lighting units, suitably protected for use near the aquarium, are expensive and bulky, however, and may not be suitable for beginners to marine fishkeeping. One final word on lighting and tank location—although it is not a good idea to locate a freshwater tank in direct sunlight, marine tanks can prosper in sunlight, and a warm conservatory or similar situation makes an ideal location.

## Heating a marine aquarium

Marine aquarium systems need to be kept at the same temperature as freshwater ones, i.e. 24°C (75°F). But marine fish are far more intolerant of temperature fluctuations than freshwater fish, and so it is important to buy reliable heating equipment. For a centrally heated "average" home environment buy a heater/thermostat with a rating that allows five watts for every 4.5 liters (one gallon) of water in the aquarium. In a colder environment, increase this allowance to 10 watts. Since even the best heater will fail eventually, and invariably when the local shop is closed, buy two half-size heaters for all except the smallest tanks, rather than buying one main heater and one spare. Then, if one heater fails, the other will cope until you replace it or, if one heater sticks in the on position, it will take far longer to raise the temperature to dangerous levels, and give you far more advanced warning.

A word here about thermometers: glass thermometers are available filled with spirit or mercury. Both sorts are

*Right: (Step One) With the main decorations in place, add the required amount of dry salt mix (see the panel opposite).*

Above: (Step Two) Add warm water to the aquarium slowly so as not to disturb the decor already in place and allow a margin for adding further items.

Above: (Step Three) Fit a cover glass or plastic condensation tray to prevent fish jumping out and water evaporation. On larger tanks you can fit more than one cover glass.

inconvenient to read, and mercury thermometers are lethal if they break, while spirit models are usually unreliable. The stick-on digital thermometers are the best to choose for marine tanks as they are for freshwater ones. Although their reading is not too accurate, they will record temperature fluctuations fairly accurately. But it is a good idea to check their accuracy with a mercury thermometer briefly suspended in the tank.

## What do "specific gravity" and "salinity" mean?

Both terms reflect the saltiness of water. Basically, the more salt in the water—and here the word "salt" refers to a mix of salts, in which sodium chloride dominates—the higher is its specific gravity and salinity. The two measurements are quite distinct, however, and are expressed in different units.

Specific gravity: this is the ratio of the density of a liquid compared to the density of distilled water, which is said to

*Left: This is a swing-needle type of hydrometer that shows the specific gravity of your aquarium water. Simply place this device in the tank and tap it gently to dislodge any air bubbles on the needle. Make sure that you test the tank water at its recommended operating temperature. Ideally, aim for a reading of 1.020.*

have a specific gravity of one. In the marine aquarium, "healthy" values hover around 1.020, and very small changes in specific gravity represent significant variations in salt concentration for the marine creatures in the tank.

Salinity: this is a measure of the salt concentration in water, and is expressed in grams/liter. There is a close relationship between salinity and specific gravity, but it alters with temperature. At 24°C (75°F), for example, a specific gravity of 1.020 is equivalent to a salinity of 29.8 gm/liter. As the temperature rises, the salinity required to maintain a specific gravity of 1.020 also rises. This is why it vital to measure and stabilize the specific gravity of the water in your aquarium at the final operating temperature. Salinity varies slightly around the world. The Pacific near the Philippines, for example, has a salinity of 30–34gm/liter, the Caribbean 35gm/liter, and the Mediterranean 36–38gm/liter.

Synthetic seawater: It may be difficult to understand why natural sea water is inferior to artificial sea water, after all, it is obviously good enough for the fish that live in it! Let us assume that you live near the coast, and collecting seawater would not be expensive or inconvenient—big assumptions! Firstly, natural seawater is usually polluted, especially near the shore, so it would be necessary to collect it offshore. Secondly, natural seawater is full of "life," including plankton, much of which would die in a home environment, thus creating a pollution problem. It is also likely that a great deal of the life forms would be disease organisms, which would attack your tank's future inhabitants.

*Right: At this stage you can fit the protein skimmer, but do not start it, and run any power filters with biological media, not chemical. Let the system run for 24 hours. By the next day, the water should be clear, the temperature should be stable, and the specific gravity should be around 1.020. The system will take ten days to a month to mature. A bacterial culture will hasten the process. If you have a friend with a marine tank, "borrow" a cup of mature sand. Measure the nitrite level regularly. At first there should be no reading, but after you add the culture, it will increase. Wait until it peaks and remains high, then falls to zero.*

# DECORATING A MARINE AQUARIUM

The decor you choose may be either "dead" or "alive." The former refers to dead coral and shells, and various types of both natural and man-made rocks. Live decoration includes "living rock" and various living but generally stationary invertebrates. You may wish to start with dead decor and graduate to living decor at a later stage.

## Arranging decorations within the tank

When you arrange the decor, remember that your fish will not be bright enough to understand which is the front of the tank and which is the rear. Therefore, although you need to give the fish some places to hide, do leave plenty of free-swimming places at the front, so that the fish will choose this area as their natural gathering and exercise territory. Take time and trouble to ensure that any rocks are solidly placed so that they will not tumble if the base sand is disturbed. A surprising number of fish and invertebrates seem to delight in rearranging your carefully placed sand. And do not lean any rocks against equipment such as heaters or filters; you will regret it when you need to change or adjust these devices. If you choose to bury an air diffuser within a piece of coral or a shell, remember to put a convenient join in the airline so that you can change the diffuser easily—they block up amazingly frequently.

## Using rockwork

A sensible approach to decorating the marine tank is to use rockwork. Suitable natural rocks include tufa rock, slates, sandstones, and most types of granite. Ensure that the rocks you choose are clean; often a good clean with a stiff brush is all that is required. If you feel that granites and similar rocks do not look sufficiently exotic, there are man-made materials that have a more realistic "submarine" appearance. These are also far more porous, and therefore do not displace so much water as the real thing. One in particular, called grotto rock, is ideal to intermix with living rock, and another, lava rock, has a red hue particularly effective under a red light. You can also buy simulated rock pieces and low walls that can be useful to hide equipment and create ledges. Use aquarium silicone sealant to fix pieces together to make interesting shapes.

## Corals and shells

Dead coral and shells were once a popular method of decoration in marine aquariums, but our awareness of the problems of habitat destruction has radically changed our thinking. Hard corals, whether dead or alive, are now listed under the CITES regulations (the Convention on International Trade in Endangered Species) to prevent their international export, and are therefore becoming increasingly less available to the hobbyist. Nevertheless, pieces are still around and available for aquarists' use. Unless you are assured that the pieces have been pre-treated, then you should treat any chosen piece yourself to ensure that the coral, or in particular the shell, does not contain any of the original living inhabitant. To do this immerse the corals for 24 hours in a solution of 50ml of household bleach per liter of water (equivalent to one cup in a gallon). In the case of shells, ensure that the bleach gets right into the core. After this period of soaking, put the pieces under running water for 48 hours or so, until there is not the slightest smell of chlorine in the air. Again, ensure that the inner crevices of the shells are thoroughly washed.

## Using "living rock"

The ideal decoration is known as "living rock," and is in fact pieces of coral rock hewn from the coral beds, the best pieces coming from the Red Sea. Every piece is different, often interestingly shaped and full of small holes and caves, and each contains a host of sea life, including corals, polyps, algae, crustaceans, and sea urchins. These creatures may be in a planktonic form, which often develop into adult forms if the tank's other inhabitants allow them to. There is no doubt that living rock is the most natural, beautiful, useful, and the healthiest type of decoration to choose for a marine aquarium.

*Left: In somewhat more restrained surroundings, a flame angelfish (Centropyge loriculus) wends its way over tufa rocks festooned with red algae and among the green, almost artificial looking fronds of a seaweed called Caulerpa. This plant is surprisingly easy to raise in a brightly lit marine aquarium. There are several species to choose from.*

*Right: The well-known regal tang (Paracanthurus hepatus) has been described as the bluest thing on earth. This is a truly gorgeous fish that rarely grows to more than 7.5–10cm (3–4in) in an aquarium. It is a good feeder, and mixes with anything. Once you have progressed beyond the damsel and clownfish stage, this is one of the safest marine fish to try, always bearing in mind the advice to provide adequate vegetable matter in the diet.*

If you do choose living rock, then do not buy it until the tank is fully ready. However, you can use it to mature the tank naturally instead of a chemical agent. If you buy a large amount, you will find that you will get a very high and protracted nitrite reading, and you will need to perform a large water change after the tank is matured, before introducing the fish. If you use only a small amount of living rock to mature a tank, it is still better to buy at least most of the required amount before introducing sensitive marine creatures, and avoid continually disturbing them in their new environment.

Living rock has a few disadvantages, not least its high cost, which rules it out as an option for many aquarists. One way of reducing the financial strain is to lay a foundation of cheaper rockwork and then cover this with living rock, from where at least some of the life will travel and encrust the dead pieces. A second drawback of living rock is that you have no control over the types of life it contains. It is no use complaining afterward if you discover that you have inadvertently introduced a vicious predator, such as a mantis shrimp, or unleashed a colony of bristle worms. These worms are harmless but incredibly fertile, and quite a few aquarists have ended up with a tank literally seething with a mass of irremovable worms. A third problem with living rock is that since it contains life, it is counted as an invertebrate, and thus prevents medication being used in disease prevention. With these points in mind, setting up a fish-only aquarium is in many ways far easier and far cheaper than a more natural mixed fish/invertebrate system, especially for beginners to the hobby.

### ARTIFICIAL CORALS

*Artificial corals made from fiberglass are an ideal substitute for the real thing. Not only are these environmentally safe, but they are also available in the natural colors of the original live coral, rather than just in bleached white. While white corals look very attractive at first, they soon become coated with algae and slime in the tank; artificial corals overcome both the moral and aesthetic objections.*

Apart from propagating their line, marine fish spend their lives either finding food or ensuring that they are not part of another fish's meal. Usually there is no shortage of either choice or quantity of food available, because the coral reefs represent an almost perfect model of a well-balanced food chain.

Fish naturally divide into various types of feeders—damselfish, clownfish, and gobies, for example, are filter feeders, almost automatically passing minute particles of food into their stomachs. Tangs are grazers; butterflyfish are pickers; angelfish both graze and pick; triggers, lionfish, and groupers are predators; and wrasses and goatfish are scavengers. Some fish are vegetarian—tangs in particular; whereas some are carnivorous, such as lionfish; most are omnivorous, taking a range of foods.

Fulfilling all the marine fish's' natural dietary demands in the home aquarium is not always easy, especially bearing in mind the need to carefully monitor feeding levels and to ensure that no excess food is ever introduced into the system. Not only is it vital never to leave uneaten food in the water because of pollution, but also it is important not to allow the fish to over-indulge themselves. It is quite a skill to ensure that shyer fish get their fair share of food to meet their dietary requirements; while there are more aggressive fish in the tank eating everything available. Every successful marine fishkeeper needs to develop this skill. Some fish are nocturnal in their natural habitats, for example, and these may not be so willing to venture out into the brightly lit open areas of the aquarium to take their share of the food available.

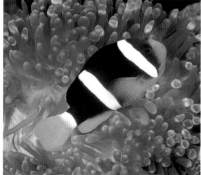

Many of the fish in the home aquarium, such as damsels, clowns, wrasses, most angels, a few butterflies, and most tangs, will readily take either flake or granular food. These are obviously the most convenient of foodstuffs as

*Left: This is* Amphiprion clarkii, *one of the chocolate, or sebae, clownfish. These delightful and fascinating marine fish will accept a wide range of small live foods, shrimp, fish, meat-based foods, vegetable foods, and 'flakes in the aquarium.*

far as the aquarist is concerned, but even if all the tank's inhabitants take them readily, it is important to vary the diet by also feeding a range of frozen foods. As well as being fresher and richer in vitamins, which are important for the fish's well-being, such foods also offer a variety of tastes, textures, and shapes that a single processed food cannot.

Frozen foods can be bought as individual types, such as Mysis shrimp, brine shrimp, lancefish, mussel meat, etc., or preferably as complete diets. If access to frozen food is impossible, it is important to feed a variety of different dry foods, and to add a vitamin supplement more often than if using frozen foods. Freeze-dried krill, bloodworm, and Gammarus shrimps can all be used as additions to flake and granules. As with freshwater fish, the frozen and freeze-dried foods for marine fish provide a safe and disease-free way of feeding.

## Regular maintenance

It is especially important to concentrate on two areas of regular maintenance—equipment and water quality. Check the equipment regularly. Replace fluorescent tubes on a regular basis to maintain light levels in the aquarium, and check and overhaul the air pumps, power heads, and power filters to a predetermined maintenance schedule. Always keep a supply of spare parts, such as diaphragms, rotors, and sealing rings, for these vital pieces of equipment. Check heaters for accuracy, replace airstones at the first sign of blocking, and clean or replace the filter medium as necessary.

When the aquarium is first established, we assume that the water quality is at its optimum. Certain parameters can be measured; equipment or kits are available for determining temperature, specific gravity, ammonia, nitrite, nitrate, pH, and oxygen levels. There are many more components to keep track of but these are beyond the hobbyist's scope. Experience has shown, however, that if the measurable parameters are all in order then the tank's well being is virtually assured.

The first step, therefore, is to buy and use reliable kits and testing equipment. The very minimum from the above list would be a thermometer, a hydrometer (used for determining specific gravity), plus nitrite, nitrate, and marine pH test kits. Keep a log and take action at the slightest deterioration in standards. It is vital to maintain a testing regime so that the various readings are correct on a consistent basis; it is difficult to take corrective action when the pH value of the water, for example, has strayed out of the range 8.1–8.3.

*Right: You can use a gravel washer when making partial water changes. As water flows out of the tank you can agitate the substrate with another tool or your hand. Hold the cylinder an inch above the gravel, so that debris is carried away. There is a filter at the top of the cylinder to prevent fish and substrate particles from being accidentally removed.*

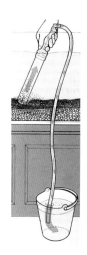

The simple, way to maintain water quality is to institute a regular regime of partial water changes. An average of 10 per cent per week is the ideal, but many factors will have an effect on the percentage, such as size of tank, sophistication of filtering equipment, number of fish, and primarily, of course, the amount of food introduced. Before adding new water to the aquarium, premix it to the correct salinity and temperature, and then aerate it for a few hours before use. To remove the appropriate amount of water from the aquarium use a siphon tube fitted with a gravel washer attachment. Do not deeply wash the gravel, however. Stir the gravel with a handled tool or your hand. Vacuum the cloudy debris from above the gravel. As part of this regular maintenance routine keep the cover glass clean and make sure that you keep the front glass of the aquarium clear of algae.

## MAINTENANCE CHECK LIST

- *Keep a written record of all equipment and aquarium maintenance. Record stock additions, lightbulb changes, test results, and any unusual fish or invertebrate behavior you have seen in the aquarium.*

- *Check your aquarium water on a regular basis so that you can keep it in top condition all the time.*

- *Maintain the pH value of the water in the range 8.1–8.3.*

- *Always keep the specific gravity between 1.019 and 1.021.*

- *Never allow any nitrite to appear, nor allow nitrates to exceed 30ppm (parts per million/equivalent to milligrams per liter). If you have live rock or other invertebrates, do not allow nitrates to exceed 12ppm.*

- *Be sure to carry out regular water changes (a minimum of the equivalent of 25% per month).*

- *Keep your fluorescent tubes fresh. On the average, they should be changed every six months, on a schedule.*

- *Always have a ready supply of replacement air diffusers.*

- *Never be tempted to use unsterilized sea foods in the aquarium, such as prawns and mussels, including live wild shrimps.*

- *Check and replace filter media when necessary to maintain efficiency.*

## BASIC MARINE HEALTH CARE

Maintaining a healthy marine aquarium is so much easier if you take a few elementary steps to prevent diseases occurring in the first place. Always buy your fish carefully from a respected and proven shop, where the livestock is well cared for and quarantined before sale. Never buy a fish that has not been in the country for at least two weeks, try and see it feeding before you buy it, and inspect it closely before taking it home. If the fish has any marks, spots, irregularities, tears, blemishes, in fact, if it is any way less than perfect, save your money!

Once the fish has been bagged, leave it in darkness until you get it home; do not keep inspecting it to see if it is all right. Once home, switch off the tank lights and expose the fish to dim daylight. Place the whole sealed plastic bag into the aquarium water and leave it there for 30 minutes, in order for the two water temperatures to equalize. Then tip the water and fish into a clean, clear, plastic container that can float in the top of the aquarium. For the next 60 minutes gradually add aquarium water to the plastic container. Finally, net the fish into the aquarium and discard all the water in the container. Leave the tank lights off until the following day.

However carefully you try to stick to any guidelines to reduce stress and prevent disease organisms entering the aquarium, sooner or later; a disease will appear. Since all marine fish are so intolerant of changing surroundings, and since every marine fish should be regarded as a swimming time bomb full of potential disease, eventually disease will break out. In simplest terms, diseases can be divided into two categories— a few readily recognizable, treatable diseases, and all the rest. Fortunately, it is the recognizable and treatable diseases that are often highly contagious, whereas most other diseases are often limited to the original host fish.

The recognizable diseases include marine white spot, coral fish disease, and flukes. All of them are characterized by spots of different sizes and colors on the fish, and all can be treated, fairly simply, by adding proprietary medications based on copper sulphate to the tank water. Almost without exception these medications work effectively and fairly quickly. However, they all have one drawback—they may not be used in an aquarium containing invertebrates.

This is why it is best to start with a fish-only system. If a disease breaks out in a fish-only tank, then you can treat the whole tank immediately. If the marine system contains both fish and invertebrates, however, and one of the above diseases appears, then the only way of treating the fish is to remove them to a separate treatment tank. And since all these diseases are contagious, it often means treating all the fish from the affected tank. So, if you intend to establish a mixed fish and invertebrate system, it is vital to first establish a small, separate quarantine tank in which you can hold all newly purchased fish for a week or two in order to quarantine them and to treat any fish that do become affected. This tank can be very simple, without a substrate and with just a heater, external power filter (no carbon) and strong aeration. A lower specific gravity (1.015) in your quarantine tank can reduce the spread of marine parasites.

## Some diseases that may affect tropical marine fish

*Marine white spot:* This is caused by the single-celled parasite *Cryptocaryon irritans* and can be recognized by the appearance of small, pinhead-sized white spots, quite regular and round, evenly distributed over the body. If left untreated, the spots increase in number, until after about two weeks the fish will become distressed and die. White spot is very contagious—but not as quickly as other diseases— and can be slow to respond to treatment (often based on copper compounds). The life cycle of the parasite involves the release of hundreds of free-swimming spores from cysts that fall to the tank floor.

    *Coral fish disease:* Caused by the single-celled parasite *Amyloodinium*, this disease also produces spots, but they are far smaller, giving a dusted velvety appearance. ("Velvet" in freshwater fish is caused by the related parasite *Oodinium*.) Often the spots can only be

seen at a certain angle. About 48 hours after developing the disease, the affected fish invariably develops a high gill rate. If it is not treated very soon after this stage, death will follow, not only to the original fish, but also to all the fish in the aquarium. Your aquarium

*Left: If left untreated fin rot, as shown on this silver angelfish, can cause a secondary fungal infection. The fins are damaged by bacteria, but can be treated with bactericide. Check stress factors and the water conditions and temperature. There are many possible health problems that marine fish can fall prey to but a cure is not always possible in every case.*

dealer will be able to supply suitable anti-parasite remedies for treating both marine white spot and coral fish disease.

*Flukes:* Flukes take many guises, and are often difficult to diagnose. The spots (i.e. the flukes adhering closely to the skin) are irregular, both in color and shape, often being off-white and smudgy. They are just as likely to be on the fins rather than on the body. The number of flukes can vary during different times of the day and, indeed, this variation is a good indicator that flukes are present. Flukes can be very debilitating, often marked by frequent scratching by the affected fish.

"Black flukes" are also not unusual, especially on yellow sailfin tangs, and occasionally on other yellow fish or on other tangs. Black flukes do not respond to copper medications, and need to be treated in a formalin bath. Seek expert advice about this. Once completed, transfer the fish to a new tank for two weeks, not the original aquarium, otherwise the flukes may reappear and you will need to treat the fish again.

*Lymphocystis:* The virus disease lymphocystis is the only other marine disease that is fairly easy to recognize and at least partly curable. The disease usually occurs on flat-sided fish, often angels, and looks like fluffy white growths on the sides of the body and fins. You can try tackling the condition by improving aquarium conditions and/or adding a suitable aquarium disinfectant.

---

### A BASIC MARINE MEDICINE CHEST

*The following items are useful for treating most health and disease problems and are worth keeping in stock.*

- *A bowl for administering a freshwater bath to newly caught (and purchased) marine fish. Match temperature to tank by floating the bag while you prepare the bath. Allow the fish to swim in clean, dechlorinated fresh water at tank temperature for 2 to 5 minutes. Observe carefully for signs of stress. Net the fish and release into the quarantine tank or his new home. There will be a balance disturbance and possibly a color change upon release, but the dip is not fatal. Marine parasites and chemical treatments can be fatal.*

- *A proprietary copper based treatment for white spot or flukes.*

- *A copper testing kit to monitor the use of the above medication.*

- *A disinfectant/bactericide to treat wounds or infections.*

- *Formalin in a 36% solution, obtainable from your chemist, for treating certain flukes and some other external parasites. This has a limited shelf life; replace it if a deposit occurs in the bottle.*

- *An oxygen bath, which is excellent for treating all those unrecognizable diseases not treatable with copper. This comes as a salt that you dissolve in a separate container.*

# FRESHWATER FISH FOR YOUR AQUARIUM

Walking into a specialist tropical fish shop and being faced with the bewildering array of fish on offer can be a daunting prospect. Which fish can I keep together? What do they eat? Which ones will eat each other? This section of the book deals with each of the main groups of freshwater fish that you are likely to encounter. It includes not only examples of small fish that will safely live together, but also discusses large cichlids and catfish that are best housed on their own or in a single species tank. 103 species are listed, with a photograph. Feeding and water requirements, mating habits, compatible tankmates, and related species are given for each.

When shopping, if you are in doubt about the identity of a fish, ask the shopkeeper. Most are willing and able to give sound advice—after all, it is in their interest to help you so that you return to buy more stock. And if you don't ask, you may find that a very attractive 5cm (2in) fish grows to become a 30cm (12in) drab-colored bully that uproots every plant in the aquarium and kills or eats several of the inmates!

The breeding requirements of many of the fish are included, and although these may not be of major concern at first, you may find that the fish breed without you having to lift a finger. If you are lucky and your fish multiply, this could well be the beginning of a long association with this fascinating hobby.

*Right: Blue-eyed plec (Panaque suttoni)*

# ANABANTIDS— FISH THAT CAN BREATHE

Anabantids are a very popular group of fish from Asia and Africa, most of which are known as gouramis. These fish have a special extra breathing organ called the "labyrinth," which is a bunch of folded tissues with many blood vessels within it. This organ enables the fish to extract the oxygen from air taken in at the surface, which is very useful in water with low oxygen levels. However, gouramis have evolved to depend so much on this organ that now they cannot exist without regularly taking air from the surface, regardless of the water's oxygen content. The air is also used to construct what are usually described as "bubblenests." The male fish build these nests on the surface of the water with air and their saliva and attach them to any floating debris. Most anabantids are undemanding and relatively peaceful compared to other fish, although often they do not get along too well with their own kind.

A gourami or other anabantid of any variety can pine away and die of stress if he (or she) fails to establish territory and interact with the other fish successfully. This may happen regardless of what species of fish they are kept with, and without any diseases being present in the aquarium. If a gourami appears stressed and afraid to eat, rearrange the tank as needed to provide more cover and allow the fish to set territorial boundaries.

# SIAMESE FIGHTING FISH

The infamous Siamese fighting fish (*Betta splendens*) is only aggressive toward its own kind. It comes from Thailand, where it lives in small pools and ditches. Each male betta has its own small territory, where it builds and repairs its bubblenest, defending it avidly from any other male. If two males come together, they

fight so viciously that if neither retreats then at least one will die. Male bettas are easy to keep in a tank, but never keep two males together. It is also unwise to keep females with males unless the intention is to breed them. Males are often overly aggressive to females that do not wish to spawn. Female bettas are excellent community fish.

**Variations:** Siamese fighting fish (*Betta splendens*) come in many colors: green, blue, red, purple, and albino. All these colors and the extremely long fins have been developed in the aquarium from the basic wild form. Females are far less colorful and lack the enormous fins.

**Origin:** Thailand and Cambodia, where they live in warm water with little dissolved oxygen.

**Temperature:** 25°C (77°F) minimum. Bettas (and gouramis) can tolerate temperatures up to 33°C (90°F).

**GH:** tolerates a range. A bit of non-iodized salt to harden the water can clear up minor skin or scale disturbances.

**pH:** 7.5 is ideal, but will tolerate 7.0 to 8.0 well.

**Hardiness:** The betta is a hardy species that will tolerate poor water conditions during cycling, as long as oxygen and temperature requirements are met.

**Feeding:** Bettas are strictly carnivorous. Freeze-dried tubifex worms, freeze-dried bloodworms, and live mosquito larvae are favorites. In an aquarium with filtration, feed daily. If the betta is kept in a bowl, feed every other day.

**Special requirements:** A betta must have access to air at the water's surface. Provide filtration or regular water changes. In a community aquarium, provide a castle or cave for your betta to claim as home.

**Compatible tankmates:** Tetras, corydoras catfish, other peaceful community fish in a planted aquarium.

**Avoid these tankmates:** Barbs or gouramis. Avoid baby fish or small neons as bettas will eat them.

**Related species:** Gouramis, paradise fish.

**Breeding:** To breed Siamese fighting fish, set up a tank with a low water level about 15cm (6in) and no filtration. Add hiding places and a tight lid to trap a layer of warm air. Place the male and female in the tank with a divider between them and feed them heavily with live food. Raise the temperature to 28°C (83°F). The male will build a nest of bubbles in one of the top corners and then search for the female. At this point, lift the divider and, if all goes well, they will embrace under the nest, with the male wrapped around the female. She then expels her eggs and the male fertilizes them. As they fall to the bottom, the male catches them in his mouth and places them within the bubblenest. The female lies motionlessly on her side under the nest, and the sequence is repeated until all the eggs are laid. Remove the female. The male tends the nest, and the fry hatch after about two days. Remove the male three days later. Feed the fry infusoria, to begin with, graduating to newly hatched brine shrimp. After another week, the labyrinth gland starts to develop and there may be many losses at this point. After a further two weeks you can safely separate them into their own little jars.

The lovely dwarf gourami (*Colisa lalia*) only grows to about 6.5cm (2.5in) in total and is relatively peaceful—a superb aquarium subject. Males are more colorful, and more frequently sold, than females. Male dwarf gouramis are a pale blue with orange vertical stripes. Females are a pale blue with silvery stripes. Water conditions are not critical, but maintain the temperature at about 25.5°C (78°F) and avoid acidic water. Dwarf gouramis often live in one of the top corners of the tank and prefer a little shade, so if their tank is brightly lit, provide some floating plants, such as duckweed, for cover.

**Variations:** The honey gourami (*Colisa sota*) is similar in size and care, but males are a warm golden shade with a blue throat and a touch of black on the anal fin. Female honey gouramis are a drab brown.

**Origin:** India and Bangladesh, Borneo. They live in warm water with little dissolved oxygen.

**Temperature:** 25.5°C (78°F) is ideal, but they will tolerate temperatures from 22°C (72°F) to 27.8°C (82°F).

**GH:** For breeding: 15°dGH, hard. Tolerates a range.

**pH:** 7.5 is ideal, but will tolerate 6.5 to 7.8 well.

**Hardiness:** The dwarf gourami is more delicate than other members of the anabantid family and is somewhat sensitive to nitrite. Be sure oxygen and temperature requirements are met. He must be able to breathe a bit of air at the water surface.

**Feeding:** Dwarf gouramis are omnivorous, requiring a mixed diet. They relish live foods as well as flake, dried, and frozen foods. They will enjoy the occasional frozen green bean. Live mosquito larvae are a treat. Feed daily.

**Special requirements:** Observe how your gouramis interact and feed regularly. Tall plants near the lift tubes can make them feel more secure.

**Compatible tankmates:** Most community fish. Dwarf gouramis do very well in planted aquariums.

**Avoid these tankmates:** Aggression can be a problem when there are multiple gouramis in the same aquarium. If it becomes a problem, rearranging the aquarium decorations may help to lessen the fighting. Any gourami that is too stressed and bullied may die, without any disease being present. Do not put any gourami in with small fry of any variety. He (or she) will eat them.

**Related species:** Bettas, other gouramis, paradise fish.

**Breeding:** Sexing gouramis—in addition to color differences, the back of the dorsal fin (on the male gourami) is slightly pointed and extends just past the point where the tail meets the body. The female's dorsal fin is rounded, and ends before the tail begins. When the female has a more rounded appearance, she may be carrying eggs. Feed live food for several days. Raise the temperature to 28°C (83°F). The male may build a nest of bubbles reinforced with bits of plants and algae in one of the top corners, then go in search of the female. If she is ready to breed, the female will be enticed under the nest. If breeding is successful, the male will tend the eggs, and the female should be removed. Once the eggs hatch, the male should be removed to breeder nets, or separate tanks, or he will eat the fry. Feed live infusoria for the first few days, then newly hatched brine shrimp.

# RED FLAME DWARF GOURAMI

The lovely red flame dwarf gourami (*Colisa lalia fire*) only grows to about 6.5cm (2.5in) in total and is relatively peaceful—a superb aquarium subject. Male red flame dwarf gouramis are a brilliant red-orange with a neon blue strip just behind the head and widening to include the dorsal fin. Females are rarely sold. Water conditions are not critical, but maintain the temperature at about 25.5°C (78°F) and avoid acidic water. Like other dwarf gouramis, they often live in one of the top corners of the tank and prefer a little shade, so if their tank is brightly lit, provide some floating plants, such as duckweed, for cover.

**Origin:** Thought to be a deliberate cross between the dwarf gourami and the honey gourami.

**Temperature:** 25.5°C (78°F) is ideal, but they will tolerate temperatures from 22°C (72°F) to 27.8°C (82°F).

**GH:** For breeding, 15°dGH, hard. Tolerates a range.

**pH:** 7.5 is ideal, but will tolerate 6.5 to 7.8 well.

**Hardiness:** The red flame dwarf gourami is more delicate than other members of the anabantid family. It is sensitive to nitrite and very sensitive to aggression from other gouramis. Be sure that oxygen and temperature requirements are met. It must be able to breathe a bit of air at the water surface.

**Feeding:** Red flame dwarf gouramis are omnivorous and require a mixed diet, with both plant and animal matter. They relish live foods and accept flake, dried, and frozen foods. They will nibble on the occasional frozen green bean. Live mosquito larvae are a gourmet treat. Feed daily.

**Special requirements:** Observe how your gouramis interact and feed regularly. A gourami can pine away and die of stress if he (or she) fails to establish territory and interact with the other fish successfully. Tall plants near the lift tubes can make them feel more secure.

**Compatible tankmates:** Most community fish. Red flame dwarf gouramis do very well in planted aquariums.

**Avoid these tankmates:** Aggression can be a problem when there are multiple gouramis in the same aquarium. If it becomes a problem, rearranging the aquarium decorations may help to lessen the fighting. Any gourami that is too stressed and bullied may die, without any disease being present. Do not put any gourami in with small fry of any variety as it will eat them.

**Related species:** Bettas, other gouramis, and paradise fish.

**Breeding:** Dwarf gouramis are egg-layers, but the author has never seen a female red flame dwarf gourami. The male might be bred to an ordinary female dwarf gourami. This species is thought to be a deliberate cross between the dwarf gourami and the honey gourami, so it may be genetically compatible with either.

Kissing gourami (*Helostoma temmincki*) adults range from 15cm (6in) to 30cm (12in). Because of their adult size, an aquarium at least 120x38x45cm (48x15x 18in), 209 liters (46 gallons) is required. These fish are most remarkable for their kissing behavior, which is not affection. The males will strive for dominance by pressing mouth to mouth until the weaker fish gives in. Kissing gouramis are usually a soft pink color with almost no markings, but there is a green variety that comes from Thailand. They prefer cover for retreat, but also require a large open swimming area for exercise. Cluster

plastic or silk aquarium plants in several areas near the back wall of the aquarium, but a couple of inches away. Leave enough room for a large fish to swim behind the plants. Kissing gouramis dig, so mix plenty of large gravel in with the fine, to reduce damage.

**Origin:** The commonly seen pink morph comes from Java. The less common green variety is from Thailand.

**Temperature:** 25.5°C (78°F) is ideal, but they will tolerate temperatures from 22°C (72°F) to 27.8°C (82°F).

**GH:** For breeding, 8°dGH, fairly soft. Tolerates a range from 5°dGH to 30°dGH.

**pH:** 7.5 is ideal, but will tolerate 6.5 to 7.8 well.

**Hardiness:** The kissing gourami requires good filtration, which becomes more critical as the fish gets larger. It is sensitive to nitrite. Be sure that oxygen and temperature requirements are met. It must be able to breathe a bit of air at the water surface.

**Feeding:** Kissing gouramis are omnivores, but require plenty of plant matter. Feed extra lettuce or other fresh vegetables. Live plants are considered snack food. In a community aquarium, observe to see whether they got to the daily food before it went. Plants will often be eaten, the best species to try are Java fern and Java moss.

**Special requirements:** Observe how your gouramis interact and feed regularly. A gourami can pine away and

die of stress if he (or she) fails to establish territory and interact with the other fish successfully. Males will "kiss" often. If they are about the same size and strength they may share the tank for years. If one is much smaller or weaker, it may need to be moved to a different tank.

**Compatible tankmates:** Most large community fish. Kissing gouramis rarely fight with other species of gourami.

**Avoid these tankmates:** Do not put any gourami in with small fry of any variety as it will eat them. Kissing gouramis can consume most of the plants in a planted aquarium rapidly.

**Related species:** Other labyrinth fish, but the relationship isn't genetically close.

**Breeding:** Kissing gouramis are egg-layers. Identifying the sex of your kissing gouramis may be difficult. The female kissing gourami pursues the male and convinces him it is time to spawn. Males and females will not exhibit kissing behavior. Lay a lettuce leaf on the water's surface for breeding material. If your kissing gouramis lay eggs, the eggs will float near the surface. The lettuce and the bacteria and infusoria feeding on it will feed the fry.

# MOONLIGHT GOURAMI

Moonlight gouramis (*Trichogaster microlepis*) can reach 15cm, (6in) to 20cm (8in). Because of their adult size, an aquarium at least 90x38x45cm (36x15x18in), 156 liters (34 gallons) is required. These fish are most remarkable for their quiet beauty. Both males and females feature a smooth silver finish, with their color highlighting sexual differences. The males are more aggressive than the females, and multiple males in a tank will cause some conflict. They require cover for retreat, but also need a large open swimming area

for exercise. Cluster real or artificial plants in several areas near the back wall of the aquarium, but a couple of inches away, giving enough room for a large fish to swim behind the plants and hide. Moonlight gouramis will claim an area as their home, which they may defend, but overall aggression is usually limited to other gouramis.

**Origin:** Thailand and Cambodia. They live in slow-moving, warm water with little dissolved oxygen.

**Temperature:** 28°C (83°F) is ideal, but they will tolerate temperatures from 26°C (79°F) to 30°C (86°F).

**GH:** For breeding, 8°dGH, fairly soft. Tolerates a range from 5°dGH to 25°dGH.

**pH:** 7.2 is ideal, but will tolerate 6.5 to 7.8 well.

**Hardiness:** The moonlight gourami requires good filtration, which becomes more critical as the fish gets larger. It is sensitive to nitrite. Be sure temperature requirements are met. It must be able to breathe a bit of air at the water surface.

**Feeding:** Moonlight gouramis are omnivores, but require plenty of plant matter, so feed extra lettuce or other fresh vegetables. Fine leaved live plants are considered snack food, or used for nest building. Flake or pellet food is acceptable, but it should contain some vegetable content. Feed daily.

**Special requirements:** Observe how your moonlight gouramis interact and eat, especially when they are new to the aquarium. A gourami can pine away and die of stress if it fails to establish territory and interact with the other fish successfully. If a gourami appears stressed and

afraid to eat, rearrange the tank to provide cover and territorial boundaries.

**Compatible tankmates:** Most community fish. Moonlight gouramis rarely fight with other species, or even other species of gourami. As fine leaved plants will be eaten or nipped at, the best plant species to try are giant vallisneria and java fern.

**Avoid these tankmates:** Do not put any gourami in with small fry of any variety as it will eat them.

**Related species:** Snake-skinned, pearl, and three-spot (or blue) gourami, other labyrinth fish.

**Breeding:** Moonlight gouramis are egg-layers. Gender can be ascertained from color differences and the back of the dorsal fin, which on the male gourami, is slightly pointed and extends just past the point where the tail meets the body. The pelvic fins of the male may be orange to red. The female's dorsal fin is rounded, and ends before the tail begins. Her pelvic fin may be yellow, or may be silver. Her feelers are often the only yellow area.

The male builds a bubble nest, but a strong current at the surface will destroy it, so lower water level or reduce current to encourage breeding. The male may use bits of fine leaved plants to reinforce the nest. Feed the fry infusoria, which was grown on lettuce leaves and banana skins.

# PEARL GOURAMI

The pearl, or leeri, gourami (*Trichogaster leeri*) grows to 10cm (4in). Its long, compressed body is blue-brown with a smothering of pearl spots. Because of their adult size, an aquarium at least 90x30x38cm (36x12x15in), 104 liters (23 gallons) is required to keep a single pearl gourami. A larger tank is best for a group. Both males and females feature the shimmering pearl spots. The male has an orange throat, while the female's throat is creamy white. The male pearl gourami is less aggressive toward females than most male labyrinth fish. They require cover for retreat, and do well in a heavily planted tank with lots of cover. Pearl gouramis are very shy if the tank has too much open space.

**Origin:** Borneo and Sumatra, where they live in slow-moving, warm water with a lot of plants.

**Temperature:** 25.5°C (78°F) is ideal, but they will tolerate temperatures from 24°C (74°F) to 28°C (82°F).

**GH:** For breeding, 10°dGH, moderate. Tolerates a range from 5°dGH to 30°dGH.

**pH:** 7.2 is ideal, but will tolerate 6.5 to 8.0 well.

**Hardiness:** The pearl gourami requires good filtration, which becomes more critical as the fish gets larger. It is sensitive to nitrite. Be sure the tank is warm enough. The fish must be able to breathe a bit of air at the water surface.

**Feeding:** Pearl gouramis are omnivores, but they relish live food such as mosquito larvae or brine shrimp. Offer lettuce occasionally. Flake or pellet food is acceptable, but it should contain some vegetable content. Feed daily.

**Special requirements:** Observe how your pearl gouramis interact and eat, especially when they are new to the aquarium. A gourami can pine away and die of stress if it fails to establish territory and interact with the other fish successfully. If a gourami appears stressed and

afraid to eat, rearrange the tank to provide more cover, and allow the fish to set territorial boundaries.

**Compatible tankmates:** Most community fish, such as tetras, clown loaches, and kuhli loaches. Pearl gouramis can be shy or defensive, but they rarely fight with other species. Provide a wide variety of live plants for cover. Some may be nibbled if the male builds a bubble nest, but generally these fish do well in planted aquariums.

**Avoid these tankmates:** Do not put pearl gouramis in with aggressive fish such as barbs or cichlids. If your pearl gouramis seem stressed, rearrange and add more plants or driftwood for cover. Baby livebearers will probably be snack food for the gouramis.

**Related species:** Moonlight, snake-skinned, and three-spot (or blue) gourami, other labyrinth fish.

**Breeding:** Pearl gouramis are egg-layers. In addition to color differences, the back of the dorsal fin, on the male gourami, is slightly pointed and extends just past the point where the tail meets the body. The throat and chest area of the male is orange to red. The throat and chest area is rounded, and ends before the tail begins. Her throat and chest area is creamy white. The male builds a bubble nest between plants. Feed the fry infusoria, or liquid fry food.

# THREE-SPOT GOURAMI

The three-spot gourami (*Trichogaster trichopterus*) grows to 15cm (6in). Because of their adult size, an aquarium at least 90x30x38cm (36x12x15in), 104 liters (23 gallons) is best to keep a single gourami with smaller community fish. A larger tank is best for a group of three or more three-spot gouramis. The body is light blue with several darker vertical patches. There is a black spot in the middle of the body and at the base of the tail, and the eye makes up the third spot. Take care when keeping this species in pairs, as males can be very aggressive toward females and may bully them to death if there

is no escape. Keeping multiple females with a single male may provide a more stable group. Provide plants for cover and some open space for the fish to swim around in. These fish accept all foods, but prefer live food.

**Variations:** There are several color variants of this species, including gold specimens, and light blue specimens with no spots. The blue gouramis without spots are often sold as "opaline" gouramis.

**Origin:** Burma, Malaysia, Southeast Asia, Thailand, Vietnam, Borneo, Sumatra, and the Indo-Australian Archipelago. They live in warm water low in dissolved oxygen.

**Temperature:** 25.5°C (78°F) is ideal, but they will tolerate temperatures from 22°C (72°F) to 30°C (86°F).

**GH:** For breeding, 12°dGH, moderate. Tolerates a range from 5°dGH to 35°dGH.

**pH:** 7.2 is ideal, but will tolerate 6.5 to 8.5 well. Sudden, large pH changes can be fatal.

**Hardiness:** The three-spot gourami prefers good filtration, but may be the sole survivor in a tank without it. Be sure the tank is warm enough. The fish must be able to breathe a bit of air at the water surface.

**Feeding:** Three-spot gouramis will eat everything from dried oatmeal to bits of earthworm and plants. They relish live food such as mosquito larvae or brine shrimp. Offer lettuce occasionally. Flake or pellet food is acceptable, but should have some vegetable content. Feed daily.

**Special requirements:** Observe how your three-spot gouramis interact and eat, especially when they are new to the aquarium. Either a single gourami, or a group of three or more is best.

**Compatible tankmates:** Most community fish, such as tetras, clown loaches, and kuhli loaches. For a more active tank, barbs of all types, red-tailed sharks, giant danios, and a geophagus make good tank-mates. Provide plenty of caves and plants for cover.

**Avoid these tankmates:** Do not put three-spot gouramis in with aggressive fish such as an oscar, jack dempsey, or African cichlids. Baby fish of any kind will be snack food for the gouramis.

**Related species:** Moonlight, snake-skinned, and pearl gourami, other labyrinth fish.

**Breeding:** Three-spot gouramis are egg-layers. There are usually no color differences between males and females. The back of the dorsal fin, on the male, is slightly pointed and extends just past the point where the tail meets the body. The female's dorsal fin is rounded, and ends before the tail begins. The male builds a bubble nest. Lower the water level and prevent surface agitation from destroying the nest. Remove the female after spawning and the male after the eggs hatch. Feed the fry infusoria, or liquid fry food.

# PARADISE FISH

Paradise fish (*Macropodus opercularis*) are often available, but males can be quite aggressive toward one another during the breeding season, so they do not mix very well. Females are slightly smaller and less colorful than males. This very hardy little Asian fish can survive in water temperatures as low as 13°C (55°F), although at these temperatures it is nowhere near as colorful. The fish appreciate some plant cover and subdued lighting. These fish accept all foods, but prefer live food.

**Variations:** There are several color variants of this species, including black and albino forms. Albino paradise fish are pink with red stripes.

**Origin:** Burma, Malaysia, Southeast Asia, Thailand, Vietnam, Borneo, Sumatra, and the Indo-Australian Archipelago. They live in shallow water low in dissolved oxygen.

**Temperature:** 21°C (70°F) is ideal, but they will tolerate temperatures from 16°C (61°F) to 26°C (79°F).

**GH:** For breeding, 12°dGH, moderate. Tolerates a range from 5°dGH to 30°dGH.

**pH:** 7.2 is ideal, but will tolerate 6.0 to 8.0 well.

**Hardiness:** Paradise fish are very hardy. They will tolerate a wide range of temperatures, and usually survive poor water conditions due to cycling. Paradise fish must be able to breathe a bit of air at the water surface.

**Feeding:** Paradise fish are omnivores, eating large flakes and tablets, but relishing live food such as mosquito larvae. Feed daily.

**Special requirements:** Observe how your paradise fish interacts and eats, especially when it is new to the aquarium. Either a single paradise fish or a group of two females and one male is best.

**Compatible tankmates:** Most community fish, such as gouramis, tetras, clown loaches, a red-tailed shark, catfish. Provide plenty of caves and plants for cover.

**Avoid these tankmates:** Do not put paradise fish in with aggressive fish such as an oscar, jack dempsey, or African cichlids. Putting two male paradise fish in the same tank should be avoided. If your paradise fish seems stressed, rearrange and add more plants or driftwood for cover. Baby fish of any kind will probably be snack food for the paradise fish. If a tank isn't working out, the paradise fish can be kept in a bowl, like a betta. The bowl should be large, have air space above the water, and be covered to keep the fish from jumping out.

**Related species:** Gouramis and bettas. Not a close genetic relationship.

**Breeding:** Paradise fish are egg-layers. The male paradise fish generally shows brighter colors, but the difference can be subtle. The back of the dorsal fin, on the male gourami, is slightly more pointed, and a bit longer. The tail on the male may be double. The female's dorsal fin is slightly shorter, and the tail may be less full and shorter. The male builds a bubble nest beneath a large leaf. Lower the water level, and raise the temperature to 24°C (75°F) to encourage spawning. Prevent surface agitation from destroying the nest. Remove the female after spawning, or the male may bully her to death. Remove the male after the eggs hatch. Feed the fry infusoria, then brine shrimp.

# GIANT GOURAMI

The very impressive giant gourami (*Osphronemus gorami*) can grow to 67.5cm (27in) long and is best kept as a single specimen "pet" in a very large tank or with other large species. It is vital to keep the water clean, which may be a problem as the fish eats a great deal of food and creates a lot of waste. Good biological filtration is essential; for best results, couple this with an external mechanical filter.

**Variations:** When young, may be confused with the chocolate gourami due to similar coloring. The similarity ends there.

**Origin:** China, eastern India, Java, and Malaysia. They are sometimes raised as food fish.

**Temperature:** 25°C (77°F) is ideal, but they will tolerate temperatures from 20°C (68°F) to 30°C (86°F).

**GH:** For breeding, 12°dGH, moderate. Tolerates a range from 5°dGH to 25°dGH.

**pH:** 7.2 is ideal, but will tolerate 6.5 to 8.0 well. Sudden, large pH changes can be fatal.

**Hardiness:** Giant gouramis are relatively hardy, but good filtration is required due to their size, the quantity they eat, and the sheer volume of waste. Like most labyrinth fish, they must be able to breathe air at the water surface.

**Feeding:** Giant gouramis will readily eat everything from vegetables and fruit to worms, beef heart, and raw fish. They will also eat large quantities of large flakes, tablets, and smaller fish. Feed daily.

**Special requirements:** A very large aquarium, preferably 150cm (60in) long, holding about 400 liters (100 gallons) of water.

**Compatible tankmates:** Larger fish when the "giant" is young. As it gets older, most of them will become dinner. Provide plenty of floating plants for cover.

**Avoid these tankmates:** Smaller fish. Giant gouramis will start eating smaller tankmates when the "giant" is only 10cm (4in) long. It can grow to 67.5cm (27 in) in length.

**Related species:** Gouramis, bettas, paradise fish.

**Breeding:** Giant gouramis are egg-layers. The dorsal and anal fins of the male are pointed. On the female, these are rounded. Due to their size, breeding is not recommended. If they do breed, the male builds a round nest using bits of plants. The eggs will be laid near and pushed into the nest. He will guard the nest until the young fish are ready to leave it, in about two weeks.

# CHARACINS TETRAS TO PIRANHAS

This group of fish comes mainly from the Southern American continent, with a lesser number originating in Africa. They are varied in size and shape, and diverse in their behavior and feeding habits. Most characins shoal in nature. They often come from the slow-moving rivers of the rainforests, where the water is soft and acidic. Many are carnivorous, but most are omnivorous, taking a wide range of foods.

Tetras are some of the smallest and most beautiful aquarium fish; in fact, they include some of the smallest fish in the world. Tetras are shoaling fish in nature and will shoal in the aquarium too, if given the chance. They are midwater swimmers and feeders and very active. In a gentle mixed community, Corydoras catfish, livebearers, and other small, non-aggressive fish make good tankmates for tetras.

Hatchetfish are members of the Characin family. They are surface-feeders and dwellers. They can rise progressively above the surface in much the same way as a hydrofoil and often skim over the surface of the water for up to 2m (6.5ft). This is because they have developed long pectoral fins that they can "beat" like wings. A tight fitting cover on their tank is needed.

Pencilfish are also characins. They are very slim with pointed mouths. They originate from the soft waters of the South American rainforests, so set up their tank accordingly.

Piranhas and pacus are the largest characins. Both can reach 30cm (12in) long. Provide an aquarium at least 120cm (48in) long, with immaculate filtration, for these shy, retiring creatures. But don't keep them with smaller fish.

# BLACK NEON TETRA

The black neon tetra (*Hyphessobrycon herbertaxelrodi*) enjoys an ever-growing popularity due to its harmonious temperament and graceful schooling behavior. Black neons reach only 4cm (1.5in) in length. They are not actually related to true neons, and demand better water quality and a more varied diet.

**Origin:** South America. Now generally captive-bred.

**Temperature:** 25°C (77°F) is ideal, but they will tolerate temperatures from 23°C (73°F) to 27°C (81°F).

**GH:** 6°dGH, soft. Tolerates from 5°dGH to 15°dGH.

**pH:** 6.5 is ideal, but will tolerate 5.5 to 7.5 well. Avoid sudden changes in pH.

**Hardiness:** Black neons demand excellent water quality. Water filtered through peat may be desirable, although they tolerate higher pH and hardness if it rises gradually. They are intolerant of nitrite, and should not be used to cycle a tank.

**Feeding:** A high quality flake alternated with small live foods such as mosquito larvae or brine shrimp. The species requires a varied diet. Feed daily.

**Compatible tankmates:** Gentle tankmates such as other tetras, bala sharks, dwarf gouramis, loaches, and corydoras catfish. Can be kept with discus. Enjoys a densely planted aquarium with a variety of plants included for cover.

**Avoid these tankmates:** Silver dollars or other large mouthed fish. Also, avoid barbs, giant danios, and more aggressive fish.

**Breeding:** Black neon tetras are egg-layers. The female has a slightly more prominent stomach, while males are slimmer. To prepare fish for breeding, feed ample live food such as mosquito larvae. Move the adults to a separate breeding tank with a sponge filter, a pH of 6.0, and soft water. After eggs are laid and fertilized, move the parents back to the main tank. The young will hatch in about three days. Feed the fry infusoria or liquid fry food, gradually moving up to larger food.

# BLACK PHANTOM TETRAS

Black phantom tetras (*Megalamphodus megalopterus*) are an elegant, adaptable addition to any community aquarium. They grow to about 4cm (1.6in)—maybe a little more. They do not demand perfect conditions and will tolerate harder water than their more delicate cousins. Black phantoms should be kept in shoals of at least five fish. In a group, they are calmer and tolerant of many different tank-mates. They are ideal in a peaceful community aquarium containing fish that are not too large. Dense plants or thickets of fine-leaved plants, such as cabomba make the fish feel at home.

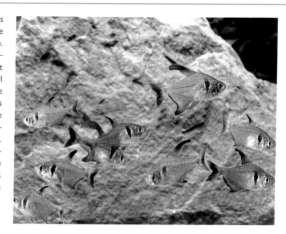

**Origin:** Brazil, South America.

**Temperature:** 25°C (77°F) is ideal, but they will tolerate temperatures from 22°C (72°F) to 28°C (82°F).

**GH:** 10°dGH, moderate. Tolerates a range from 6°dGH to 18°dGH.

**pH:** 6.8 is ideal, but will tolerate 6.0 to 7.8 well. Avoid sudden changes in pH.

**Hardiness:** Black phantoms prefer good water quality, and should not be used to cycle a tank.

**Feeding:** A high quality flake alternated with small live foods such as mosquito larvae or brine shrimp. Will nibble on bottom-feeder's pellets. Feed daily.

**Compatible tankmates:** Virtually any community fish. Black phantoms can be kept with livebearers, gouramis, other tetras, angelfish, loaches, corydoras catfish, red-tailed sharks. They can be kept with barbs and fast-swimming danios as well. Enjoys a densely planted aquarium with a variety of plants for cover.

**Avoid these tankmates:** African cichlids, large-mouthed fish such as oscars, adult geophagus, etc.

**Breeding:** Black phantom tetras are egg-layers. The female black phantom has a slightly more prominent stomach, and may have a reddened area on her adipose fin. Males are slimmer. To prepare fish for breeding, feed ample live food such as mosquito larvae. Prepare a separate breeding tank, without gravel, just a sponge filter (with a live biological filter cultured in it), a pH of 6.0 and soft water. Temperature should be between 24°C (75°F) and 26°C (79°F). Provide spawning material such as anchored fine-leaved plants, floating ferns, or green nylon wadding. When courtship seems to have begun, move the adults to the breeding tank. Feed the minimum live food necessary to encourage breeding. About 50 to 300 eggs will be released. After eggs are laid and fertilized, move the parents back to the main tank. The young will hatch in about three days. Feed the fry infusoria, followed by brine shrimp, gradually moving up to very small flake food. If feeding only flake food, feed a small portion several times a day.

# BLEEDING HEART TETRA

Bleeding heart tetras (*Hyphessobrycon erythrostigma*) are a delicate jewel of the tetra family. They require fairly precise environmental conditions and rarely breed in an aquarium of any size. They grow to about 4cm (1.6in)—maybe a little more. They require very soft water, a tank located in a quiet room, and gentle tankmates. They are ideal in a peaceful community aquarium containing fish that are not too large, too small, or too nippy and are happiest if kept in a shoal in soft, slightly acidic water.

**Origin:** Peru, South America.

**Temperature:** 25°C (77°F) is ideal, but they will tolerate temperatures from 23°C (73°F) to 28°C (82°F).

**GH:** 6°dGH, soft to moderate. Tolerates a range from 4°dGH to 12°dGH.

**pH:** 6.4 is ideal, but will tolerate 6.0 to 7.2. Avoid sudden changes in pH.

**Hardiness:** Bleeding heart tetras are delicate. Under no circumstances should they be used to cycle a tank.

**Feeding:** A high quality flake alternated with small live foods such as mosquito larvae or brine shrimp. Will nibble on bottom-feeder's pellets. Feed daily.

**Compatible tankmates:** Many gentle community fish. Bleeding heart tetras can be kept with livebearers, dwarf gouramis, other tetras, angelfish, loaches, corydoras cat-fish, red-tailed sharks. Watch for aggression problems, even with gentle species. If the bleeding hearts are picked on, they may die of stress. Have an extra tank ready, in case they, or an aggressive fish, needs to be removed. Bleeding heart tetras enjoy a densely planted aquarium with a variety of plants for cover.

**Avoid these tankmates:** African cichlids, large-mouthed fish such as oscars or adult geophagus. Also avoid barbs or other fish that nip fins regularly.

**Breeding:** Bleeding heart tetras are egg-layers, rarely bred in captivity. This may contribute to their scarcity in pet stores. Once a commonly kept tropical fish, it has been several years since the author has seen a bleeding heart tetra for sale in a pet shop.

# BLUE FLAME TETRA

The blue flame tetra was formerly sold as the red/blue Colombian tetra, but the name was too long. A latin name has not been assigned yet, but they will probably belong to the Hyphessobrycon Genus. They have only been available in pet shops since about 1996, and may be difficult to locate, though the search is well worth the effort. They are as undemanding and adaptable as the black phantom, but their shimmering pale blue accented by flame fins provides a delightful accent to any community aquarium. Blue flame tetras should be kept in shoals of at least five fish. In a group, they are calmer, and tolerant of many different tankmates.

**Origin:** South America. Species breeding and refinement done in aquariums in Germany.

**Temperature:** 25°C (77°F) is ideal, but they will tolerate temperatures from 22°C (72°F) to 28°C (82°F).

**GH:** 10°dGH, moderate. Tolerates from 6°dGH to 18°dGH.

**pH:** 6.8 is ideal, but will tolerate 6.5 to 7.8 well. Avoid sudden changes in pH.

**Hardiness:** Blue flame tetras prefer good water quality, and should not be used to cycle a tank.

**Feeding:** A high quality flake alternated with small live foods such as mosquito larvae or brine shrimp. May nibble on bottom-feeder's pellets. Feed daily.

**Compatible tankmates:** Virtually any community fish. Blue flame tetras can be kept with livebearers, gouramis, other tetras, angelfish, loaches, corydoras catfish, red tailed sharks. Enjoys a densely planted aquarium with a variety of plants for cover. Can also be kept with neon blue dwarf rainbowfish, Congo tetras, and discus.

**Avoid these tankmates:** Should not be kept with African cichlids, large-mouthed fish such as oscars, adult geophagus, etc.

**Breeding:** Blue flame tetras are egg-layers. The female blue flame has a slightly more prominent stomach and swim bladder. Males are slimmer. To prepare fish for breeding, feed ample live food such as mosquito larvae. Prepare a separate breeding tank, without gravel, just a sponge filter (with a live biological filter cultured in it), a pH of 6.5 and soft water. Temperature should be between 24°C (75°F) and 26°C (79°F). Provide spawning material such as anchored fine-leaved plants, floating ferns, or green nylon wadding. When courtship seems to have begun, move the adults to the breeding tank. Feed the minimum live food necessary to encourage breeding. About 50 to 300 eggs will be released. After eggs are laid and fertilized, move the parents back to the main tank. The young will hatch in about three days. Feed the fry infusoria, followed by brine shrimp, gradually moving up to very small flake food. If feeding only flake food, feed a small portion several times a day.

# CARDINAL TETRA

A school of cardinal tetras (*Paracheirodon axelrodi*) can add a splash of glowing color to the cool greens of a planted aquarium. Surprisingly hardy, for such a small fish, they may live for years in good water conditions.

Keep a shoal of at least four fish. Cardinals have a full-length red stripe along their body, while neon tetras have a half-length red stripe.

**Origin:** South America, in slow or standing water.

**Temperature:** 25°C (77°F) is ideal, but they will tolerate temperatures from 23°C (73°F) to 27°C (81°F).

**GH:** 4°dGH, very soft. Tolerates a range from 4°dGH to perhaps 10°dGH. Do not add calcium or magnesium salts, or stones that might leach these minerals into your water.

**pH:** In the wild, a pH of 5.8 is ideal for cardinals. However, tank-bred cardinal tetras seem to accept an average pH of 7.0 without a problem, and they may adapt to 7.6 well. Check dealer's pH before adjusting your tank pH. Avoid sudden changes in pH.

**Hardiness:** Cardinal tetras require excellent water quality, and should not be used to cycle a tank.

**Feeding:** A high quality flake alternated with small live foods such as very small mosquito larvae or brine shrimp. Feed daily.

**Compatible tankmates:** Black neon tetras, dwarf gouramis, corydoras catfish, loaches, bala sharks, and other gentle community fish that prefer soft water. Once the cardinals are large enough they may be kept with discus. Enjoys a densely planted aquarium with a variety of plants for cover.

**Avoid these tankmates:** Cardinals should not be kept with large mouthed or aggressive fish.

**Breeding:** Cardinal tetras are egg-layers. The female cardinal is somewhat heavier, males are slimmer. To prepare fish for breeding, feed ample live food such as small mosquito larvae. Prepare a separate breeding tank, without gravel, just a sponge filter (with a live biological filter cultured in it), a pH of 6 and soft water, only 1–2°dGH. Temperature should be 24°C (75°F). Provide a green nylon mat for spawning material. The male embraces the female as she spawns, turning her almost vertical. Remove the adults after spawning. Leave the tank darkened. About 130 eggs will be laid. After 24 hours the fry will hatch. Feed small live foods, gradually moving up to very small flake food.

The beautiful congo tetras (*Phenacogrammus interruptus*) grow to about 9cm (3.5in) and adults have very long flowing fins. All the fins, especially the tail, the anal fin, and the pectoral fins, have a ragged appearance and a whitish edge. These fins are longest in males. Keep Congo tetras in a shoal of at least four fish. They will do best in an aquarium in a quiet room, with little human traffic, and no one tapping on the glass.

**Origin:** Zaire, Africa.

**Temperature:** 25°C (77°F) is ideal, but they will tolerate temperatures from 24°C (75°F) to 27°C (81°F).

**GH:** 4°dGH, soft. Tolerates a range from 4°dGH to 18°dGH. Do not add calcium or magnesium salts, or stones that might leach these minerals into your water.

**pH:** In the wild, a pH of 6.2 is ideal for Congo tetras. However, they seem to accept an average pH of 7.0 without a problem, and they may adapt to 7.6 well. Check dealer's pH before adjusting your tank. Avoid sudden changes in pH.

**Hardiness:** Congo tetras require excellent water quality, and should not be used to cycle a tank.

**Feeding:** A high quality flake alternated with small live foods such as very small mosquito larvae or brine shrimp. Feed daily. Congo tetras will often wait and not touch the food while the keeper is near the tank.

**Compatible tankmates:** Black neon tetras, loaches, dwarf gouramis, corydoras catfish, bala sharks, and other gentle community fish that like soft water. Congo tetras may be kept with discus. Enjoys a fairly slow moving, densely planted aquarium with a various plants for cover.

**Avoid these tankmates:** Congo tetras should not be kept with fast-swimming, large mouthed, or aggressive fish. Avoid barbs, most sharks, and danios. They should not be kept with African cichlids.

**Breeding:** Congo tetras are egg-layers. The female congo is somewhat heavier. Males are slimmer, and the anal fin is shaped differently. To prepare fish for breeding, turn up the light to simulate sunlight. They are more likely to spawn in shallow water, so preparing a breeding tank with a bright light, low water level, without gravel, just an air driven sponge filter (with a live biological filter cultured in it), a pH of 6.2, and soft water, about 4°dGH. Temperature should be 25°C (77°F). About 300 eggs should drop to the bottom. Remove the adults after spawning. After six days the fry will hatch. Feed infusoria the first week, brine shrimp the second week, and graduate to very small flake food the third week.

# GLOWLIGHT TETRA

The elegant glowlight tetra (*Hemigrammus erythrozonus*) grows to a maximum of 5cm (2in) and then only rarely. Its long, slim body is transparent, with a glowing orange line running along it. This color is also evident at the base of the dorsal fin and all the fins have touches of white on the edges. Like all tetras, it likes to shoal and makes an attractive display if kept in a large group. Glowlight tetras prefer softly lit, heavily planted tanks with plenty of small, peaceful fish for company.

**Origin:** Guyana, South America. Most are now tank-bred.

**Temperature:** 25°C (77°F) is ideal, but they will tolerate temperatures from 24°C (74°F) to 28°C (82°F).

**GH:** 6°dGH, soft. Tolerates a range from 4°dGH to perhaps 15°dGH. Do not add calcium or magnesium salts, or stones that might leach these minerals into your water.

**pH:** 6.8 is ideal, but will tolerate 6.5 to 7.8 well. Avoid sudden changes in pH.

**Hardiness:** Glowlight tetras require excellent water quality, and should not be used to cycle a tank.

**Feeding:** They happily accept most foods. A high quality flake alternated with small live foods such as very small mosquito larvae or brine shrimp is recommended. Feed daily.

**Compatible tankmates:** Neon or black neon tetras, cardinal tetras, dwarf gouramis, corydoras catfish, loaches, bala sharks, and other gentle community fish that prefer soft water. Enjoys a variety of plants for cover.

**Avoid these tankmates:** Glowlight tetras should not be kept with large mouthed or aggressive fish.

**Breeding:** Glowlight tetras are egg-layers. The female glowlight is larger and more muscular. Males are slimmer. To prepare fish for breeding, feed ample live food such as small mosquito larvae. Prepare a separate breeding tank, without gravel, just a sponge filter (with a live biological filter cultured in it), with soft, peaty water, and a temperature of 28°C (82°F). Provide several vertical, pinnate plants. Put a school in the tank at a time. The pairs will spawn between the plants. Remove the adults after spawning. When the fry hatch, feed small live foods, gradually moving up to very small flake food.

Lemon tetras (*Hyphessobrycon pulchripinnis*) are attractive, versatile community fish. They are not overly delicate, but should not be used to cycle a tank. Purchase a shoal of at least seven lemon tetras for their comfort, and to see true schooling or shoaling behavior. Their colors are pale when they are unhappy or nervous. As they become accustomed to the aquarium, their pale yellow brightens. They do best in shoals of seven or more. A large shoal of 20 is delightful in a large planted aquarium, and spontaneous egg laying often occurs.

**Origin:** Brazil, South America.

**Temperature:** 25°C (77°F) is ideal, but they will tolerate temperatures from 22°C (72°F) to 28°C (82°F).

**GH:** 8°dGH, moderate. Tolerates a range from 6°dGH to 18°dGH.

**pH:** 7.0 ideal, but will tolerate 6.5 to 7.8 well. Avoid sudden changes in pH.

**Hardiness:** Lemon tetras prefer good water quality, and should not be used to cycle a tank.

**Feeding:** A high quality flake alternated with small live foods such as mosquito larvae or brine shrimp. Will nibble on bottom-feeder's pellets. Feed daily.

**Compatible tankmates:** Virtually any community fish. Lemon tetras can be kept with livebearers, gouramis, other tetras, angelfish, loaches, corydoras catfish, red-tailed sharks. They can also be kept with rams or kribensis, or a betta. Their versatility in community tanks is part of their charm. Enjoys a variety of plants for cover. Lemon tetras will nibble soft-leaved plants.

**Avoid these tankmates:** African cichlids, large-mouthed fish such as oscars, adult geophagus, etc.

**Breeding:** Lemon tetras are egg-layers. Male lemon tetras will dance, noses down, fins on display, to impress the females. Eggs and sperm are scattered liberally in the water, some finding attachment on live plants. If the plants with fertilized eggs are moved to another tank, the eggs will hatch. Left in the tank, the eggs will be eaten by the lemon tetras. The fry will feed on tender plants, such as elodea. Supplement with a tiny amount of crumbled flake.

# NEON TETRA

Neon tetras (*Paracheirodon innesi*) originate in the Amazon and only grow to about 4cm (1.5in) or a little more in length. They are among the slimmest tetras and are renowned for their colors. The top of the back is olive green and below this runs an electric blue line from the top of the tail through the eye. Below this line is a bright silver belly and behind this is a bright blood-red anal section.

**Origin:** Amazon, South America. Generally captive-bred.

**Temperature:** 25°C (77°F) is ideal, but they will tolerate temperatures from 23°C (73°F) to 27.5°C (82°F).

**GH:** 6°dGH, soft. Tolerates a range from 5°dGH to 15°dGH.

**pH:** 7.0 is ideal, but will tolerate 6.0 to 8.0 well. Avoid sudden changes in pH.

**Hardiness:** Neon tetras demand excellent water quality. Water filtered through peat may be desirable, although they tolerate higher pH and hardness if it rises gradually. They are intolerant of nitrite, and should not be used to cycle a tank. Poor water conditions promote neon tetra disease, which begins with fading colors and ends with death. Perform regular water changes.

**Feeding:** Neon tetras will accept most flake foods, along with freeze-dried tubifex worms, brine shrimp, and daphnia, although they much prefer frozen or live foods. A high quality flake alternated with small live foods such as mosquito larvae or brine shrimp. Feed daily.

**Compatible tankmates:** Gentle tankmates such as other small tetras, bala sharks, dwarf gouramis, loaches, and corydoras catfish. Can also be kept with discus. Enjoys a densely planted aquarium with a variety of plants for cover.

**Avoid these tankmates:** Silver dollars, bettas, angelfish, gouramis, or other large mouthed fish. Also, avoid barbs, giant danios, and more aggressive fish.

**Breeding:** Neon tetras are egg-layers. The female has a slightly more prominent stomach, while males are slimmer. To prepare fish for breeding, feed ample live food such as mosquito larvae. Move the adults to a separate breeding tank with a sponge filter, a pH of 6.4, and soft water. After eggs are laid and fertilized, move the parents back to the main tank. The young will hatch in about three days. Feed the fry infusoria or liquid fry food, gradually moving up to larger food.

# RED SERPAE TETRA

Red serpae tetras (*Hyphessobrycon serpae*) are a brilliant addition to most community aquariums. Their color varies, from a ruddy orange to an almost brilliant red-orange depending on their diet. Feed live foods weekly to see their true color. They grow to about 4cm (1.6in)—maybe a little more. They do not demand perfect conditions and will tolerate harder water than their more delicate cousins. Red serpae tetras should be kept in shoals of at least six fish. In a group, they are calmer, and tolerant of many different tankmates. They are ideal in a community aquarium containing fish about their size. A roomy tank, broad rather than tall, with dense plantings of real or artificial plants can make the fish feel at home. They are nippy toward other species when they are nervous.

**Origin:** Paraguay, South America.

**Temperature:** 25°C (77°F) is ideal, but they will tolerate temperatures from 22°C (72°F) to 28°C (83°F).

**GH:** 8°dGH, moderate. Tolerates 6°dGH to 18°dGH.

**pH:** 6.6 is ideal, but will tolerate 6.0 to 7.8 well. Avoid sudden changes in pH.

**Hardiness:** Red serpae tetras prefer good water quality, and should not be used to cycle a tank.

**Feeding:** A high quality flake alternated with small live foods such as mosquito larvae or brine shrimp. Will nibble on bottom-feeder's pellets. Feed daily.

**Compatible tankmates:** Red serpae tetras should always be kept in a group of at least six. As a shoal, they can be kept with livebearers, gouramis, other large tetras, loaches, corydoras catfish, and red-tailed sharks. They can be kept with barbs and fast-swimming danios as well. Their versatility in community tanks is part of their charm. Enjoys a roomy, densely planted aquarium with a variety of plants for cover. They have been known to nip the fins of angels and other slow-moving, large fish.

**Avoid these tankmates:** Do not keep red serpae tetras with neon, cardinal, or other small tetras as they are aggressive toward the smaller species. Also to be avoided are angelfish, bettas, African cichlids, large-mouthed fish such as oscars, adult geophagus, etc.

**Breeding:** Red serpae tetras are egg-layers. The female red serpae has a slightly more prominent stomach. Males are slimmer. To prepare fish for breeding, feed ample live food such as mosquito larvae. Prepare a separate breeding tank, without gravel, just a sponge filter (with a live biological filter cultured in it), a pH of 6.4 and soft water. Temperature should be between 24°C (75°F) and 26°C (79°F) Provide spawning material such as anchored fine-leaved plants, floating ferns, or green nylon wadding. When courtship seems to have begun, move the adults to the breeding tank. Feed the minimum live food necessary to encourage breeding. About 50 to 300 eggs will be released. After eggs are laid and fertilized, move the parents back to the main tank. The young will hatch in about three days. Feed the fry infusoria, followed by brine shrimp, gradually moving up to very small flake food. If feeding only flake food, feed a small portion several times a day.

# RED-EYED TETRA

Red-eyed tetras, also known as yellow-banded moenkhausia (*Moenkhausia sanctaefilomenae*) are a very popular community fish. Their silvery bodies are marked only with a wide black band across the tail, but their eyes are a brilliant red. They grow to about 4cm (1.6in)—maybe a little more. They do not demand perfect conditions and will tolerate harder water than their more delicate cousins. Red-eyed tetras should be kept in shoals of at least six fish. In a group, they are calmer and tolerant of many different tankmates. They are ideal in a community aquarium containing fish about their size, or larger. A roomy tank, with several areas of plantings surrounding an open swim area will help them to feel comfortable.

**Origin:** Paraguay, South America. Most are captive-bred.

**Temperature:** 25°C (77°F) is ideal, but they will tolerate temperatures from 24°C (75°F) to 28°C (83°F).

**GH:** 8°dGH, moderate. Tolerates a range from 6°dGH to 18°dGH.

**pH:** 7.2 is ideal, but will tolerate 6.0 to 8.5 well. Avoid sudden changes in pH.

**Hardiness:** Red-eyed tetras prefer good water quality, and should not be used to cycle a tank.

**Feeding:** A high quality flake alternated with small live foods such as mosquito larvae or brine shrimp. Will nibble on bottom-feeder's pellets. Feed daily.

**Compatible tankmates:** Red-eyed tetras should always be kept in a group of at least four. As a shoal, they can be kept with livebearers, gouramis, other large tetras, loaches, corydoras catfish, and red tailed sharks. They can be kept with barbs and fast-swimming danios as well. Enjoys a roomy aquarium with a variety of plants for cover.

**Avoid these tankmates:** Do not keep with neon, cardinal, or other small tetras. They are aggressive toward the smaller species. Angelfish, bettas, African cichlids, large-mouthed fish such as oscars, adult Geophagus, etc, should also be avoided.

**Breeding:** Red-eyed tetras are egg-layers. The female has a slightly more prominent stomach. Males are slimmer. To prepare fish for breeding, feed ample live food such as mosquito larvae. Prepare a separate breeding tank, without gravel, just a sponge filter (with a live biological filter cultured in it), a pH of 6.4 and soft water. Temperature should be between 24°C (75°F) and 26°C (79°F). Provide spawning material such as anchored fine-leaved plants, floating ferns, or green nylon wadding. When courtship seems to have begun, move the adults to the breeding tank. Feed the minimum live food necessary to encourage breeding. About 50 to 300 eggs will be released. After eggs are laid and fertilized, move the parents back to the main tank. The young will hatch in about one or two days. Feed the fry powdered flake food. After a week, feed brine shrimp, gradually moving up to very small flake food. If feeding only flake food, feed a small portion several times a day.

# WEST AFRICAN RED-EYED CHARACIN

The West African red-eyed characin, (*Arnoldichthys spilopterus*) is completely peaceful and makes an ideal community fish. They can reach 7.5cm (3in) in length. Some of the scales on this fish are dark, creating a lattice pattern. The dorsal fin is quite tall and square, with a black to charcoal gray blotch in the middle, and a black line runs horizontally through the tail. The body colors of this fish are quite subtle, the top half being purple and brown, the bottom yellow and green. Males tend to be far more splendid in coloration than the females. This fish requires a shallow tank, 30cm (12in) deep, with a dark bottom. When frightened, the fish will dive for cover, so choose gravel without sharp edges. Provide some plantings but plenty of open swimming area. Do not keep West African red-eyed characins with aggressive fish; they are very timid. Their tank should be in a room without a lot of human traffic.

**Origin:** West Africa.

**Temperature:** 25°C (77°F) is ideal, but they will tolerate temperatures from 22°C (72°F) to 28°C (82°F).

**GH:** 12°dGH, moderate. Tolerates a range from 6°dGH to 18°dGH.

**pH:** 6.6 is ideal, but will tolerate 6.0 to 7.5 well. Avoid sudden changes in pH.

**Hardiness:** Requires good water quality, and should not be used to cycle a tank.

**Feeding:** A high quality flake alternated with small live foods such as mosquito larvae or brine shrimp. Will nibble on bottom-feeder's pellets. Feed daily.

**Compatible tankmates:** Other quiet community fish with similar living requirements. Congo tetras, black phantom tetras, loaches, and corydoras catfish would make good tankmates.

**Avoid these tankmates:** Do not be keep with aggressive or fast-swimming fish, such as danios, cichlids, or barbs.

**Breeding:** West African red-eyed characins are egg-layers. The male's anal fin is convex, or rounded, with stripes of red, yellow, and black. The female's is straight with a black tip. To prepare fish for breeding, feed ample live food, such as mosquito larvae. Prepare a breeding tank, without gravel, just a sponge filter (with a live biological filter cultured in it), a pH of 6.6, soft water, and one or two live plants. The breeding tank bottom should have a soft surface such as sand. After eggs are laid and fertilized, move the parents back to the main tank. The young will hatch in about 30 hours. Feed them finely crumbled flake, brine shrimp, gradually moving up to crumbled egg yolk, then very small flake food. Offer small amounts several times a day.

# RED-BELLIED PACU

The red-bellied pacu (*Piaractus brachypomum*) from northern South America, is a real giant that grows to over 45cm (18in). A single specimen requires a large aquarium, 120x38x45cm (48x15x18in), 209 liters (46 gallons). It is a fruit eater, enjoying any fruit or vegetable, but it is not a vegetarian; pacus will eat virtually anything that is put into the tank, demolishing live plants, and even damaging plastic plants trying to eat the algae built up on them. They are large, laterally compressed fish, with a black back, gray belly, and red-orange throat. Aquarium water should be soft and acidic and kept very clean. Pacus are shoaling fish in their natural habitat, but a group in captivity

will need a very large tank, perhaps 600cm (240in) long. A single fish kept in a "pet aquarium" often becomes quite friendly toward its owners, and readily snacks on whole grapes. A startled or frightened adult pacu can break his tank. Do not treat a tank containing a pacu with malachite green. The pacu will die of copper poisoning. They are quite sensitive to salt as well, so avoid adding it to their aquarium.

**Origin:** Amazon, South America.

**Temperature:** 26°C (79°F) is ideal, but they will tolerate temperatures from 22°C (72°F) to 28°C (82°F).

**GH:** 6°dGH, soft. Tolerates a range from 6°dGH to 12°dGH.

**pH:** 6.8 is ideal, but will tolerate 6.5 to 7.5 well. Avoid sudden changes in pH.

**Hardiness:** A red bellied pacu requires a large tank and good water quality, and should not be used to cycle a tank. They produce a lot of waste, and do not tolerate nitrates well, so partial water changes should be weekly.

**Feeding:** Fruits and vegetables in bite size pieces, romaine lettuce hung from a clip, high quality flake or pellet food, occasional small live foods, such as insects. Feed amply daily.

**Compatible tankmates:** Large, fairly gentle fish, such as catfish.

**Avoid these tankmates:** Expensive live plants. Live plants are fine, but they will all be snack food, down to the roots. Also avoid very aggressive fish, such as African cichlids, or any fish small enough to eat.

**Breeding:** Pacus are egg-layers. The size of the aquarium required to breed them is impractical for most situations. Females have a rounder body, more coloring on the tail, less coloring on the anal fin.

Red hook silver dollars (*Metynnis hypsauchen*) are also related to the piranha. But their size is easier to accommodate in an average sized aquarium. They are a shoaling fish, and single specimens are very nervous. A shoal of silver dollars requires a large aquarium, 120x38x45cm (48x15x18in), 209 liters (46 gallons). Silver dollars can eat almost any fish food, but will demolish live plants in a tank trying to get their vegetables. They may also damage plastic plants trying to eat the algae built up on them. They are large, laterally compressed fish, with a smooth, silver skin that is extremely sensitive to medication. Do not treat a tank containing silver dollars with malachite green, as the fish will die of copper poisoning. They are quite sensitive to salt as well, so avoid adding it to their aquarium.

**Origin:** Amazon, South America.

**Temperature:** 26°C (79°F) is ideal, but they will tolerate temperatures from 22°C (72°F) to 29°C (84°F).

**GH:** 6°dGH, soft. Tolerates a range from 4°dGH to 12°dGH.

**pH:** 6.8 is ideal, but will tolerate 6.5 to 7.8 well. Avoid sudden changes in pH.

**Hardiness:** Silver dollars are so sensitive to nitrite that they detect it before a nitrite kit gives evidence. Gasping silver dollars, with their mouths moving, are a sign of biological filtration problem. They are also extremely sensitive to salt. Silver dollars should not be used to cycle a tank. They do not tolerate nitrates well, so partial water changes should be done about every 10 days.

**Feeding:** Silver dollars are herbivores, although they will eat fish food containing protein from fish meal. A balanced diet for silver dollars consists mainly of fruits and vegetables in bite size pieces, romaine lettuce hung from a clip, and high quality spirulina flake or pellet food. Feed amply, daily.

**Compatible tankmates:** Silver dollars are best kept in a school, or even in a pair. A single fish is very nervous, and may injure itself. Good companions include calm tetras, gouramis, loaches, and a geophagus or a red-tailed shark. Silver dollars may be kept with barbs if the aquarium is large enough, and if the barb school doesn't attack.

**Avoid these tankmates:** Expensive live plants. Live plants are fine, but they will all be eaten, down to the roots. Also avoid very small fish, such as neon tetras, fry of any species, African cichlids, or really aggressive fish.

**Breeding:** Red hook silver dollars are egg-layers. A mature pair in a clean tank will attempt breeding often, carelessly scattering their eggs. Females have an orange coloring on the gill and very end of the tail. Males have a pointed anal fin, which forms a bright red-orange "hook." The female pursues the male, nipping at his anal fin, to encourage mating. The pursuit goes on for some time, until they swim side by side, "shimmying," their anal fins barely touching. The eggs, perhaps 2,000 at a time, will drop to the bottom. Silver dollars will not eat their own eggs. The fry hatch in three days and are free-swimming within seven days. The baby fish will anchor themselves to the tank glass and catch minute food, preferably plankton, as it goes by.

# THREE-LINED PENCILFISH

The three-lined pencilfish (*Nannostomus trifasciatus*) is a small, very peaceful fish from South America that grows to about 5cm (2in). The body shape is very long and slim, with a pointed snout and tiny mouth. The water should be kept at about 26°C (79°F) and be soft and very slightly acidic. It is most at home in a well-planted aquarium with gentle tankmates.

**Origin:** Brazil, South America.

**Temperature:** 26°C (79°F) is ideal, but they will tolerate temperatures from 22°C (72°F) to 28°C (82°F).

**GH:** 4°dGH, soft. Tolerates a range from 6°dGH to 12°dGH.

**pH:** 6.4 is ideal, but will tolerate 5.5 to 7.0 well. Avoid sudden changes in pH.

**Hardiness:** Three-lined pencilfish require good water quality, and should not be used to cycle a tank. They do not tolerate nitrates well, change water regularly.

**Feeding:** A high quality flake alternated with small live foods such as mosquito larvae or brine shrimp. Feed in the evening.

**Compatible tankmates:** Small tetras, loaches, and corydoras catfish would make good tankmates. Adult pencilfish can be kept with discus.

**Avoid these tankmates:** Large mouthed fish or aggressive fish, especially top-feeding large mouthed fish. Barbs, angelfish, and gouramis are not suitable tankmates.

**Breeding:** Three-lined pencilfish are egg-layers. Females have a rounder body with less pronounced coloring. Offer live food such as black mosquito larvae in the evening, to prepare the adults for breeding. A breeding tank should be used, with soft water, not over 2°dGH, and a pH of 6.0. The water may be darkened slightly with peat, and the tank light should be turned off. A nylon mesh 3 to 4mm, should be placed in the tank, so that the eggs fall through to the bottom, or on plants placed below the mesh. Choose a pair of fish to attempt breeding with. They may lay only a few eggs at one time, perhaps a dozen. Once the eggs fall to the bottom the parents should be removed. The eggs hatch in one to three days. Feed infusoria or rotifers. After the seventh day, the fry should eat brine shrimp.

The marbled hatchetfish (*Gasteropelecus strigatus*) has become the most common hatchetfish in the aquarium hobby. It grows to about 8cm (3.2in) and thrives in soft, slightly acidic water at a temperature of about 26°C (79°F). Provide floating plants for cover.

**Origin:** South America.

**Temperature:** 26°C (79°F) is ideal, but they will tolerate temperatures from 22°C (72°F) to 30°C (86°F).

**GH:** 8°dGH, moderate. Tolerates a range from 6°dGH to 15°dGH.

**pH:** 6.8 is ideal, but will tolerate 6.0 to 7.5 well. Avoid sudden changes in pH.

**Hardiness:** Marbled hatchetfish require good water quality, and should not be used to cycle a tank.

**Feeding:** A high quality flake alternated with small live foods such as insects, mosquito larvae, or brine shrimp. Feed daily.

**Compatible tankmates:** Other community fish that live at lower levels. A combination of fish such as tetras, loaches, a red tailed shark, and corydoras catfish would make good tankmates.

**Avoid these tankmates:** Large mouthed fish or aggressive fish, especially top-feeding large mouthed fish. Angelfish and gouramis have been known to pick on them.

**Breeding:** Marbled hatchetfish are egg-layers. Females are fuller, and will swell with eggs prior to spawning. Offer live food such as fruit flies and mosquito larvae to prepare the adults for breeding. A breeding tank should be used, with soft water, not over 5°dGH, and a pH of 6.0. The water may be darkened with peat until it resembles strong tea. The fish will spawn on floating plants after a long courtship. Once the eggs fall to the bottom the parents should be removed. The eggs hatch in about 30 hours. Feed powdered foods. After the seventh day, the fry should eat brine shrimp.

# CYPRINIDS BARBS
# TO "SHARKS"

The Cyprinid family includes tropical barbs and sharks, as well as coldwater goldfish and carp. These species vary greatly in size; some barbs only grow to 7.5cm (3in) or less, whereas carp can grow to over 60cm (24in) and weigh as much as 22.5kg (50lb). Many of these fish live in shoals, although the sharks are often loners. Many cyprinids eat plants, so choose inexpensive, hardy live plants or plastic plants.

**Barbs:** Barbs vary from deep-bodied to long and slim. They vary in size from 5–40cm (2–16in) and are best kept in small groups of a single species. Barbs nip other fish's fins, so don't keep them with angelfish or bettas.

**Danios and Rasboras:** Danios and rasboras are top swimming cyprinids. They swim in shoals and eat near the water's surface. Danios have a reputation for nipping the fins of other species.

**Sharks:** Sharks have an erect dorsal fin and similar swimming pattern to the marine terror but the resemblance ends there. They are active swimmers but generally do not harm the other fish.

**Loaches and Botias:** Loaches are a small group of scavengers that make up the Cobitidae family of fish. They are very active, nocturnal bottom-dwellers. The botias and some cobitids possess a spine in front of the eye that they can raise to inflict considerable damage on other fish or on the unwary aquarist. Most loaches seen in aquariums are from Southeast Asia, where they live in muddy, oxygen-depleted waters. They gulp air at the surface and absorb oxygen in the gut lining to compensate.

Checkered barbs (*Barbus oligolepis*) are non-demanding members of the barb family. They are a peaceful fish when kept in small shoals. They can reach 6in (15cm) in length, but should be kept in a group of at least four fish to reduce aggression. They still should not be kept with long-finned fish such as angelfish or a betta.

**Origin**: Indonesia, Sumatra.

**Temperature**: 22.8°C (73°F) is ideal, but they will tolerate temperatures from 20°C (68°F) to 24°C (74°F).

**GH**: 6°dGH, soft. Tolerates a range from 4°dGH to 10°dGH.

**pH**: 6.4 is ideal, but will tolerate 6.0 to 7.0 well. Avoid sudden changes in pH.

**Hardiness**: Checkered barbs are relatively hardy, but should not be used to cycle a tank. Perform regular partial water changes.

**Feeding**: Checkered barbs will enjoy a high quality flake alternated with small live foods such as fresh algae, frozen green beans, and mosquito larvae. They require fresh vegetable bits to display their best color. If fresh algae isn't available, offer an algae or Spirulina wafer. Feed daily.

**Compatible tankmates**: Gouramis, a red-tailed or rainbow shark, and tetras would all be acceptable tankmates.

**Avoid these tankmates**: Expensive live plants. Live plants are fine, but they may be nipped occasionally. Also avoid very small fish, such as neon tetras, or fry of any species, African cichlids, or really aggressive fish.

**Breeding**: Checkered barbs are egg-layers. Females are fuller, and will swell with eggs prior to spawning. Offer live food, as suggested above, to prepare the adults for breeding. A breeding tank should be used, with soft water, temperature 24°C (76°F), hardness not over 5°dGH, and a pH of 6.2. Thick plantings of myriophyllum or nitella are recommended. Spawning will happen above the plants, near the surface, one egg at a time. Select a single male and female for the breeding tank. When spawning is complete, the parents should be removed. The eggs hatch in about 3 to 4 days. Feed powdered foods, followed by crumbled flake.

# ROSY BARB

The shoaling rosy barbs (*Barbus conchonius*) are excellent community fish. Their coloration is best seen in reflected light. Adult males are gold to olive-green along the back with pink flanks, their fins are tinged with pink and the dorsal fin has a deep black tip. Adult females are gold to olive-green all over, with a very slight flush of pink on the flanks. When breeding, the males take on a deep red color as they chase the egg-scattering females through thickets of plants. The fish are sexually mature at about 6cm(2.4in) and do not usually exceed 10cm (4in) in the aquarium. Provide plenty of fine-leaved plants and ample swimming space.

**Origin**: India, Bengal.

**Temperature**: 20°C (68°F) is ideal, but they will tolerate temperatures from 17.8°C (64°F) to 22°C (72°F).

**GH**: 6°dGH, soft. Tolerates a range from 4°dGH to 10°dGH.

**pH**: 6.5 is ideal, but will tolerate 6.2 to 7.4 well. Avoid sudden changes in pH.

**Hardiness**: Rosy barbs are relatively hardy, but should not be used to cycle a tank. Perform regular partial water changes.

**Feeding**: Rosy barbs will enjoy all live foods, such as bloodworms, mosquito larvae, and brine shrimp, alternated with a high quality flake food, frozen green beans, or an algae or Spirulina wafer occasionally. Feed daily.

**Compatible tankmates**: Gouramis, a red-tailed or rainbow shark, and tetras would all be acceptable tankmates.

**Avoid these tankmates**: Angelfish, bettas, other large fish with trailing fins. Expensive live plants. Live plants are fine, but they may be nipped occasionally. Also avoid very small fish, such as neon tetras, or fry of any species, African cichlids or really aggressive fish.

**Breeding**: Rosy barbs are egg-layers. Females are fuller and have less color than the males. Males develop a brilliant "rosy" abdomen when ready to spawn. Offer live food, as suggested above, to prepare the adults for breeding. A small breeding tank should be used, with only a few inches of water. The temperature should be 23°C (75°F), hardness not over 5°dGH, pH of 6.4. The bottom can have either coarse gravel, marbles, or be bare with a plastic grid for the eggs to drop through. Select a male and 2 females for breeding. Mock breeding and play will precede actual spawning. The eggs will drop to the bottom. If a grid is used, the parents can be left in the breeding tank. 400 eggs may be laid. If marbles or coarse gravel are used, remove the parents when spawning seems to be complete. The eggs will hatch in about 30 hours. Feed powdered foods, followed by crumbled flake.

# TIGER BARB

The tiger, or Sumatran, barb (*Barbus tetrazona*) only reaches about 5cm (2in) in the aquarium. These delightful, colorful little fish like to shoal, so keep them in small groups. Be sure you have at least four, or more tiger barbs. This increases the odds of having a female in the group. She seems to be a calming influence on the males, and reduces their tendencies to nip fins. Lone tiger barbs can be very nervous, which makes them aggressive and nippy. Never buy just one or two tiger barbs and add them to a community tank. Provide plenty of fine-leaved plants and ample swimming space.

**Origin**: Indonesia, Sumatra, Borneo.

**Temperature**: 25°C (77°F) is ideal, but they will tolerate temperatures from 20°C (68°F) to 28°C (83°F).

**GH**: 6°dGH, soft. Tolerates a range from 4°dGH to 12°dGH.

**pH**: 6.8 is ideal, but will tolerate 6.5 to 8.0 well. Avoid sudden changes in pH.

**Hardiness**: Tiger barbs are hardy. A group of four can be used to cycle a tank. Perform regular partial water changes.

**Feeding**: Tiger barbs require a high quality flake food, supplemented with live foods for variety. They will enjoy all live foods, such as bloodworms, mosquito larvae and brine shrimp, alternated with a high quality flake food, frozen green beans, or an algae or Spirulina wafer occasionally. Feed daily.

**Compatible tankmates**: Gouramis, other barbs, a red-tailed or rainbow shark, and tetras would all be acceptable tankmates.

**Avoid these tankmates**: Angelfish, bettas, other large fish with trailing fins. Expensive live plants. Live plants are fine, but they may be nipped occasionally. Also avoid very small fish, such as neon tetras, or fry of any species, African cichlids or really aggressive fish.

**Breeding**: Tiger barbs are egg-layers. Females are fuller-bodied than the males. Males are thinner and have slightly brighter coloring. Males may conduct a mating dance to display their readiness to mate. A group of males, three or more, may swim nose-to-nose while the entire group whirls in a horizontal circle, like an aquatic "ring-of-roses." The female may display little interest, or watch from a quiet corner of the tank. A small breeding tank with a sponge filter should be used, with only a few inches of water. The temperature should be 27°C (80°F), hardness not over 12°dGH, pH 6.8. The bottom can have either marbles, or be bare with a plastic grid for the eggs to drop through. Put the female in a day or two early, with some floating plants to make her feel secure. Feed live foods, as suggested above, or brine shrimp. Select a male with good color definition and add him to the tank in the evening. Mock breeding and play will precede actual spawning. Check for eggs in the morning. About 200 eggs will drop to the bottom. If a grid is used, the parents can be left in the breeding tank. If marbles are used, remove the parents when spawning seems to be complete. The eggs will hatch in about 30 hours. Feed powdered foods, followed by crumbled flake. The breeding tank will require good filtration and regular water changes while the fry grow.

# TIN FOIL BARB

The tin foil barb (*Barbus schwanefeldi*) is one of the fastest growing tropical aquarium fish. They can reach 35cm (13in), so choose a large aquarium, at least 120 x 38 x 45cm (48 x 15 x 18in) 209 liters (46 gallons). These delightful large fish are not suited for planted aquariums, at least not if you value your plants. They are, however, very dramatic in a large tank with plenty of swimming room. They may be happiest in a shoal, but they do equally well in a community tank with large fast-swimming tankmates. Provide plenty of plants along the sides and back of the tank for smaller fish to hide in. Be sure there is a large, open area with ample swimming space.

**Origin:** Thailand, Sumatra, Borneo, Southeast Asia, Malayan Peninusula.

**Temperature:** 22°C (72°F) is ideal, but they will tolerate temperatures from 21°C (70°F) to 27°C (81°F).

**GH:** 6°dGH, soft. Tolerates a range from 4°dGH to 12°dGH.

**pH:** 6.8 is ideal, but will tolerate 6.5 to 8.0 well. Avoid sudden changes in pH.

**Hardiness:** Tin foil barbs are hardy. They can be used to cycle a large 220 liters (55 gallons) tank. Perform regular partial water changes.

**Feeding:** Tin foil barbs require a high quality flake food, supplemented for variety. They particularly enjoy sinking pelleted food, such as Spirulina wafers. The tin foil barbs will cheerfully steal pellets from the bottom feeders and use them for "sport" before eating them. Frozen green beans are also popular. They enjoy larger live foods, insects, as well as bloodworms, mosquito larvae, and brine shrimp. Feed daily.

**Compatible tankmates:** Giant danios, gouramis, other barbs, a red-tailed or rainbow shark, large tetras, geophagus, clown loaches, and a pleco would all be acceptable tankmates.

**Avoid these tankmates:** Delicate plants, small fish, angelfish, bettas, other large fish with trailing fins. Expensive live plants. Live plants are fine, but they may be nipped occasionally. Also avoid very small fish, such as neon tetras, or fry of any species, African cichlids, or really aggressive fish.

**Breeding:** Tin foil barbs are egg-layers that have not been bred in an aquarium yet. There are no external differences between male and female.

The harlequinfish, or harlequin rasbora, (*Rasbora heteromorpha*) is a small, peaceful fish, often seen in tropical aquariums. It is quite deep toward the front of the body around the belly, but tapers to a very narrow tail. All the fins are clear and the body has a lovely pinkish-blue hue. The rear half of the body is distinguished by a black marking that follows the body shape. These beautiful little community fish only grow to about 4cm (1.6in) and do best when kept in a shoal. They make good tankmates for danios and livebearers and thrive in the same conditions. Harlequins eat flake and live or

freeze-dried foods, such as Daphnia or brine shrimp. They do not spawn as readily as danios and will need soft acidic water in the aquarium for breeding to be successful.

**Origin**: Thailand.

**Temperature**: 20°C (68°F) is ideal, but they will tolerate temperatures from 23°C (73°F) to 28°C (82°F).

**GH**: 6°dGH, soft. Tolerates a range from 4°dGH to 12°dGH.

**pH**: 6.5 is ideal, but will tolerate 6.2 to 7.2 well. Avoid sudden changes in pH.

**Hardiness**: Harlequin rasboras are delicate and should not be used to cycle a tank. Perform regular partial water changes.

**Feeding**: Harlequin rasboras enjoy small live foods, such as bloodworms, mosquito larvae, and brine shrimp, alternated with a high quality flake food. They may nibble on frozen green beans, or an algae or Spirulina wafer occasionally. Feed daily.

**Compatible tankmates**: Live-bearers (except mollies), zebra danios, neon tetras or other small tetras. Adult rasboras can be kept with discus. Clown loaches, bala sharks and corydoras catfish are also acceptable tankmates.

**Avoid these tankmates**: Aggressive fish with large mouths.

**Breeding**: Harlequin rasboras are egg-layers, and can be very difficult to breed. Females are fuller and have less color than the males. Offer live food listed above to prepare the adults for breeding. A small breeding tank should be used, with plenty of fine-leaved plants. The temperature should be 21°C (70°F), hardness not over 10°dGH, pH of 6.4. The bottom can have fine, dark gravel. Select a male and a female for breeding. Eggs will be laid on the plants. The parents should be removed after spawning seems to be complete. The eggs will hatch in about 36 hours. Feed liquid fry food, then powdered foods, followed by live baby brine shrimp.

# GIANT DANIO

At 10cm (4in) the giant danio (*Brachydanio malabaricus*) is the largest commonly sold danio. It is also the least suited to a gentle community tank. Giant danios should be kept in a shoal, in a tightly covered aquarium. These fish are jumpers. Giant danios will shoal, at high speeds, startling quieter fish. As a group they will pick at and disturb fish their own size, smaller or larger. If no other species are present, the largest giant danio will ceaselessly pick on the smaller ones. Choose giant danios for a large aquarium with sturdy, diverse occupants, to distract the other fish from aggressive behavior (see below for tankmates).

**Origin:** Thailand.

**Temperature:** 27°C (81°F) is ideal, but they will tolerate temperatures from 23°C (73°F) to 28°C (82°F).

**GH:** 6°dGH, soft. Tolerates a range from 4°dGH to 12°dGH.

**pH:** 7.2 is ideal, but will tolerate 6.5 to 8.0 well. Avoid sudden changes in pH.

**Hardiness:** Giant danios are hardy enough to cycle a tank. Perform regular partial water changes.

**Feeding:** Giant danios aren't fussy eaters. A high quality flake food can be supplemented with most live foods, such as bloodworms, mosquito larvae and brine shrimp. They may nibble on frozen green beans, or an algae or Spirulina wafer occasionally. Feed daily.

**Compatible tankmates:** Tiger barbs, zebra danios, gouramis, geophagus, other large cichlids, Chinese algae eaters, and a red-tailed or rainbow shark. The other occupants should be diverse, at least three species. Giant danios should be kept in a shoal, with enough territorial tankmates to keep any one giant danio from becoming "king."

**Avoid these tankmates:** Slow-swimming, peaceful community fish. The giant danios will chase and stress quiet tankmates, often to death.

**Breeding:** Giant danios are egg-layers, and may not be easy to breed. Females are fuller and have slightly less color than the males. Offer live food, as suggested above, to prepare the adults for breeding. A tightly covered breeding tank should be used, with a grid for the eggs to drop to the bottom, or a thick layer of marbles. The temperature should be 23°C (74°F), hardness not over 10°dGH, pH of 7.2. Choose a group of fish that don't fight too much and probably contains a male and two females. The parents should be removed after spawning seems to be complete. The eggs will hatch in about four days. Feed liquid fry food, then powdered foods, then live baby brine shrimp.

The pearl danio (*Brachydanio albolineatus*) from the dark, muddy rivers of Burma and Indo-China is a superb beginner's fish. These lovely little fish are quite hardy for their size—only 5cm (2in)—and very active. The body is very long and slim, all the fins are clear, and the fish feeds from the surface with its small, upturned mouth. Toward the back half of the body are two or three pink lines that run horizontally over pastel blue scales to produce a pearl effect, hence the common name. This species also has a golden form. Males are usually more brightly colored and not as plump as females. Pearl danios prefer to live in shoals. In the wild, they have a great many predators and if

attacked they all disperse in different directions to create confusion and avoid being eaten. The water temperature should be about 23°C (74°F) and the tank should be brightly lit and well planted.

**Origin**: Southeast Asia, Burma, Thailand, Sumatra.

**Temperature**: 23°C (74°F) is ideal, but they will tolerate temperatures from 20°C (68°F) to 25°C (77°F).

**GH**: 6°dGH, soft. Tolerates a range from 4°dGH to 12°dGH.

**pH**: 7.0 is ideal, but will tolerate 6.5 to 7.8 well. Avoid sudden changes in pH.

**Hardiness**: Pearl danios are hardy, but should not be used to cycle a tank. Perform regular partial water changes.

**Feeding**: Pearl danios aren't fussy eaters. A high quality flake food can be supplemented with most live foods, such as bloodworms, mosquito larvae, and brine shrimp. They may nibble on frozen green beans, or an algae or Spirulina wafer occasionally. Feed daily.

**Compatible tankmates**: Pearl danios do well in planted aquariums. They get along well with most community fish such as live-bearers, tetras, small barbs, zebra danios, gouramis, loaches, corydoras catfish, a red-tailed or rainbow shark.

**Avoid these tankmates**: Large-mouthed, aggressive fish, such as geophagus, oscars, and other south American cichlids. Do not put danios in with discus. Danios may be small, but they are nippy.

**Breeding**: Pearl danios are egg-layers. Although pearl danios originate from soft water areas, they are one of the few cyprinids that will spawn in hard water. Set up a tank with a bunch of plants at one end, and marbles in the bottom. Feed the prospective pair well for a few days before placing them in the breeding aquarium and raising the temperature slowly to 26°C (79°F). The spawning should take place during the next morning, particularly if the tank receives some direct sunlight. The pair chase through the plants, where the eggs are released and fertilized. Once the spawning is over, remove the parents or they will eat the eggs. The eggs hatch some time the following day, depending on the temperature, and the fry will be free-swimming four to five days later. Feed them on a liquid fry food at this time.

# ZEBRA DANIO

The zebra danio (*Brachydanio rerio*) is a superb beginner's fish. These lovely little fish are quite hardy for their size—only 5cm (2in)—and very active. The body is very long and slim, all the fins are delicately striped and the fish feeds from the surface with its small, upturned mouth. Males are usually not as plump as females. Zebra danios prefer to live in shoals, swimming just below the surface of the water. In the wild, they have a great many predators and if attacked they all disperse in different directions to create confusion and avoid being eaten. The tank should be covered, brightly lit and well planted.

**Origin**: Eastern India.

**Temperature**: 21°C (70°F) is ideal, but they will tolerate temperatures from 18°C (64°F) to 24°C (74°F).

**GH**: 6°dGH, soft. Tolerates a range from 4°dGH to 12°dGH.

**pH**: 7.0 is ideal, but will tolerate 6.5 to 7.8 well. Avoid sudden changes in pH.

**Hardiness**: Zebra danios are very hardy, and can be used to cycle a tank. Perform regular partial water changes.

**Feeding**: Zebra danios aren't fussy eaters. A high quality flake food can be supplemented with most live foods, such as bloodworms, mosquito larvae, and brine shrimp. They may nibble on frozen green beans, or an algae or Spirulina wafer occasionally. Feed daily.

**Compatible tankmates**: Zebra danios do well in planted aquariums and can live with most community fish such as live-bearers, tetras, small barbs, pearl danios, gouramis, loaches, corydoras catfish, a red-tailed or rainbow shark.

**Avoid these tankmates**: Large-mouthed, aggressive fish, such as geophagus, oscars, and other south American cichlids. Do not put danios in with discus. Danios may be small, but they are nippy.

**Breeding**: Zebra danios are egg-layers, and relatively easy to breed. Although zebra danios originate from soft water areas, they are one of the few cyprinids that will spawn in hard water. Set up a tank with plants at one end, and marbles in the bottom. The tank should be placed where it will receive some sun. Feed the prospective pair well for a few days before placing them in the breeding aquarium and raising the temperature slowly to 26°C (79°F). The spawning should take place during the next morning, particularly if the tank receives some direct sunlight. The pair chase through the plants. Many of the eggs may be dropped into the marbles. Feed them enchytraea during spawning. Once the spawning is over, remove the parents or they will eat the eggs. About 400 eggs will be laid. They will hatch in three to four days, depending on the temperature, and the fry will be free-swimming four to five days later. Feed them baby flake food, fine Enchytraea, or crumbled egg yolk at this time.

The white cloud mountain minnow (*Tanichthys albonubes*) is another of the really easy care danios. It will thrive in hard or soft water, with a temperature on the low side, about 22°C(72°F) is warm enough. The tank should be covered, brightly lit and well planted.

**Origin**: China.

**Temperature**: 21°C (68°F) is ideal, but they will tolerate temperatures from 18°C (64°F) to 22°C (72°F).

**GH**: 6°dGH, soft. Tolerates a range from 4°dGH to 12°dGH.

**pH**: 7.0 is ideal, but will tolerate 6.5 to 7.5 well. Avoid sudden changes in pH.

**Hardiness**: White cloud mountain minnows are relatively hardy as long as their temperature requirements are met. They should not be used to cycle a tank. Perform regular partial water changes.

**Feeding**: These fish aren't fussy eaters. A high quality flake food can be supplemented with most live foods, such as bloodworms, mosquito larvae, and brine shrimp. They may nibble tiny bites from a frozen green beans, or an algae or Spirulina wafer occasionally. Feed daily.

**Compatible tankmates**: White cloud mountain minnows are a gentle species that do well in shoals in planted aquariums. They get along well with most community fish such as live-bearers, tetras, small barbs, pearl danios, gouramis, loaches, corydoras catfish, a red-tailed or rainbow shark. Adult white cloud mountain minnows can share a tank with neon or cardinal tetras and discus.

**Avoid these tankmates**: Large-mouthed, aggressive fish, such as geophagus, oscars, and other cichlids.

**Breeding**: White cloud mountain minnows are egg-layers. Set up a breeding tank with plants. Be sure the temperature stays cool, between 20°C (68°F) and 22°C (72°F). Choose a single male and female to introduce for breeding. The eggs will be laid on the plants. Once spawning is over, remove the parents or they will eat the eggs. About 400 eggs will be laid. They will hatch in three days, depending on the temperature. Feed fine micro-food or liquid fry food.

# BALA SHARK

Slim and horizontally compressed, the silver shark or bala shark (*Balantiocheilus melanopterus*) is one of the largest sharks, growing to 30cm (12in). These very active fish need a tank at least 90cm (36in) long, ideally 120cm (48in). The water temperature should be about 24°C (75°F), but otherwise the water composition is unimportant. They are a fast-swimming species, but totally non-aggressive. Bala sharks often act as a barometer for water quality or disease. They are usually the first fish to display symptoms of ich, visible as black patches where they've scraped off their scales.

They are often the first fish to die if the tank is contaminated. They are shy and sensitive, and may die of stress if battered by giant danios or other aggressive or nippy fish. Like most sharks, this species is a jumper, so always cover the tank.

**Origin:** Thailand, Borneo, Sumatra, and Southeast Asia.

**Temperature:** 24°C (75°F) is ideal, but they will tolerate temperatures from 22°C (72°F) to 27°C (81°F).

**GH:** 6°dGH, soft. Tolerates a range from 4°dGH to 12°dGH.

**pH:** 7.0 is ideal, but will tolerate 6.5 to 7.8 well. Avoid sudden changes in pH.

**Hardiness:** Bala sharks do not tolerate nitrite, and should never be used to cycle a tank. Perform regular partial water changes.

**Feeding:** Offer a varied diet, including a high quality flake food, freeze-dried Tubifex, and live foods, such as chopped earthworms. Feed daily.

**Compatible tankmates:** Bala sharks do well in planted aquariums. They get along well with most community fish such as live-bearers, tetras, small barbs, pearl danios, gouramis, loaches, corydoras catfish, a red-tailed or rainbow shark. They can be kept with shoals of neon tetras, clown loaches, and discus.

**Avoid these tankmates:** Aggressive fish, such as geophagus, and oscars. Avoid giant danios, lone barbs, chain fish, or other moderately aggressive fish that pursue and nip constantly. Do not put them in with African cichlids.

**Breeding:** Bala or silver sharks are egg-layers that do not breed in a home aquarium. The female may be a little fuller bodied during spawning season, but there are no color differences.

# RED-FINNED SHARK

The red-finned shark (*Epalzeorhynchus frenatus* or *Labeo erythrurus*) is a close cousin of the red-tailed black shark and also stems from Asia. The body, care, and feeding is virtually the same, except that this species is slightly more slender than its cousin, and all the fins are orange or red. This fish grows to about 15cm (6in). The red-finned shark is a bottom-feeder, browsing along the gravel for bits of food and algae, using its barbels as food-finding sensors. This fish prefers to spend bright days in shady, dark caves. He will claim a cave as his own and defend it, although his mouth is not large enough to seriously harm another fish. Like most sharks, this species is a jumper, so always cover the tank. These very active fish need a tank at least 90cm (36in) long, ideally 120cm (48in). The bottom should have fine gravel. Don't put two sharks of this family, whether red-finned or red-tailed or both, in the same tank. Unless the tank is very large, with many shady hiding places, one will murder the other.

**Origin**: Northern Thailand.

**Temperature**: 24°C (75°F) is ideal, but they will tolerate temperatures from 22°C (72°F) to 26°C (79°F).

**GH**: 6°dGH, soft. Tolerates a range from 4°dGH to 15°dGH.

**pH**: 7.0 is ideal, but will tolerate 6.5 to 7.8 well. Avoid sudden changes in pH.

**Hardiness**: Red-finned sharks do not tolerate nitrite, and should never be used to cycle a tank. Perform regular partial water changes.

**Feeding**: Red-finned sharks need a varied diet, including a high quality flake food, live bloodworms, and live vegetable foods, such as romaine lettuce, peas, frozen green beans,

or spinach. Algae or Spirulina pellets are also welcomed. Feed daily.

**Compatible tankmates**: Red-finned sharks get along well with most community fish such as live-bearers, tetras, small barbs, pearl danios, gouramis, loaches, corydoras catfish, shoals of neon tetras, clown loaches, giant danios, and even some African cichlids.

**Avoid these tankmates**: Live plants as they will eat them. Avoid aggressive fish with large mouths, such as oscars. Red-finned sharks are too bullying to be kept with discus or very nervous fish.

**Breeding**: Red-finned sharks are egg-layers. The male is thinner, with a black line on the anal fin. They are occasionally bred in an aquarium, but the territorial intolerance of their own species makes breeding very difficult.

# RED-TAILED BLACK SHARKS

The red-tailed black sharks (*Epalzeorhynchus bicolor* or *Labeo bicolor*) from Thailand are probably the most popular of the sharks. Red-tailed sharks are best kept as individual fish in a community tank. This very active fish can grow as large as 18cm (7in); a 90cm (36in) tank will suffice when the fish is juvenile, but adults need a 120cm (48in) tank. The bottom should have fine gravel. This fish is a jumper, so keep the tank well covered with fairly thick, heavy glass. Like his cousin, the red-tailed shark is a bottom- feeder, browsing along the gravel for bits of food and algae, using its barbels as food-finding sensors. This fish prefers to spend bright days in shady, dark caves. He will claim a cave as his own and defend it, although his mouth is not large enough to seriously harm another fish. Like most sharks, this species is a

jumper, so always cover the tank. Do not put two sharks of this family, whether red-finned or red-tailed or both, in the same tank. Unless the tank is very large, with many shady hiding places, one will often kill the other.

**Origin**: Central Thailand.

**Temperature**: 24°C (75°F) is ideal, but they will tolerate temperatures from 22°C (72°F) to 26°C (79°F).

**GH**: 6°dGH, soft. Tolerates a range from 4°dGH to 15°dGH.

**pH**: 7.0 is ideal, but will tolerate 6.5 to 7.8 well. Avoid sudden changes in pH.

**Hardiness**: Red-tailed sharks do not tolerate nitrite, and should never be used to cycle a tank. Perform regular partial water changes.

**Feeding**: Offer a varied diet, including a high quality flake food, live bloodworms, and live vegetable foods, such as romaine lettuce, peas, frozen green beans, or spinach. Algae or Spirulina pellets are also welcomed. Feed daily.

**Compatible tankmates**: Red-tailed sharks get along well with most community fish such as live-bearers, tetras, small barbs, pearl danios, gouramis, loaches, corydoras cat-fish, shoals of neon tetras, clown loaches, giant danios, and even some African cichlids.

**Avoid these tankmates**: Live plants as red-tailed sharks will eat them. Avoid aggressive fish with large mouths, such as oscars. Red-tailed sharks are too bullying to be kept with discus or very nervous fish.

**Breeding**: Red-tailed sharks are egg-layers that have occasionally been bred in an aquarium, but the territorial intolerance of their own species makes breeding very difficult. Success is rare. The male's dorsal fin comes to a point, while the female's dorsal fin forms a right angle. Ideal conditions for breeding are: soft water filtered through peat, at a temperature of 26°C (79°F) to 29°C (82°F). Be sure plenty of cover, such as roots and caves, are available for the fish to choose from. If successful, the fry hatch in about two days, and are free-swimming two days after hatching. Feed bits of frozen or blanched spinach, or fine Spirulina flake.

The weather loach or "dojo" sold in pet stores may belong to either of two species. The Chinese weather loach (*Misgurnus anguillicaudatus*) comes from Asia, specifically Siberia, China, Korea, and Japan. The Chinese weather loach has a light brown background with dark brown blotches, giving the fish a mottled appearance. It can reach 20cm (8in) in length, and is also available in a pale gold color without spots.

The second common species of weather loach, (*Misgurnus fossilis*), originates in northern Europe. It can reach 30cm (11.75in) but rarely achieves that size in an aquarium. Its markings are bands of tan and cream running lengthwise along its body.

Behaviorally, the two species are indistinguishable, and they require the same water conditions. Weather loaches are friendly, curious fish, whose common name derives from the fish's alleged sensitivity to changes in air pressure. Be sure to keep the aquarium cover tightly closed if you have a weather loach. They are avid, muscular, jumpers. They will also burrow through the gravel or sand, under the plants, in pursuit of snails or to hide from the other fish. Provide shady caves or rocks and plastic tubes to hide in. If you keep more than one weather loach in the tank, they will sometimes sleep in a "pile" at the back of the tank, entwined together.

**Origin**: Siberia, China, Korea, Japan (*Misgurnus anguillicaudatus*); Northern Europe (*Misgurnus fossilis*).

**Temperature**: 18°C (65°F) is ideal, but they will tolerate temperatures from 4°C (39°F) to 25°C (77°F).

**GH**: 6°dGH, soft. Tolerates a range from 4°dGH to 15°dGH.

**pH:** 7.0 is ideal, but will tolerate 6.5 to 7.8 well. Avoid sudden changes in pH.

**Hardiness**: Weather loaches do not tolerate nitrite, and should never be used to cycle a tank. Perform regular partial water changes.

**Feeding**: Offer a varied diet, including a high quality flake food, live bloodworms, and live vegetable foods, such as romaine lettuce, peas, frozen green beans, or spinach. Algae or Spirulina pellets are also welcomed. Feed daily

unless snails are a problem. Weather loaches will supplement their diet with fresh snails.

**Compatible tankmates:** Weather loaches get along well with most community fish that enjoy cooler water temperatures. They are curious, not aggressive, and do not bully the other fish. They can be kept with tetras, barbs, danios, gouramis, other gentle loaches, corydoras catfish, shoals of neon tetras, clown loaches, giant danios, and red-tailed or red-finned sharks.

**Avoid these tankmates**: Avoid aggressive fish with large mouths, such as geophagus or oscars. Do not keep weather loaches with African cichlids.

**Breeding**: Weather loaches are egg-layers that have been accidentally spawned in an aquarium. The eggs are laid on plants, usually from April to July. The male weather loach is smaller and thinner, and his pectoral fin is somewhat thicker. The female is slightly more full-bodied.

# CLOWN LOACH

Like most botia species, clown loaches (*Botia macracantha*) are quite timid in the tank at first. Provide a fast flowing current in the aquarium where the fish can swim head-on into the flow and exercise their muscles. A fairly warm tank with soft water and shady hiding places will make clown loaches feel at home. They can reach 30cm (11.75in) in the wild, but rarely exceed 16cm (6.5in) in an aquarium. They relish live foods and will gobble up chopped earthworms and Daphnia. These bottom-dwellers feed by scavenging with their little feelers. They can do a remarkable job of eliminating snails in an aquarium. They are happiest kept in groups, and sometimes make audible

clicking noises as they explore the tank. Be sure to keep the aquarium cover tightly closed when you have loaches. They will jump, sometimes out of small openings. The barb near the clown loaches' eye can become tangled in a net, or stab an aquarist, so care in handling is recommended.

**Origin**: Borneo, Indonesia, Sumatra.

**Temperature**: 27°C (81°F) is ideal, but they will tolerate temperatures from 25°C (77°F) to 30°C (86°F).

**GH**: 6°dGH, soft. Tolerates a range from 4°dGH to 10°dGH. Avoid sudden changes in GH. Do not add salt to their aquarium.

**pH**: 7.0 is ideal, but will tolerate 6.5 to 7.8 well. Avoid sudden changes in pH.

**Hardiness**: Clown loaches do not tolerate ammonia or nitrite, and should never be used to cycle a tank. Perform regular partial water changes. Clown loaches are prone to ich, but copper can be fatal to them. If ich must be treated, raise the tank temperature to 28.3°C (83°F) and treat with a non-copper preparation.

**Feeding**: Offer a varied diet, with high quality flake food, live bloodworms, and live vegetable foods, such as romaine lettuce, peas, frozen green beans, or spinach. Algae or Spirulina pellets are also welcomed. Feed daily, unless you have snails as clown loaches will devour these.

**Compatible tankmates**: Clown loaches get along well with most community fish that enjoy warm water temperatures. They are curious, not aggressive, and do not bully the other fish. They can be kept with tetras, barbs, danios, gouramis, other gentle loaches, corydoras catfish, shoals of neon tetras, discus, giant danios, and red-tailed or red-finned sharks. Clown loaches can be kept with African cichlids if the GH in the tank isn't too high.

**Avoid these tankmates**: Clown loaches have been known to nip the leaves from plants, possibly out of boredom, since they don't seem to eat them. Avoid expensive live plants. Avoid aggressive fish with large mouths, such as oscars.

**Breeding**: Clown loaches are egg-layers that have not been successfully spawned in a home aquarium, where it is very difficult to imitate rapidly flowing, and foaming streams. The male clown loach is thicker and broader tailed, with tiny notched irregularities on the inner edges of the tail's points. The female is smaller and thinner.

# ORANGE-FINNED LOACH

The orange-finned loach (*Botia modesta*) is an interesting fish similar to the clown loach. Take care when purchasing, that yours is its natural silvery or brownish gray color, with orange fins. Dealers sometimes dye these fish to brighten their body color to pink, purple, or aqua, and the dye is a poison. The orange-finned loach does not grow quite as large; 20cm (8in) is an excellent size. This little bottom-dweller is an undemanding tank occupant, happiest when kept with others of his own kind. He is an ideal scavenger, chasing greedily after all foods. Kept without others of his species, he may bully the other fish. Like most loaches, he is equipped with a barb near each eye, which he uses to defend against predators, (and sometimes aquarists). They sometimes make audible clicking noises as they explore the tank. Be sure to keep the aquarium cover tightly closed when you have loaches. They will jump, sometimes out of very small openings.

**Origin**: India, Thailand, Vietnam, and Malaysia.

**Temperature**: 27°C (81°F) is ideal, but they will tolerate temperatures from 25°C (77°F) to 30°C (86°F).

**GH**: 6°dGH, soft. Tolerates a range from 4°dGH to 10°dGH. Avoid sudden changes in GH. Do not add salt to their aquarium.

**pH**: 7.0 is ideal, but will tolerate 6.5 to 7.8 well. Avoid sudden changes in pH.

**Hardiness**: Orange-finned loaches do not tolerate ammonia or nitrite, and should never be used to cycle a tank. Perform regular partial water changes. They are prone to ich, but copper can be fatal to them. If ich must be treated, raise the tank temperature to 28.3°C (83°F), and treat with a non-copper preparation.

**Feeding**: Offer a varied diet, including a high quality flake food, live or frozen bloodworms, and live vegetable foods, such as romaine lettuce or peas. Sinking carnivore or algae pellets are also welcomed. Feed daily unless snails are a problem. Orange-finned loaches will supplement their diet with fresh snails.

**Compatible tankmates**: Orange-finned loaches get along well with most large community fish that enjoy warm water temperatures. They are a bit more dominant than clown loaches, and can share a tank with African cichlids if the water is not too hard. They can also be kept with tetras, barbs, giant danios, gouramis, clown loaches, and red-tailed or red-finned sharks.

**Avoid these tankmates**: Avoid small, easily injured fish. Orange finned loaches have been known to burrow under plants, up-rooting them, so protect plants with pots, or avoid expensive live plants.

**Breeding**: Orange-finned loaches are egg-layers that have not been successfully spawned in captivity.

# CHAINFISH

The chainfish (*Botia lohachata*) is an interesting fish similar to the clown loach. His markings are repetitive, providing protective coloration when he hides near the base of a plant. The chainfish rarely exceeds 10cm (4in), but he is a bit more aggressive than his relatives. This bottom-dweller cares little for water chemistry. He spends his days in his cave, and his nights chasing the other fish around. The chainfish is not intimidated by larger fish. Like most loaches, he is equipped with a barb near each eye, which he uses to defend against predators, (and sometimes aquarists). They sometimes make audible clicking noises as they explore the tank. Be sure to keep the aquarium cover tightly closed when you have loaches. They will jump, sometimes out of very small openings.

**Origin:** India, Bangladesh.

**Temperature:** 27°C (81°F) is ideal, but they will tolerate temperatures from 24°C (75°F) to 30°C (86°F).

**GH:** 6°dGH, soft. Tolerates a range from 4°dGH to 12°dGH. Avoid sudden changes in GH. Do not add a lot of salt to your aquarium.

**pH:** 7.0 is ideal, but will tolerate 6.5 to 7.8 well. Avoid sudden changes in pH.

**Hardiness:** Chainfish do not tolerate ammonia or nitrite, and should never be used to cycle a tank. Perform regular partial water changes. They are prone to ich, but copper can be fatal to them. If ich must be treated, raise the tank temperature to 28.3°C (83°F), and treat with a non-copper preparation.

**Feeding:** Offer a varied diet, including a high quality flake food, live or frozen bloodworms, and live vegetable foods, such as romaine lettuce, or peas. Sinking carnivore or algae pellets are also welcomed. Feed daily unless snails are a problem. Chainfish may supplement their diet with fresh snails.

**Compatible tankmates:** Chainfish get along well with most large community fish that enjoy warm water temperatures. They are a bit more dominant than clown loaches, and can share a tank with African cichlids if the water is not too hard. They can also be kept with barbs, giant danios, gouramis, clown loaches, and red-tailed or red-finned sharks.

**Avoid these tankmates:** Avoid small, easily injured, or timid fish. Chainfish are nocturnal bullies that can harass bala sharks or angel fish to death. They have been known to burrow under plants, uprooting them, so protect plants with pots, or avoid expensive live plants.

**Breeding:** Chainfish are egg-layers that have not been successfully spawned in captivity.

# KUHLI LOACH

The kuhli loach (*Pangio kuhli* or *Acanthophthalmus kuhlii*) is a nocturnal, solitary fish requiring a dark, soft bottom and plenty of shade. The kuhli loach rarely exceeds 8cm (3in). He prefers soft, acidic water and live food.

Be sure to keep the aquarium cover tightly closed when you have loaches. They will jump, sometimes out of very small openings.

**Origin**: Borneo, Java, Malaysia, Singapore, Southeast Asia, Sumatra, Thailand.

**Temperature**: 28°C (83°F) is ideal, but they will tolerate temperatures from 24°C (75°F) to 30°C (86°F).

**GH**: 8°dGH, soft. Tolerates a range from 4°dGH to 12°dGH. Avoid sudden changes in GH. Do not add a lot of salt to their aquarium.

**pH**: 7.0 is ideal, but will tolerate 6.5 to 7.8 well. Avoid sudden changes in pH.

**Hardiness**: Kuhli loaches do not tolerate ammonia or nitrite, and should never be used to cycle a tank. Perform regular partial water changes. They are prone to ich, but copper can be fatal to them. If ich must be treated, raise the tank temperature to 28.3°C (83°F), and treat with a non-copper preparation.

**Feeding**: Offer a varied diet, including a lot of live or frozen bloodworms, live mosquito larvae, and other live foods. May eat some snails. Kuhli loaches sometimes accept sinking carnivore pellets.

**Compatible tankmates**: Kuhli loaches get along well with most smaller community fish that enjoy acidic water. They can be kept with small danios, tetras, barbs, dwarf gouramis, and other upper-water fish.

**Avoid these tankmates**: Aggressive, large mouthed fish such as oscars.

**Breeding**: Kuhli Loaches are egg-layers that have been spawned in captivity, but it is challenging. Provide floating plant cover, in addition to a heavily planted tank. The eggs are bright green and will be laid on the plants.

# CATFISH—
# FISH WITH WHISKERS

Tropical aquarium catfish come from all over. Most are rather drably colored, mainly because they need good camouflage to avoid predators and most are bottom-dwellers. To compensate for poor vision, catfish have developed barbels, which are covered in taste receptors. Barbels may be long and used for hunting, as in the pimelodids or, as in the corydoras catfish, short and used to burrow and tease their way into the gravel to detect food or insects.

Some catfish scavenge at the bottom for tasty morsels; others are midwater swimmers that feed mainly on insect larvae. Large predatory species hunt for small live fish. Some catfish have large, rubbery, sucker-type mouths, which they use to remove the algae from aquarium glass, plants, rocks, or gravel.

All catfish are highly sensitive to medicines. They are scaleless fish, and malachite green penetrates their skin, causing death within hours of treatment. Methylene blue is also best avoided. Corydoras catfish prefer shady corners of a tropical community tank, but are quite active. They have a small mouth and scavenge the bottom for flake food or pellets. Suckermouth and whiptail catfish generally eat algae and need a supplement to their diet of peas, lettuce or a slice of zucchini.

All carnivorous catfish require some live food in their diets. Many of them will eat small fish. Carnivorous species include the Zebra plec, banjo catfish, pictus catfish, Raphael catfish, upside-down catfish, pangasius catfish, Colombian shark catfish, and shovelnose catfish. Synodontis catfish are natives of the great African lakes, Lake Tanganyika and Lake Malawi. Most synodontis catfish have not been bred in captivity and are now protected species.

Bronze or "green" corydoras catfish (*Corydoras aeneus*) have quite a bit of metallic green coloration as well. They are completely peaceful and probably best kept in groups of three or more. Even in a mixed community, males often follow the females about. Males are usually smaller and less robust than females. Bronze catfish are very popular miniature aquarium subjects, reaching only about 7cm (2.8in).

**Origin:** Amazon, South America.

**Temperature:** 24°C (75°F) is ideal, but they will tolerate temperatures from 22°C (72°F) to 28°C (83°F).

**GH:** 8°dGH, moderate. Tolerates a range from 4°dGH to 12°dGH.

**pH:** 7.3 is ideal, but will tolerate 6.8 to 8.0 well. Avoid sudden changes in pH.

**Hardiness:** Bronze Corydoras do not tolerate ammonia or nitrite, and should never be used to cycle a tank. Perform regular partial water changes.

**Feeding:** Offer a varied diet. They will scavenge for flake that falls to the bottom, but enjoy live or frozen bloodworms, sinking "catfish" pellets, and sinking shrimp or algae pellets.

**Compatible tankmates:** Corydoras catfish get along well with most community fish. They are a charming addition to any community aquarium with good conditions. They can be kept with live-bearers, tetras, small barbs, gouramis, and loaches.

**Avoid these tankmates:** Cichlids, particularly African or large-mouthed cichlids. Large mouthed catfish will compete for territory and may harm corydoras.

**Breeding:** Corydoras will breed in the home aquarium, although some species are easier than others. They are best bred in an aquarium of their own, with two males and one female. The female is pestered by the two males and lays her eggs on the plants and glass. The males then fertilize the eggs, which hatch after three or four days or so and fall to the bottom. There they live off a yolk sac for a few more days and then you can feed them on fine fry foods or newly hatched brine shrimp.

# LEOPARD CORYDORAS

Leopard corydoras (*Corydoras julii*) are a very popular corydoras species, growing to about 6cm (2.4in). Add three or more to your aquarium and watch them establish a catfish convention in the back corner of the tank. They certainly seem to be communicating harmoniously as they sit in a circle, heads at the center. Provide good water conditions, good company, and good food, and they are happy fish.

**Origin:** Brazil, South America.

**Temperature:** 24°C (75°F) is ideal, but they will tolerate temperatures from 22°C (72°F) to 28°C (83°F).

**GH:** 8°dGH, moderate. Tolerates a range from 4°dGH to 12°dGH.

**pH:** 7.3 is ideal, but will tolerate 6.8 to 8.0 well. Avoid sudden changes in pH.

**Hardiness:** Leopard corydoras do not tolerate ammonia or nitrite, and should never be used to cycle a tank. Perform regular partial water changes.

**Feeding:** Offer a varied diet. They will scavenge for flake that falls to the bottom, but enjoy live or frozen bloodworms, sinking "catfish" pellets, and sinking shrimp or algae pellets.

**Compatible tankmates:** Corydoras catfish get along well with most community fish. They are a charming addition to any community aquarium with good conditions. They can be kept with live-bearers, tetras, small barbs, gouramis, and loaches.

**Avoid these tankmates:** Cichlids, particularly African or large-mouthed cichlids. Large mouthed catfish will compete for territory and may harm corydoras.

**Breeding:** Corydoras will breed in the home aquarium, although some species are easier than others. They are best bred in an aquarium of their own, with two males and one female. The female is pestered by the two males and lays her eggs on the plants and glass. The males then fertilize the eggs, which hatch after three or four days or so and fall to the bottom. There they live off a yolk sac for a few more days and then you can feed them on fine fry foods or newly hatched brine shrimp.

Panda corydoras (*Corydoras panda*) are also a popular corydoras species, growing to about 6cm (2.4in). Their markings are distinctive. Add three or more to your aquarium and watch them scurry around together, searching for tasty morsels in the gravel. They also enjoy a quiet cave behind a plant for the community nap.

**Origin:** Amazon, South America.

**Temperature:** 24°C (75°F) is ideal, but they will tolerate temperatures from 22°C (72°F) to 28°C (83°F).

**GH:** 8°dGH, moderate. Tolerates a range from 4°dGH to 12°dGH.

**pH:** 7.3 is ideal, but will tolerate 6.8 to 8.0 well. Avoid sudden changes in pH.

**Hardiness:** Panda corydoras do not tolerate ammonia or nitrite, and should never be used to cycle a tank. Perform regular partial water changes.

**Feeding:** Offer a varied diet. They will scavenge for flake that falls to the bottom, but also enjoy live or frozen bloodworms, sinking "catfish" pellets, sinking shrimp or algae pellets.

**Compatible tankmates:** Corydoras catfish get along well with most community fish. They are a charming addition to any community aquarium with good conditions. They can be kept with live-bearers, tetras, small barbs, gouramis, and loaches.

**Avoid these tankmates:** Cichlids, particularly African or large-mouthed cichlids. Large mouthed catfish will compete for territory and may harm corydoras.

**Breeding:** Corydoras will breed in the home aquarium, although some species are easier than others. They are best bred in an aquarium of their own, with two males and one female. The female is pestered by the two males and lays her eggs on the plants and glass. The males then fertilize the eggs, which hatch after three or four days or so and fall to the bottom. There they live off a yolk sac for a few more days and then you can feed them on fine fry foods or newly hatched brine shrimp.

# PEPPERED CORYDORAS

The plated catfish, or peppered corydoras (*Corydoras paleatus*) is peaceful and a good community fish. He can reach 7cm (2.8in) in length. It is brown with a slightly purple tinge and a number of black blotches over the body. Plated catfish prefer quite cool conditions of about 22°C(72°F), When females of this species are ripe with eggs they become really plump. This is probably the commonest of all the available Corydoras catfish and one of the easiest to breed in captivity.

**Origin:** Amazon, South America.

**Temperature:** 22°C (72°F) is ideal, but they will tolerate temperatures from 21°C (70°F) to 26°C (79°F).

**GH:** 8°dGH, moderate. Tolerates a range from 4°dGH to 12°dGH.

**pH:** 7.3 is ideal, but will tolerate 6.8 to 8.0 well. Avoid sudden changes in pH.

**Hardiness:** Peppered corydoras do not tolerate ammonia or nitrite, and should never be used to cycle a tank. Perform regular partial water changes.

**Feeding:** Offer a varied diet. They will scavenge for flake that falls to the bottom, but enjoy live or frozen bloodworms, sinking "catfish" pellets, and sinking shrimp or algae pellets.

**Compatible tankmates:** Corydoras catfish get along well with most community fish. They are a charming addition to any community aquarium with good conditions. They can be kept with live-bearers, tetras, small barbs, gouramis, and loaches.

**Avoid these tankmates:** Cichlids, particularly African or large-mouthed cichlids. Large-mouthed catfish will compete for territory and may harm corydoras.

**Breeding:** Corydoras will breed in the home aquarium, although some species are easier than others. They are best bred in an aquarium of their own, with two males and one female. The female is pestered by the two males and lays her eggs on the plants and glass. The males then fertilizes the eggs, which hatch after three or four days or so and fall to the bottom. There they live off a yolk sac for a few more days and then you can feed them on fine fry foods or newly hatched brine shrimp.

Punctatus corydoras (*Corydoras punctatus*) resemble the leopard corydoras from a distance, but their spots are a bit smaller and rounder. They are another popular corydoras species, growing to about 6cm (2.4in). Like other corydoras, they keep a varied schedule. They scurry around the tank looking for food, make a few gravel to surface exercise runs, then take an afternoon nap. Provide a shady corner for their nap, and they will be happy.

**Origin:** Amazon, South America.

**Temperature:** 24°C (75°F) is ideal, but they will tolerate temperatures from 22°C (72°F) to 28°C (83°F).

**GH:** 8°dGH, moderate. Tolerates a range from 4°dGH to 12°dGH.

**pH:** 7.3 is ideal, but will tolerate 6.8 to 8.0 well. Avoid sudden changes in pH.

**Hardiness:** Punctatus corydoras do not tolerate ammonia or nitrite, and should never be used to cycle a tank. Perform regular partial water changes.

**Feeding:** Offer a varied diet. They will scavenge for flake that falls to the bottom, but enjoy live or frozen bloodworms, sinking "catfish" pellets, and sinking shrimp or algae pellets.

**Compatible tankmates:** Corydoras catfish get along well with most community fish. They are a charming addition to any community aquarium with good conditions. They can be kept with live-bearers, tetras, small barbs, gouramis, and loaches.

**Avoid these tankmates:** Cichlids, particularly African or large-mouthed cichlids. Large mouthed catfish will compete for territory and may harm corydoras.

**Breeding:** Corydoras will breed in the home aquarium, although some species are easier than others. They are best bred in an aquarium of their own, with two males and one female. The female is pestered by the two males and lays her eggs on the plants and glass. The males then fertilize the eggs, which hatch after three or four days or so and fall to the bottom. There they live off a yolk sac for a few more days and then you can feed them on fine fry foods or newly hatched brine shrimp.

Hypostomus (photo: *Hypostomus punctatus*) have three rows of plates along their flanks, covered in fine dermal denticles that make the surface feel like sandpaper. They have a large dorsal and forked tail and small eyes on top of the head. They are quite timid and may hide in a brightly lit tank, but will live happily in most safe temperature and water conditions. If two of these fish are kept together in the same tank they may bicker a little, but rarely do one another harm. They may reach 30cm (12in) in length if well-fed.

**Origin:** Brazil, South America.

**Temperature:** 24°C (75°F) is ideal, but they will tolerate temperatures from 22°C (72°F) to 28°C (83°F).

**GH:** 8°dGH, moderate. Tolerates a range from 1°dGH to 25°dGH.

**pH:** 7.3 is ideal, but will tolerate 6.5 to 8.0 well. Avoid sudden changes in pH.

**Hardiness:** Hypostomus do not tolerate ammonia or nitrite, and should never be used to cycle a tank. Perform regular partial water changes.

**Feeding:** Offer a varied diet. Apart from algae, they also accept green foods such as lettuce, spinach, and zucchini slices. They will scavenge for flake that falls to the bottom, sinking "catfish" pellets or algae pellets.

**Compatible tankmates:** Hypostomus get along well with most community fish. They are a useful addition to any community aquarium with enough algae to support them. They can be kept with live-bearers, tetras, barbs, gouramis, cichlids, other catfish, and loaches.

**Avoid these tankmates:** Larger and more aggressive fish. A hypostomus or pleco that will be sharing a tank with an oscar should be a very large pleco. Provide plenty of cover such as a large plastic tube or adequate rocky cave before putting in with African cichlids or large South American cichlids.

**Breeding:** Unsuccessful in home aquariums.

Quite a few types of bristlenose such as ancistrus (photo: *Ancistrus dolichopterus*) are offered for sale. These non-aggressive fish remain quite small, reaching only 13cm (5in) in length. Males are distinguished by the many fleshy bristles over the front of the head. In females, shorter bristles fringe the snout. Body colors and markings vary between individual species, some being brown, and many being black. Bristlenoses make excellent algae cleaners; if there are no plants in the tank feed them peas or blanched lettuce. They are happiest in moderately hard water with a neutral pH level and a temperature maintained at about 24°C (75°F).

**Origin:** Brazil, South America.

**Temperature:** 24°C (75°F) is ideal, but they will tolerate temperatures from 22°C (72°F) to 26°C (79°F).

**GH:** 8°dGH, moderate. Tolerates a range from 2°dGH to 25°dGH.

**pH:** 7.3 is ideal, but will tolerate 6.5 to 8.0 well. Avoid sudden changes in pH.

**Hardiness:** Bristlenoses do not tolerate ammonia or nitrite, and should never be used to cycle a tank. Perform regular partial water changes.

**Feeding:** Bristlenoses need to be offered a varied diet. Apart from algae, they also accept green foods such as lettuce, spinach, and zucchini slices. They will scavenge for flake that falls to the bottom, sinking "catfish" pellets, or algae pellets.

**Compatible tankmates:** Bristlenoses get along well with most community fish. They are a useful addition to any community aquarium with enough algae to support them. They can be kept with live-bearers, tetras, barbs, gouramis, cichlids, other catfish, and loaches.

**Avoid these tankmates:** Larger and more aggressive fish, such as the African cichlids or the large South American cichlids.

**Breeding:** Bristlenoses lay eggs in roots. The male guards the eggs and aerates the water above them. Water values during breeding should be pH 6.5 to 7.0, with a hardness of 4°dGH to 10°dGH. After the egg sac is gone offer fine Spirulina flake or baby fry food.

# SAILFIN PLEC

As its name suggests, the sailfin plec (*Pterygoplichthys gibbiceps*) has a very large dorsal fin. Its body is covered in round black spots that are usually bolder in juvenile fish. The bright copper base color may also fade with age. This fish can grow to about 40cm (16in) in a large tank. Provide plenty of shady hideouts with plants, roots, or rock.

**Origin:** Peru, South America.

**Temperature:** 24°C (75°F) is ideal, but they will tolerate temperatures from 22°C (72°F) to 27°C (81°F).

**GH:** 8°dGH, moderate. Tolerates a range from 4°dGH to 20°dGH.

**pH:** 7.3 is ideal, but will tolerate 6.5 to 8.0 well. Avoid sudden changes in pH.

**Hardiness:** Sailfin plecs do not tolerate ammonia or nitrite, and should never be used to cycle a tank. Perform regular partial water changes.

**Feeding:** Feed at night. Apart from algae, they may also accept green foods such as blanched lettuce, spinach, and zucchini slices. Offer large fish several sinking algae or Spirulina pellets if all the algae is eaten. They will scavenge for flake that falls to the bottom, sinking "catfish" pellets.

**Compatible tankmates:** Sailfin plecs get along well with most community fish. They are a useful addition to any community aquarium with enough algae to support them. They can be kept with live-bearers, tetras, barbs, gouramis, cichlids, other catfish, and loaches.

**Avoid these tankmates:** Larger and more aggressive fish. A Sailfin pleco that will be sharing a tank with an oscar should be a very large pleco. Provide plenty of cover such as a large plastic tube or adequate rocky cave before putting in with African Cichlids or large South American cichlids.

**Breeding:** Unsuccessful in home aquariums.

The clown plec (*Pterygoplichthys vittata*), and most dwarf plecs belong to the Pterygoplichthys family, a group of quite decorative, small suckermouths that never grow much more than about 10cm (4in) long. They are superb little algae cleaners and very peaceful fish in the aquarium, only becoming argumentative if another fish tries to muscle in on their hiding places, which they guard quite fiercely for their size. Clown plecs like to hide during the daytime and come out to feed at night, so you may not see them too often. Females are duller in coloration than the males. Clown plecs will not burrow or bother plants. They require plenty of algae.

**Origin:** Amazon, South America.

**Temperature:** 24°C (75°F) is ideal, but they will tolerate temperatures from 22°C (72°F) to 26°C (79°F).

**GH:** 8°dGH, moderate. Tolerates a range from 2°dGH to 20°dGH.

**pH:** 7.0 is ideal, but will tolerate 6.5 to 8.0 well. Avoid sudden changes in pH.

**Hardiness:** Clown plecs do not tolerate ammonia or nitrite, and should never be used to cycle a tank. Perform regular partial water changes.

**Feeding:** Feed at night. Apart from algae, they may also accept green foods such as blanched lettuce, spinach, and zucchini slices. They may scavenge for flake that falls to the bottom and sinking "catfish" pellets.

**Compatible tankmates:** Clown plecs get along well with most community fish. They are a useful addition to any community aquarium with enough algae to support them. They can be kept with live-bearers, tetras, barbs, gouramis, cichlids, other catfish, and loaches.

**Avoid these tankmates:** Larger and more aggressive fish, such as the African cichlids or the large South American cichlids.

**Breeding:** Unsuccessful in home aquariums.

# ROYAL PLECO

An exceptionally beautiful catfish, the royal pleco, (*Panaque nigrolineatus*), can be very difficult to acclimatize. Provide clean, well-filtered, highly oxygenated water in a planted aquarium. Offer newly acquired specimens green foods, as their digestive system seems unable to cope with high-protein foods at this time.

They may browse on aquarium plants. You can add chopped prawns to their diet once acclimatized. The royal pleco can be territorial toward its own kind. This fish can grow quite large—up to about 45cm (18in). Provide plenty of shady cover.

**Origin:** Colombia, South America.

**Temperature:** 24°C (75°F) is ideal, but they will tolerate temperatures from 22°C (72°F) to 26°C (79°F).

**GH:** 8°dGH, moderate. Tolerates a range from 2°dGH to 15°dGH.

**pH:** 7.0 is ideal, but will tolerate 6.5 to 7.5 well. Avoid sudden changes in pH.

**Hardiness:** Royal plecs do not tolerate ammonia or nitrite, and should never be used to cycle a tank. Perform regular partial water changes.

**Feeding:** Feed at night. Apart from algae, they may also accept green foods such as blanched lettuce, spinach, and zucchini slices. Once accustomed to the tank, they may scavenge for flake that falls to the bottom, sinking algae or catfish pellets.

**Compatible tankmates:** Royal plecs get along well with most community fish. They are a useful addition to any community aquarium with enough algae to support them. They can be kept with live-bearers, tetras, barbs, gouramis, cichlids, other catfish, and loaches.

**Avoid these tankmates:** Larger and more aggressive fish, such as the African cichlids or the large South American cichlids.

**Breeding:** Unsuccessful in home aquariums.

There are many types of farlowella catfish but most are very much alike. The twig catfish (*Farlowella gracilis*) shown here is quite armoured, with a pointed, slightly upturned snout. In the aquarium it prefers a steady temperature of 24°C(75°F), water with a high oxygen content, and plenty of shade. It dislikes many of the standard aquarium disease remedies, so take care when adding chemicals to the water.

**Origin:** Colombia, South America.

**Temperature:** 24°C (75°F) is ideal, but they will tolerate temperatures from 22°C (72°F) to 26°C (79°F).

**GH:** 8°dGH, moderate. Tolerates a range from 2°dGH to 15°dGH.

**pH:** 7.0 is ideal, but will tolerate 6.5 to 7.5 well. Avoid sudden changes in pH.

**Hardiness:** Twig catfish do not tolerate ammonia or nitrite, and should never be used to cycle a tank. Perform regular partial water changes using a good water conditioner or well-filtered water.

**Feeding:** Feed at night. Apart from algae, they may also accept green foods such as blanched lettuce, spinach, and zucchini slices. Once accustomed to the tank, they may scavenge for flake that falls to the bottom, sinking algae or "catfish" pellets.

**Compatible tankmates:** Twig catfish get along well with most community fish. They are a useful addition to any community aquarium with enough algae to support them. They can be kept with live-bearers, tetras, barbs, gouramis, cichlids, other catfish, and loaches.

**Avoid these tankmates:** Larger and more aggressive fish, such as the African Cichlids or the large South American cichlids.

**Breeding:** Unsuccessful in home aquariums.

# PANAMA WHIP

The Panama whip (*Sturisoma panamense*) is plain brown with darker brown flanks. It has a very high dorsal fin and usually two whips on the tail. These ray extensions grow much longer with age. Like most suckermouth catfish, the panamense is quite armour plated for protection. It lives happily in a range of waters from soft to hard, but changes from one to the other should be gradual.

**Origin:** Panama, Colombia, and Ecuador.

**Temperature:** 21°C (70°F) is ideal, but they will tolerate temperatures from 20°C (68°F) to 22°C (72°F).

**GH:** 8°dGH, moderate. Tolerates a range from 2°dGH to 20°dGH.

**pH:** 7.0 is ideal, but will tolerate 6.5 to 7.2 well. Avoid sudden changes in pH.

**Hardiness:** The panama whip species does not tolerate ammonia or nitrite well, and so they should never be used to cycle a tank. You need to perform regular partial water changes using a good water conditioner or well-filtered water.

**Feeding:** Feed at night. Apart from algae, they may also accept green foods such as blanched lettuce, spinach, and zucchini slices. Once accustomed to the tank, they may scavenge for flake that falls to the bottom, sinking algae or "catfish" pellets.

**Compatible tankmates:** Panama whips get along well with most community fish. They are a useful addition to any community aquarium with enough algae to support them. They can be kept with live-bearers, tetras, barbs, gouramis, cichlids, other catfish, and loaches.

**Avoid these tankmates:** Larger and more aggressive fish, such as the African cichlid or large South American cichlids.

**Breeding:** Unsuccessful in home aquariums.

The Chinese or Indian algae eater (photo: *Gyrinocheilus aymonieri*) has become very popular in aquarium shops. A variety of species may be offered under the same name, but all of them remain much smaller than plecs. They may reach 28cm (11in) in the wild, but rarely exceed 15cm (6in) in aquariums. Chinese algae eaters are hardier than plecs, and survive well in African cichlid tanks. They are also more aggressive when hungry, and may seek out and consume small fish if sufficient algae is not available.

**Origin:** Asia.

**Temperature:** 25°C (77°F) is ideal, but they will tolerate temperatures from 21°C (70°F) to 28°C (83°F).

**GH:** 8°dGH, moderate. Tolerates a range from 2°dGH to 20°dGH.

**pH:** 7.0 is ideal, but will tolerate 6.5 to 8.0 well. Avoid sudden changes in pH.

**Hardiness:** Chinese algae eaters do not tolerate ammonia or nitrite, and should never be used to cycle a tank. Perform regular partial water changes.

**Feeding:** Feed at night. Apart from algae, they may also accept green foods such as blanched lettuce, spinach, and zucchini slices. They will scavenge for flake that falls to the bottom, sinking algae or "catfish" pellets.

**Compatible tankmates:** Chinese algae eaters get along well with most community fish. They are a useful addition to any community aquarium with enough algae to support them. They can be kept with live-bearers, tetras, barbs, gouramis, cichlids, other catfish, and loaches. They can also be kept with African cichlids. They may survive with South American cichlids.

**Avoid these tankmates:** Discus, or any gentle, slow-moving small fish. If algae runs low, they may eat tender live plants.

**Breeding:** Unsuccessful in home aquariums.

# OTOCINCLUS

Otocinclus (Photo: *Otocinclus affinis*) are the fishkeeper's dream algae eater. They are far more delicate than their larger cousins, but they are always hungry. Their small mouths clean plants as well as glass walls. Their small size 5cm (2in) makes them easy prey for large fish, so choose several of them for aquariums stocked with smaller community fish and lots of plants for cover.

**Origin:** South America.

**Temperature:** 25°C (77°F) is ideal, but they will tolerate temperatures from 21°C (70°F) to 27°C (81°F).

**GH:** 8°dGH, moderate. Tolerates a range from 5°dGH to 19°dGH.

**pH:** 7.0 is ideal, but will tolerate 6.5 to 8.0 well. Avoid sudden changes in pH.

**Hardiness:** Otocinclus do not tolerate ammonia or nitrite, and should never be used to cycle a tank. Perform regular partial water changes using a good water conditioner or well-filtered water.

**Feeding:** Feed at night. Apart from algae, they may also accept green foods such as fresh romaine lettuce, spinach, and zucchini slices. They will scavenge for flake that falls to the bottom, sinking algae or "catfish" pellets.

**Compatible tankmates:** Otocinclus are not aggressive. They are safest in aquariums with community fish. They can be kept with live-bearers, tetras, small barbs, gouramis, corydoras catfish, discus and loaches.

**Avoid these tankmates:** African cichlids, large south American cichlids.

**Breeding:** Unsuccessful in home aquariums.

The flying fox (*Epalzeorhynchus kallopterus*) is included with the algae eaters because it eats some algae. It is actually closely related to the red-tailed and red-finned labeo sharks. Provide good water quality, with lots of shady hiding places. The flying fox grows to 15cm (6in), and may become more aggressive with age. This species does not eat hair algae. The flying fox has dark shading on the dorsal and anal fins. (*See* Siamese flying fox. It eats hair algae.)

**Origin:** Borneo, Sumatra, Indonesia, Thailand, India.

**Temperature:** 25°C (77°F) is ideal, but they will tolerate temperatures from 24°C (75°F) to 27°C (81°F).

**GH:** 5°dGH, soft. Tolerates a range from 5°dGH to 8°dGH.

**pH:** 7.0 is ideal, but will tolerate 6.5 to 8.0 well. Avoid sudden changes in pH.

**Hardiness:** Flying foxes do not tolerate ammonia or nitrite, and should never be used to cycle a tank. Perform regular partial water changes using a good water conditioner or well-filtered water.

**Feeding:** Apart from algae, they may also accept green foods such as fresh romaine lettuce, spinach, and zucchini slices. They will scavenge for flake that falls to the bottom, sinking algae or "catfish" pellets.

**Compatible tankmates:** Flying foxes are comfortable in aquariums with community fish. They can be kept with fish such as live-bearers, tetras, barbs, gouramis, corydoras catfish, and loaches.

**Avoid these tankmates:** African cichlids, large south American cichlids.

**Breeding:** Unsuccessful in home aquariums.

The Siamese flying fox (*Crossocheilus siamensis*, aka *Epalzeorhynchus siamensis*) is included with the sucker-mouth catfish because it eats algae. Provide heavily oxygenated water, with lots of shady hiding places. The Siamese flying fox grows to 15cm (6in), and is somewhat intolerant of its own species. It does well in a community tank. It eats hair algae, and can be identified by its transparent fins.

**Origin:** Thailand, Southeast Asia

**Temperature:** 25°C (77°F) is ideal, but they will tolerate temperatures from 24°C (75°F) to 26°C (79°F).

**GH:** 5°dGH, soft. Tolerates a range from 5°dGH to 20°dGH.

**pH:** 7.0 is ideal, but will tolerate 6.5 to 8.0 well. Avoid sudden changes in pH.

**Hardiness:** Siamese flying foxes do not tolerate ammonia or nitrite, and should never be used to cycle a tank. Perform regular partial water changes using a good water conditioner or well-filtered water.

**Feeding:** Siamese flying foxes will eat algae and hair algae. Apart from algae, they may also accept green foods such as fresh romaine lettuce, spinach, and zucchini slices. They will scavenge for flake that falls to the bottom, sinking algae or "catfish" pellets.

**Compatible tankmates:** Siamese flying foxes are comfortable in aquariums with community fish. They can be kept with live-bearers, tetras, danios, barbs, gouramis, corydoras catfish, discus, and loaches.

**Avoid these tankmates:** African cichlids, large south American cichlids.

**Breeding:** Unsuccessful in home aquariums.

The Zebra plec (*Hypancistrus zebra*) does not eat much algae, and only reaches 10cm (4in) in length. While this stunning fish looks much like a plec, he is carnivorous. Zebra plecs are shy, and enjoy shady hideouts. Build one facing the front of the tank, or you may never see this fish. Keep them in a group of two or three, as long as you have enough hideouts available for each one to claim territory. They will defend their territory from their own species, but their interaction will give you a better view.

**Origin:** Brazil, South America.

**Temperature:** 25°C (77°F) is ideal, but they will tolerate temperatures from 24°C (75°F) to 26°C (79°F).

**GH:** 8°dGH, soft. Tolerates a range from 5°dGH to 15°dGH.

**pH:** 6.8 is ideal, but will tolerate 6.5 to 7.8 well. Avoid sudden changes in pH.

**Hardiness:** Zebra plecs do not tolerate ammonia or nitrite and should never be used to cycle a tank. Perform regular partial water changes using a good water conditioner or well-filtered water.

**Feeding:** These fish are nocturnal carnivores. Fresh shrimp, bloodworms, beef heart, or bits of earthworm should be offered twice a week, in the evening. The zebras will often wait until the other fish have eaten before approaching food. Feed adequately or they may miss dinner due to their timidity. Offer sinking algae or "catfish" pellets to your tank, but these may not be eaten.

**Compatible tankmates:** They can be kept with livebearers, tetras, danios, small barbs, gouramis, corydoras catfish, discus, and loaches.

**Avoid these tankmates:** African cichlids, large south American cichlids.

**Breeding:** Unsuccessful in home aquariums.

# PANTHER CATFISH

The angelicus or panther are trade names for the pictus catfish (*Pimelodus pictus*). It can reach 25cm (10in) and is more active during the day than most other puns. It appreciates some live food in its diet, so do not put it with small fish that could become a meal. The Pictus catfish is quite happy in hard water, although prefers soft, slightly acidic conditions. It is quite peaceful and a good community catfish if kept with suitably sized tankmates. Take care in handling. Do not use a net to catch, rather a plastic or glass container. Sharp spines can become tangled in the net, and inflict painful injuries to humans.

**Origin:** Colombia, Peru, South America.

**Temperature:** 25°C (77°F) is ideal, but they will tolerate temperatures from 23°C (73°F) to 27°C (81°F).

**GH:** 10°dGH, moderate. Tolerates a range from 5°dGH to 20°dGH.

**pH:** 7.2 is ideal, but will tolerate 6.5 to 8.0 well. Avoid sudden changes in pH.

**Hardiness:** Pictus catfish do not tolerate ammonia or nitrite, and should never be used to cycle a tank. Perform regular partial water changes.

**Feeding:** Offer a varied diet, including a lot of live or frozen bloodworms, live mosquito larvae, and other live foods. May eat sinking carnivore pellets, sinking algae pellets. Will eat small fish.

**Compatible tankmates:** Pictus catfish get along well with fish their own size or larger. They can be kept with large tetras, large barbs, south American cichlids, and other large catfish,

**Avoid these tankmates:** Small, tasty fish.

**Breeding:** Pictus catfish are not normally able to be bred in home aquariums.

The striped raphael (talking) catfish, (*Platydoras costatus*) is not a beginner's fish, but makes an enjoyable addition to a tank with large fish and plants. He is a large-mouthed catfish, and can reach 20cm (8in) in length. The raphael is not particular about water hardness, but is nocturnal, and rarely seen outside his cave in the daytime. Provide good water conditions and plenty of cover. Position his cave so that you can see inside of it, and he will settle right in. The "talking" nickname comes from the audible croak heard when he is caught. It is quite peaceful and a good community catfish if kept with suitably sized tankmates. Take care in handling. Do not use a net to catch, rather a plastic or glass container. Sharp spines can become tangled in the net, and inflict painful injuries to humans.

**Origin:** Peru, South America.

**Temperature:** 25°C (77°F) is ideal, but they will tolerate temperatures from 23°C (73°F) to 27°C (81°F).

**GH:** 10°dGH, moderate. Tolerates a range from 5°dGH to 20°dGH.

**pH:** 7.2 is ideal, but will tolerate 6.5 to 8.0 well. Avoid sudden changes in pH.

**Hardiness:** Raphael catfish do not tolerate ammonia or nitrite, and should never be used to cycle a tank. Perform regular partial water changes.

**Feeding:** Offer a varied diet, including a lot of live or frozen bloodworms, live mosquito larvae, and other live foods. May eat sinking carnivore pellets, sinking algae pellets. Will eat small fish.

**Compatible tankmates:** Raphael catfish get along well with fish their own size or larger. They can be kept with large tetras, large barbs, south American cichlids, and other large catfish.

**Avoid these tankmates:** Small, tasty fish.

**Breeding:** Raphael catfish are not normally able to be bred in home aquariums.

# UPSIDE-DOWN CATFISH

The upside-down catfish (*Synodontis nigriventris*) spends much of its time swimming inverted near the water surface. Its belly is darker than its back, which affords it greater protection from predators. It grows to a maximum of 10cm (4in) and is suited to water conditions in a tropical community tank. It has quite long whiskers, and the tail and dorsal fin are pointed, making it look rather squared-off in shape. Provide a fine bottom well-planted with broad-leaved plants, and plenty of shady overhangs of either roots, rocks, or both.

**Origin:** Central Africa, Central Congo basin.

**Temperature:** 24°C (75°F) is ideal, but they will tolerate temperatures from 22°C (71°F) to 26°C (79°F).

**GH:** 8°dGH, moderate. Tolerates a range from 5°dGH to 12°dGH.

**pH:** 7.2 is ideal, but will tolerate 6.5 to 8.0 well. Avoid sudden changes in pH.

**Hardiness:** Upside-down catfish do not tolerate ammonia or nitrite, and should never be used to cycle a tank. Perform regular partial water changes.

**Feeding:** Offer a varied diet, including live or frozen crustaceans, bloodworms, live mosquito larvae, and other live foods. May eat sinking carnivore or "catfish" pellets.

**Compatible tankmates:** Upside down catfish can be kept in a planted community aquarium with live-bearers, tetras, barbs, gouramis, loaches, and corydoras catfish.

**Avoid these tankmates:** Large barbs, African or South American cichlids, larger catfish.

**Breeding:** Upside-down catfish are egg-layers that have been successfully tank-bred, in their own tanks. Other species might eat the eggs, but upside-down catfish are good parents, carefully looking after their brood. The aquarium should be heavily planted with echinodorus and other broad-leaved plants. Roots and stones should be used to provide alcoves. The females are rounder, especially at spawning time. Eggs are laid in a hollow at the bottom of the tank. Feed the fry newly hatched brine shrimp after their egg-sac disappears, usually around the fourth day.

With the advent of modern tank building techniques and very strong adhesives, it is no longer a problem to build large tanks. Aquariums measuring 180cm (72in) long with a capacity of 680 litres (150 gallons) are quite common throughout the hobby. This means that the scope for keeping larger species of tropical fish is greater than ever before. Many of these fish are given a pet status by their owners, and when kept on their own they tend to develop a personality that is theirs alone. Due to their large size, it is not usually possible to decorate the tank with plants or any quantity of rockwork, as the fish soon demolish these with disastrous results! Most pet tanks are furnished with just the basics, such as a mix of fine and very large gravel and an undergravel filter, coupled with a power filter to cope with the large volume of waste that these fish produce.

The Pangasius catfish or irridescent shark (*Pangasius sutchi*) is not really an aquarium fish, but fish dealers sell many of them. In the wild, they can reach 100cm (39in) in length. In an aquarium, they rarely exceed 20cm (8in). A large aquarium, at least 120cm (48in) long, is recommended. Cover, such as plants, rocks, or caves is optional. The fish has poor eyesight and is easily startled. Avoid suddenly turning on lights, rapid movements near the tank, or tapping on the tank. When young they can be kept in shoals, but will want their own territory as they age.

**Origin:** Thailand

**Temperature:** 24°C (75°F) is ideal, but they will tolerate temperatures from 22°C (72°F) to 25°C (79°F).

**GH:** 8°dGH, soft. Tolerates a range from 2°dGH to 20°dGH.

**pH:** 7.0 is ideal, but will tolerate 6.4 to 7.8 well. Avoid sudden changes in pH.

**Hardiness:** Pangasius catfish do not tolerate ammonia or nitrite, and should never be used to cycle a tank. Perform regular partial water changes.

**Feeding:** Pangasius catfish are omnivores. They require live carnivorous food when young. Bloodworms, fresh shrimp, beef heart, or bits of earthworm should be offered twice a week. Offer sinking "catfish" pellets to your tank, but observe to see if the Pangasius eat them.

**Compatible tankmates:** They can be kept with a few sturdy upper and mid-water swimmers, perhaps gouramis or tin foil barbs.

**Avoid these tankmates:** Small fish, African Cichlids.

**Breeding:** Unsuccessful in home aquariums.

# SHARK CATFISH OR COLOMBIAN SHARK CATFISH

The shark catfish or Colombian shark catfish (*Arius see-mani* or *Arius jordani*) is a shoaling fish from the coast of Peru. Only young specimens are suitable for the aquarium. Keep them in groups in brackish water, with fish their size or larger. They can reach 35cm (14in) if well fed and in good condition. They require a fairly high salinity (SG 1.014) to really thrive, although they will live in freshwater. They are predators who will eat any fish they can catch and fit even partially into their mouth. When they are not hunting, shark catfish spend most of their days hiding in a corner, behind a lift tube, or under a rock. Like most catfish, they have spines that can injure a fishkeeper if they are handled improperly.

**Origin:** California, U.S.A. to Colombia, South America.

**Temperature:** 27°C (81°F) is ideal, but they will tolerate temperatures from 24°C (75°F) to 30°C (86°F).

**GH:** 15°dGH, hard. Tolerates a range from 10°dGH to 20°dGH or higher. They need salt or marine salt in their aquarium.

**pH:** 7.5 is ideal, but will tolerate 7.2 to 8.3 well. Avoid sudden changes in pH.

**Hardiness:** Columbian shark catfish do not tolerate ammonia or nitrite, and should never be used to cycle a tank. Perform regular partial water changes.

**Feeding:** Offer a varied diet, including a lot of live or frozen bloodworms, live mosquito larvae, and other live foods. May eat some snails, sinking carnivore pellets, sinking algae pellets. Will eat small fish.

**Compatible tankmates:** Columbian shark catfish get along well with fish their own size or larger. They can be kept with large tetras, barbs, cichlids, other large catfish, or brackish fish such as monos and scats.

**Avoid these tankmates:** Small, tasty fish.

**Breeding:** Columbian shark catfish have not been bred in home aquariums.

The shovelnose catfish or duckbill catfish, (*Sorubim lima*) is often for sale as a juvenile at 10–13cm (4–5in). However, with care it can reach at least 38cm (15in). Obviously, you must keep this highly predatory fish away from any other fish that might slip into its huge mouth. Feed it about three times a week. Raw fish is a good base food and can include whitebait, lance fish and any runts or deformities that your dealer can easily supply. The tank should offer plenty of plants, rocks and roots for cover. It is nocturnal. Like most catfish, they have spines that can injure a fishkeeper if handled improperly.

**Origin:** Amazon, South America.

**Temperature:** 27°C (81°F) is ideal, but they will tolerate temperatures from 23°C (73°F) to 30°C (86°F).

**GH:** 10°dGH, moderate. Tolerates a range from 10°dGH to 20°dGH or higher.

**pH:** 7.2 is ideal, but will tolerate 6.5 to 7.8 well. Avoid sudden changes in pH.

**Hardiness:** Duckbill catfish do not tolerate ammonia or nitrite, and should never be used to cycle a tank. Perform regular partial water changes.

**Feeding:** Offer a varied diet, including a lot of raw fish, supplemented with live or frozen bloodworms, large earthworms, and other live foods. May eat some snails, sinking carnivore pellets, and sinking algae pellets. Will eat any fish it can get in its mouth.

**Compatible tankmates:** Can be kept with fish too large to eat. When young, they can be kept with tinfoil barbs, cichlids, pacu, or other large catfish

**Avoid these tankmates:** Small, tasty fish.

**Breeding:** Duckbill catfish have not been bred in home aquariums.

# KILLIFISH EGGLAYING TOOTHCARPS

Killifish, or egg laying toothcarps as they are sometimes described, are a very colorful group of usually small, elongated fish. Most come from Africa, but some are found in the Americas, Asia, and Europe. Unfortunately, they do not make very good community fish and are certainly not the best choice for beginners. Killifish usually come from very soft water regions, which also tend to be acidic in composition, although a few are found in more alkaline and harder water areas.

The fish often live in shaded areas of rainforest, trapped in small pools, where water temperatures may fall as low as 21°C (70°F) or lower. If you wish to keep killifish in an aquarium, you must provide the appropriate water conditions; otherwise they are unlikely to survive for very long. This being so and because most other species (apart from some tetras and a few others) do not really thrive in such conditions, it is easy to see why killifish are usually kept only with their own kind.

Another problem is that they are naturally short-lived. Their life cycle revolves around a seasonal dry-out, so the adults die, the eggs harden and go dormant, then hatch at the first rainfall. It is usually possible to distinguish the sex of killifish, as males are more colorful and have more splendid fins than the females. Given their short lifespan and specialized water requirements, killifish are not often seen in aquarium shops, nor are they commonly kept.

Playfair's panchax (*Pachypanchax playfairi*) only grows to about 7.5cm (3in), and females are slightly smaller. The female's fins are usually clear, apart from the dorsal fin, which has a black blotch at the base. Males can be very aggressive during breeding time, so avoid keeping more than one male in the aquarium. Feed these killifish with small live foods if possible; otherwise offer them frozen or freeze-dried foods. The water should be kept at about 22°C (72°F), but this is one killifish that does not demand soft water. The species is a jumper, so ensure that you keep the aquarium tightly covered.

**Origin:** East Africa.

**Temperature:** 24°C (74°F) is ideal, but they will tolerate temperatures from 22°C (72°F) to 24°C (75°F).

**GH:** 8°dGH, moderate. Tolerates a range from 8°dGH to 15°dGH.

**pH:** 6.8 is ideal, but will tolerate 6.5 to 7.0 well. Avoid sudden changes in pH.

**Hardiness:** Playfair's panchax do not tolerate ammonia or nitrite, and should never be used to cycle a tank. Perform regular partial water changes.

**Feeding:** Offer a varied diet, including a lot of live or frozen bloodworms, live mosquito larvae, and other live foods. May eat some snails, sinking carnivore pellets, and sinking algae pellets. Will eat small fish.

**Compatible tankmates:** Can be kept with fish too large to eat, but recommend keeping a single male with multiple females, and no other species in the tank.

**Avoid these tankmates:** Small, tasty fish. The aggressive male may even stress larger species.

**Breeding:** Playfair's panchax are egg-layers whose eggs do not have to dry out before hatching. Females are fuller and more evenly colored. Males have a row of red dots on the side, and a black edge on the tail. Feed live food, as suggested above, to prepare the adults for breeding. A breeding tank should be used, with only 2 gallons of water, at a temperature of 25°C (77°F), with the hardness and pH as suggested above. Thick plantings of fine-leaved plants, hornfern or Java moss are recommended. Place the pair in the tank. Spawning will take several days. When spawning is complete, the parents should be removed, or they will eat the eggs. The eggs hatch in about 12 days if the tank remains at 24°C (75°F). Feed artemia and live newly hatched brine shrimp, and other small live food.

# AMERICAN FLAGFISH

The American flagfish (*Jordanella floridae*) can only be regarded as semi tropical. It reaches 6cm (2.4in). In captivity, it will accept a temperature as low as 19°C (66°F), but it is happiest at 22°C (72°F) and does quite well in hard water. Its coloration is quite variable. It has vegetarian tastes and will nibble at algae. Plant real plants interspersed with artificial ones along the sides and back of the aquarium. The gravel should be fine and dark. Plastic plants may survive better than real ones, but the flagfish requires vegetable matter in their diet. Provide plenty of the light for plants and to support some algae growth.

**Origin:** Florida, U.S.A. to Mexico, Central America.

**Temperature:** 22°C (72°F) is ideal, but they will tolerate temperatures from 22°C (72°F) to 24°C (75°F).

**GH:** 8°dGH, moderate. Tolerates a range from 8°dGH to 15°dGH.

**pH:** 6.8 is ideal, but will tolerate 6.5 to 7.0 well. Avoid sudden changes in pH.

**Hardiness:** American flagfish are not delicate. Choose three, one male and two female for a 40-liter (10-gallon) aquarium with plenty of live plants. They should survive cycling the tank. Perform regular partial water changes.

**Feeding:** Offer a varied diet, including a lot of live plant matter such as romaine lettuce, spinach as well as live mosquito larvae, and other live foods. Supplement with a high-quality flake food.

**Compatible tankmates:** If breeding, should be a single species tank. Can be kept with tetras and corydoras catfish. Recommend keeping a single male with multiple female flagfish.

**Avoid these tankmates:** Aggressive larger fish such as barbs.

**Breeding:** American flagfish are egg-layers whose eggs do not have to dry out before hatching. Females are fuller, and more yellow. Males are rather plain. Offer live food as suggested above to prepare the adults for breeding. A breeding tank should be used, at a temperature of 23°C (73°F) to 25°C (77°F), with the hardness and pH as listed above. Thick plantings of fine-leaved plants, hornfern, or Java moss are recommended. Place the pair in the tank. Spawning will take several days. When spawning is complete, remove the female. The male will guard the eggs. Eggs hatch in about seven days if the tank remains at 24°C (75°F). Feed micro-food, followed by artemia and live newly hatched brine shrimp, other small live food.

# LIVEBEARERS — FISH THAT PRODUCE LIVE YOUNG

Livebearers make an excellent introduction to the fishkeeping hobby. They are hardy, active, easy to maintain, and easy to induce into breeding in the aquarium. So what is a livebearer? Well, all the fish discussed so far are egglayers, i.e. fish that lay eggs and then fertilize them outside the female's body. In livebearers, the eggs are retained within the female's body after fertilization and the embryos develop for about one month before being released. When the fry are released, they are usually exact miniature replicas of the female. In some species this process can be repeated every two months.

In the wild, mollies are usually found in quite hard water areas and river estuaries, so it is a good idea to add a teaspoonful of sea salt to every 23 litres (5 gallons) of tank water. The guppy must be one of the best-known tropical aquarium fish, as well as one of the most beautiful and prolific. Depending on the particular aquarium-bred strain, the dorsal fin may either be small or massively flowing, but the male's tail will always be like a long flowing scarf. The tail may be one of several different shapes, depending on the breed, and will also have various names, such as "delta tail," "veiltail," or "fantail" and so on. Females are far less colorful but larger, growing to about 5cm (2in), whereas the male only reaches about 3.5cm (1.4in) in body length, which could lead you to think that these are two totally different fish.

Platies and swordtails are related species that are available in many color variations. In the male swordtail the bottom ray of the caudal fin extends to a very long point, like the blade of a sword.

# MARBLED SAILFIN MOLLY

This marbled form of the sailfin molly (*Poecilia velifera*) grows to about 7.5cm (3in) excluding the tail. Like their close relative the guppy, these fish are easy to breed but can be a little nervous. They prefer a heavily plant-ed aquarium, but choose plants that will tolerate very hard water. Supplement with artificial plants to make the fish feel secure.

**Origin:** Yucatan, Mexico.

**Temperature:** 26°C (79°F) is ideal, but they will tolerate temperatures from 22°C (72°F) to 28°C (83°F).

**GH:** 25°dGH, hard. Tolerates a range from 25°dGH to 35°dGH. Add salt or marine salt to their tank to harden the water to this range.

**pH:** 7.8 is ideal, but will tolerate 7.5 to 8.5 well. Avoid sudden changes in pH.

**Hardiness:** Sailfin mollies are relatively hardy, but should not be used to cycle a tank. Perform regular partial water changes.

**Feeding:** Choose a high-quality flake food. Offer them some vegetable matter, such as garden peas with the skins removed, romaine lettuce, and spinach as well as live mosquito larvae, bloodworms, and brine shrimp as supplements.

**Compatible tankmates:** If breeding, keep as a single species tank. In a community tank, keep with other fish that can tolerate hard water, such as platies and guppies. Recommend keeping a single male with multiple females.

**Avoid these tankmates:** Aggressive larger fish such as barbs, and South American and African cichlids.

**Breeding:** They are best bred in a tank of their own, where they produce broods of 10–40 fry. The female will release the fry near fine plants, but will also eat any that fail to hide. A breeder trap can be helpful in preserving the young fish. Feed crumbled flake food.

The silver lyretail molly (*Poecilia*) thrives and breeds well in most aquariums, so it is an excellent beginner's fish. They require less added salt than the sailfins, and are more tolerant of slight pH and hardness variations. Mollies like some plants in the tank to give them cover and to nibble at, and the occasional rocky hideaway or castle will be enjoyed. If you add salt to the tank, make sure that other fish and any plants can withstand the brackish conditions, or use plastic plants.

**Origin:** The Atlantic coast of the U.S.A. to South America.

**Temperature:** 26°C (79°F) is ideal, but they will tolerate temperatures from 22°C (72°F) to 28°C (83°F).

**GH:** 25°dGH, hard. Tolerates a range from 25°dGH to 35°dGH. Add salt or marine salt to their tank to harden the water to this range.

**pH:** 7.8 is ideal, but will tolerate 7.5 to 8.5 well. Avoid sudden changes in pH.

**Hardiness:** Most mollies are hardy and can be used to cycle a tank. Fancy varieties, and nearly wild sailfins, are less hardy. Perform regular partial water changes. Feeding: Choose a high-quality flake food. Offer them some vegetable matter, such as garden peas with the skins removed, romaine lettuce, and spinach as well as live mosquito larvae, bloodworms, and brine shrimp as supplements.

**Compatible tankmates:** If breeding, keep as a single species tank. In a community tank, keep with other community fish that can tolerate hard water, such as swordtails or guppies. Recommend keeping a single male with multiple females.

**Avoid these tankmates:** Aggressive larger fish such as barbs, and South American and African cichlids.

**Breeding:** They are best bred in a tank of their own, where they produce broods of 10–40 fry. The female will release the fry near fine plants, but will also eat any that fail to hide. A breeder trap can be helpful in preserving the young fish. Feed crumbled flake food.

# GREEN VARIEGATED DELTA TAIL GUPPIES

A pair of green variegated delta tail guppies (*Poecilia reticulata*). The lower fish is a male with a splendid tail, but even the female fish—normally drab compared to the male—has benefited from the breeding pro-

gramme and sports a striking tail. The name "guppy" comes from the naturalist Robert Guppy, who first collected the fish in Trinidad in the 1860s.

**Origin:** South America.

**Temperature:** 26°C (79°F) is ideal, but they will tolerate temperatures from 22°C (72°F) to 28°C (83°F).

**GH:** 25°dGH, hard. Tolerates a range from 25°dGH to 35°dGH. Add salt or marine salt to their tank to harden the water to this range.

**pH:** 7.8 is ideal, but will tolerate 7.5 to 8.5 well. Avoid sudden changes in pH.

**Hardiness:** Most guppies are hardy and can be used to cycle a tank. Fancy varieties are less hardy. Perform regular partial water changes.

**Feeding:** Choose a high-quality flake food. Offer them some vegetable matter, such as garden peas with the skins

removed, romaine lettuce, and spinach as well as live mosquito larvae, bloodworms, and brine shrimp as supplements.

**Compatible tankmates:** If breeding, should be a single species tank. In a community tank, keep with other fish that can tolerate hard water, such as mollies, swordtails, or platies. Recommend keeping a single male with multiple females.

**Avoid these tankmates:** Aggressive larger fish such as barbs, and South American and African cichlids.

**Breeding:** They are best bred in a tank of their own, where they produce broods of 10–40 fry. The female will release the fry near fine plants, but will also eat any that fail to hide. A breeder trap can be helpful in preserving the young fish. Feed crumbled flake food.

Red, orange, yellow, and black are the predominant colors in the platy (*Xiphophorus*), although some shimmering hybrids have been produced. These quite plump fish have slightly upturned little mouths for feeding from the surface. Provide plants and caves for cover, to help the fish feel secure. Male fish grow to a maximum length of 5cm (2in), whereas females are often a little larger. The dorsal fin and tail are very rounded. Both platies and swordtails may be descendants of the green swordtail. In the absence of members of the opposite sex of their own type, platies and swordtails will crossbreed. Try to prevent this if at all possible.

**Origin:** Central America.

**Temperature:** 22°C (72°F) is ideal, but they will tolerate temperatures from 18°C (64°F) to 25°C (77°F).

**GH:** 15°dGH, hard. Tolerates a range from 9°dGH to 20°dGH. Add a small amount of salt or marine salt to their tank to harden the water to this range.

**pH:** 7.5 is ideal, but will tolerate 7.0 to 8.0 well. Avoid sudden changes in pH.

**Hardiness:** Most platies are hardy and can be used to cycle a tank. Fancy varieties are less hardy. Perform regular partial water changes.

**Feeding:** Choose good quality flake food. You can offer them some vegetable matter, such as garden peas without skins, romaine lettuce, and spinach as well as live mosquito larvae, bloodworms, and brine shrimp as supplements.

**Compatible tankmates:** If breeding, keep as a single species tank. In a community tank, keep with other live-bearers, or tetras, loaches, and corydoras catfish. It is recommended to keep a single male with multiple females. Match tankmates to recommended water pH and hardness ranges.

**Avoid these tankmates:** Aggressive larger fish such as barbs, and South American and African cichlids.

**Breeding:** They are best bred in a tank of their own, where they produce broods of 10–40 fry. The male has a pointed anal fin whereas the female's anal fin is rounded or fan-shaped. Females also tend to be plumper than males. The platy is always ready to breed and females are rarely unfertilized. A mature female can release up to 100 young at a time, but 40 is nearer the normal brood size for these fish. She can produce a brood every 40 days, including several broods after the male is no longer in the tank. The female will release the fry near fine plants, but will also eat any that fail to hide. A breeder trap can be helpful in preserving the young fish. Feed crumbled flake food.

# SWORDTAIL

Excluding the long tail that the male develops as it matures, the swordtail (*Xiphophorus helleri*) will grow to about 7.5cm (3in), sometimes a little more. The red swordtail is a beautiful aquarium fish that has grown significantly less hardy in the last ten years due to massive inbreeding. Choose an alternate color, or platies, for the hardiest fish. Like platies, the male has a pointed anal fin, but male swordtails also have a visible sword once they reach adulthood. Swordtails can crossbreed with platies, so don't combine the two groups in a tank if you are trying to achieve pure-bred fish. The swordtail is also always ready to breed and females are rarely unfertilized. Provide plants and caves for cover, to help the fish feel secure.

**Origin:** Central America.

**Temperature:** 22°C (72°F) is ideal, but they will tolerate temperatures from 18°C (64°F) to 25°C (77°F).

**GH:** 15°dGH, hard. Tolerates a range from 9°dGH to 20°dGH. Add a small amount of salt or marine salt to their tank to harden the water to this range.

**pH:** 7.5 is ideal, but will tolerate 7.0 to 8.0 well. Avoid sudden changes in pH.

**Hardiness:** Most swordtails are hardy and can be used to cycle a tank. Fancy varieties are less hardy. Perform regular partial water changes.

**Feeding:** Choose a high-quality flake food. Offer them some vegetable matter, such as garden peas without skins, romaine lettuce, and spinach as well as live mosquito larvae, bloodworms, and brine shrimp as supplements.

**Compatible tankmates:** If breeding, should be a single species tank. In a community tank, can be kept with other live-bearers, or tetras, loaches and corydoras catfish. It is recommended to keep a single male with multiple females. Match tankmates to recommended water pH and hardness ranges.

**Avoid these tankmates:** Aggressive larger fish such as barbs, and South American and African cichlids.

**Breeding:** They are best bred in a tank of their own, where they produce broods of 10–40 fry. The male has a pointed anal fin whereas the female's anal fin is rounded or fan-shaped. Females also tend to be plumper than males. The platy is always ready to breed and females are rarely unfertilised. A mature female can release up to 100 young at a time, but 40 is nearer the normal brood size for these fish. She can produce a brood every 40 days, including several broods after the male is no longer in the tank. The female will release the fry near fine plants, but will also eat any that fail to hide. A breeder trap can be helpful in preserving the young fish. Feed them crumbled flake food.

# CICHLIDS —
# DIVERSE AND FASCINATING

Cichlids come from Africa, South and Central America, and a couple of species come from Asia. The smallest species only grow to 5cm (2in), whereas the largest reach over 60cm (24in). All cichlids are territorial, some more so than others. Most are relatively easy to breed and this is where their true attraction lies, for they look after their young with the greatest care and devotion. All cichlids are intolerant of poor water conditions, particularly nitrite. Many carry the parasite hexamita, which can flare up and kill them at the slightest stress. Metronizadole is the only effective medication for hexamita.

African cichlids from the Rift Lakes require a lot of rockwork and caves to help the fish to feel secure, and to minimize aggression. Most require a high pH and hard water. South American cichlids require aquariums with little rockwork and a lot of plants. The water quality is much softer, with a lower pH. They range in size from dwarf cichlids only 5cm (2in) long to oscars reaching 30cm (12in) or longer. Angelfish and discus aren't dwarf cichlids, but they have small mouths compared to the really large South American cichlids.

Large American cichlids require a large aquarium and plenty of food. They make a lot of mess and need large, regular water changes. Their real attraction is their intelligence. These fish will move gravel and rocks with a purpose—usually to stake out a territory and entice a mate. They eat any fish they can swallow, but charm their owner by recognizing him or her. They will often shun or try to bite strangers. Some of these fish can break an aquarium if they can lift a suitably hard ornament to throw at the glass.

# ELECTRIC YELLOW LABIDO

The electric yellow labido is the sweetheart of the Rift Lake cichlids, rarely exceeding 15cm (6in). If you put them in a community tank, you will have some seriously injured community fish. But sharing an aquarium with other species from the Rift Lakes, the electric yellow labido is the timid fish peeking out from under a rock. Provide plenty of rockwork and caves for cover, to help the fish feel secure. Rockwork should extend over most of the tank bottom, and be stacked up to about a third of the tank's height. Be sure the stacked rock is secure, and tuck the bases of plastic plants between rocks.

**Origin:** Lake Malawi, Africa.

**Temperature:** 25.5°C (78°F) is ideal, but they will tolerate temperatures from 23°C (74°F) to 28.3°C (83°F).

**GH:** 15°dGH, hard. Tolerates a range from 9°dGH to 25°dGH. Add a small amount of salt or marine salt to their tank to harden the water to this range.

**pH:** 8.2 is ideal, but will tolerate 7.7 to 8.6 well. Avoid sudden changes in pH.

**Hardiness:** Cichlids do not tolerate nitrite at all. Even low levels of nitrite are fatal within a day or so. Do not use cichlids to cycle a tank. Perform regular partial water changes.

**Feeding:** Choose a high-quality flake food and baby cichlid pellets in both vegetable and carnivorous flavors. You may need to rotate their food periodically. Offer some romaine lettuce or fresh spinach as well as live mosquito larvae, and brine shrimp as supplements. Take care not to pollute the tank, feeding only what will be eaten. Do not overfeed. (Yellow labidos will constantly beg for food.)

**Compatible tankmates:** Other African cichlids from the Rift Lakes, synodontis catfish, Chinese algae eaters. Can be mixed with large tropical fish that are gradually accustomed to a high pH, such as red hook silver dollars, angelfish, clown loaches, gouramis, geophagus, a red-tailed shark. If mixing with these community fish, provide rocky cover in one corner of a very large 120cm (48in) community tank to help the yellow labidos settle in.

**Avoid these tankmates:** Small, gentle, tropical community fish.

**Breeding:** Electric yellow labidos are mouthbrooders. Some males and some females have deep black markings on their dorsal, pelvic, and abdominal fins. Males may have white egg spots on the anal fin after they mature. Start with a group of young fish, and wait. When someone has a lower chin and a full jaw, she has a mouthful of eggs. She will not eat until the babies are free-swimming. If you have multiple females and no male, you may still see a fish holding eggs, but no babies follow. Feed the fry small live food or crumbled flake food.

# GOLDEN CICHLID

Females of the golden cichlid (*Melanochromis auratus*) from Lake Malawi have rows of black, white, and yellow stripes, whereas the base color is blue in the male. These fish are rarely more than 10cm (4in) long and females remain smaller. A dwarf species (*M. dialeptus*) is also available. They are very aggressive for their size. Provide plenty of rockwork and caves for cover, to help the fish feel secure. Rockwork should extend over most of the tank bottom, and be stacked up to about a third of the tank's height. Be sure the stacked rock is secure, and tuck the bases of plastic plants between rocks. Never add just one fish to an African cichlid tank. Rearrange the rockwork and add at least four at a time to reduce aggression, and possibly prevent deaths.

**Origin:** Lake Malawi, Africa.

**Temperature:** 27°C (81°F) is ideal, but they will tolerate temperatures from 23°C (74°F) to 28.3°C (83°F).

**GH:** 21°dGH, hard. Tolerates a range from 9°dGH to 30°dGH. Add a small amount of salt or marine salt to their tank to harden the water to this range.

**pH:** 8.1 is ideal, but will tolerate 7.7 to 8.6 well. Avoid sudden changes in pH.

**Hardiness:** Cichlids do not tolerate nitrite at all. Even low levels of nitrite are fatal within a day or so. Do not use cichlids to cycle a tank. Perform regular partial water changes.

**Feeding:** Choose a high-quality flake food and baby cichlid pellets in both vegetable and carnivorous flavors. You may need to rotate their food periodically, for variety. Offer some romaine lettuce or fresh spinach as well as live mosquito larvae, and brine shrimp as supplements. Take care not to pollute the tank, feeding only what will be eaten.

**Compatible tankmates:** Melanochromis johanni and chipokee, both tough customers from the same family. Other large African cichlids from the Rift Lakes, synodontis catfish, Chinese algae eaters.

**Avoid these tankmates:** Small, gentle, tropical community fish, small African cichlids.

**Breeding:** These cichlids are mouthbrooders and usually quite easy to breed, if the male doesn't kill the female. The female lays eggs on the gravel or a rock, while the male swims with her in a tight circle. She then turns around to pick up the eggs with her mouth. "Egg spot" markings on the anal fin of the male look like eggs to the female and she tries to collect them in her mouth. In doing so, she collects a mouthful of sperm instead and this fertilizes the eggs. The female keeps the eggs in her mouth until they become free-swimming fry, which can take 21–50 days. During this time, the female does not usually feed and it is advisable to remove her (with the fry) to a separate maternity tank to develop in peace. Once the fry are released from the female's mouth, they are fully developed, like little replicas of their mother.

# ELECTRIC BLUE JOHANNI

Male and female electric blue johannis (Melanachromis johanni) have deep blue-black bodies, with a brilliant electric blue stripe extending nearly from nose to tail. M. interruptus are frequently sold as johannis, but the blue line is broken at regular intervals. These fish are rarely more than 12cm (5in) long and females remain smaller. Males display white egg spots on the anal fin. They are very aggressive for their size. Provide plenty of rockwork and caves for cover, to help the fish feel secure. Rockwork should extend over most of the tank bottom, and be stacked up to about a third of the tank's height. Be sure the stacked rock is secure, and tuck the bases of plastic plants between rocks. Never add just one fish to an African cichlid tank. Rearrange the rockwork and add at least four at a time to reduce aggression, and possibly prevent deaths.

**Origin:** Lake Malawi, Africa.

**Temperature:** 27°C (80°F) is ideal, but they will tolerate temperatures from 23°C (74°F) to 28.3°C (83°F).

**GH:** 21°dGH, hard. Tolerates a range from 9°dGH to 30°dGH. Add a small amount of salt or marine salt to their tank to harden the water to suit.

**pH:** 8.0 is ideal, but will tolerate 7.7 to 8.6 well. Avoid sudden changes in pH.

**Hardiness:** Cichlids do not tolerate nitrite at all. Even low levels of nitrite are fatal within a day or so. You shold never use cichlids to cycle a tank. Perform regular partial water changes.

**Feeding:** Choose a high-quality flake food and baby cichlid pellets in both vegetable and carnivorous flavours. You may need to rotate their food periodically, for variety. Offer some romaine lettuce or fresh spinach as well as live mosquito larvae, and brine shrimp as supplements. Take care not to pollute the tank, feeding only what will be eaten.

**Compatible tankmates:** Melanochromis auratus and chipokee, both tough customers from the same family. Other large African cichlids from the Rift Lakes, synodontis catfish, Chinese algae eaters.

**Avoid these tankmates:** Small, gentle, tropical community fish, small African cichlids.

**Breeding:** These cichlids are mouthbrooders and usually quite easy to breed, if the male doesn't kill the female. The female lays eggs on the gravel or a rock, while the male swims with her in a tight circle. She then turns around to pick up the eggs with her mouth. 'Egg spot' markings on the anal fin of the male look like eggs to the female and she tries to collect them in her mouth. In doing so, she collects a mouthful of sperm instead and this fertilizes the eggs. The female keeps the eggs in her mouth until they become free-swimming fry, which can take 21–50 days. During this time, the female does not usually feed and it is advisable to remove her (with the fry) to a separate maternity tank to develop in peace. Once the fry are released from the female's mouth, they are fully developed, like little replicas of their mother.

# KENNYI

The kennyi (*Metriaclima lombardoi*, formerly *Pseudotropheus lombardoi*) male makes other African cichlids seem tame. All young kennyi are blue, with vertical stripes if darker blue, like the adult female. When the male approaches puberty his color changes to an odd shade of pink. A few days later he is a brilliant clear yellow-orange. And his temperament is murderous. Regardless of rockwork, deliberate overcrowding, and constant change, there may be injuries in the tank. Minimum tank size for this species should be 200 liters (50 gallons). A net-breeder should be kept in a cabinet

near the aquarium, to allow his victims time to heal. They are very aggressive for their size. Provide plenty of rockwork and caves for cover, to help the fish feel secure. Rockwork should extend over most of the tank bottom, and be stacked up to about a third of the tank's height. Be sure the stacked rock is secure, and tuck the bases of plastic plants between rocks. Never add just one fish to an African cichlid tank. Rearrange the rockwork and add at least four at a time to reduce aggression, and possibly prevent deaths.

**Origin:** Lake Malawi, Africa.

**Temperature:** 27°C (80°F) is ideal, but they will tolerate temperatures from 23°C (74°F) to 28.3°C (83°F).

**GH:** 22°dGH, hard. Tolerates a range from 9°dGH to 30°dGH. Add a small amount of salt or marine salt to their tank to harden the water to this range.

**pH:** 8.1 is ideal, but will tolerate 7.7 to 8.6 well. Avoid sudden changes in pH.

**Hardiness:** Cichlids do not tolerate nitrite at all. Even low levels of nitrite are fatal within a day or so. Do not use cichlids to cycle a tank. Perform regular partial water changes.

**Feeding:** Choose a high-quality flake food and baby cichlid pellets in both vegetable and carnivorous flavors. You may need to rotate their food periodically, for variety. Offer some romaine lettuce or fresh spinach as well as live mosquito larvae, and brine shrimp as supplements. Take care not to pollute the tank, feeding only what will be eaten.

**Compatible tankmates:** *M. johanni*, *M. auratus* and *M. chipokee*, tough customers from the Melanachromis family. Other large African cichlids from the Rift Lakes, synodontis catfish, Chinese algae eaters.

**Avoid these tankmates:** Small, gentle, tropical community fish, small African cichlids.

**Breeding:** These cichlids are mouthbrooders and usually quite easy to breed, if the male does not kill the female. The female lays eggs on the gravel or a rock, while the male swims with her in a tight circle. She then turns around to pick up the eggs with her mouth. "Egg spot" markings on the anal fin of the male look like eggs to the female and she tries to collect them in her mouth. In doing so, she collects a mouthful of sperm instead and this fertilizes the eggs. The female keeps the eggs in her mouth until they become free-swimming fry, which can take 21–50 days. During this time, the female does not usually feed and it is advisable to remove her (with the fry) to a separate maternity tank to develop in peace. Once the fry are released from the female's mouth, they are fully developed, like little replicas of their mother.

# RED ZEBRA CICHLID

The red zebra cichlid (*Metriaclima estherae*, formerly *Pseudotropheus estherae*) looks very similar to the kennyi. Zebras from Lake Malawi's rocky shores come in various colors, depending on where they are found within the lake. They are available as albinos, and at least one morph features a yellow female, while the male is pale blue marked with vertical stripes of dark blue. They reach 12cm (5.5in) in size, and are quite aggressive. Provide plenty of rockwork and caves for cover, to help the fish feel secure. Rockwork should extend over most of the tank bottom, and be stacked up to about a third of the tank's height. Ensure the stacked rock is secure, and tuck the bases of plastic plants between rocks. Never add just one fish to an African cichlid tank. Rearrange the rockwork and add at least four at a time to reduce aggression, and prevent deaths.

**Origin:** Lake Malawi, Africa.

**Temperature:** 27°C (80°F) is ideal, but they will tolerate temperatures from 23°C (74°F) to 28.3°C (83°F).

**GH:** 22°dGH, hard. Tolerates a range from 9°dGH to 30°dGH. Add a small amount of salt or marine salt to their tank to harden the water to this range.

**pH:** 8.1 is ideal, but will tolerate 7.7 to 8.6 well. Avoid sudden changes in pH.

**Hardiness:** Cichlids do not tolerate nitrite at all. Even low levels of nitrite are fatal within a day or so. Do not use cichlids to cycle a tank. Perform regular partial water changes.

**Feeding:** Choose a high-quality flake food and baby cichlid pellets in both vegetable and carnivorous flavors. You may need to rotate their food periodically, for variety. Offer some romaine lettuce or fresh spinach as well as live mosquito larvae and brine shrimp as supplements. Take care not to pollute the tank, feeding only what will be eaten.

**Compatible tankmates:** *M. johanni*, *M. auratus* and *M. chipokee*, tough customers from the Melanachromis family. Other large African cichlids from the Rift Lakes, synodontis catfish, Chinese algae eaters.

**Avoid these tankmates:** Small, gentle, tropical community fish, small African cichlids, kennyi.

**Breeding:** These cichlids are mouthbrooders and usually quite easy to breed, if the male doesn't kill the female. The female lays eggs on the gravel or a rock, while the male swims with her in a tight circle. She then turns around to pick up the eggs with her mouth. "Egg spot" markings on the anal fin of the male look like eggs to the female and she tries to collect them in her mouth. In doing so, she collects a mouthful of sperm instead and this fertilizes the eggs. The female keeps the eggs in her mouth until they become free-swimming fry, which can take 21–50 days. During this time, the female does not usually feed and it is advisable to remove her (with the fry) to a separate maternity tank to develop in peace. Once the fry are released from the female's mouth, they are fully developed, like little replicas of their mother.

# SOCOLOFI

The Socolofi or Powder Blue cichlid, (*Pseudotropheus socolofi*), is another native of Lake Malawi with an attitude. They reach 12cm (5.5in) in size, and are quite aggressive. Provide plenty of rockwork and caves for cover, to help the fish feel secure. Rockwork should extend over most of the tank bottom, and be stacked up to about a third of the tank's height. Be sure the stacked rock is secure, and tuck the bases of plastic plants between rocks. Never add just one fish to an African cichlid tank. Rearrange the rockwork and add at least four at a time to reduce aggression, and possibly prevent deaths.

**Origin:** Lake Malawi, Africa.

**Temperature:** 27°C (80°F) is ideal, but they will tolerate temperatures from 23°C (74°F) to 28.3°C (83°F).

**GH:** 22°dGH, hard. Tolerates a range from 9°dGH to 30°dGH. Add a small amount of salt or marine salt to their tank to harden the water to this range.

**pH:** 8.1 is ideal, but will tolerate 7.7 to 8.6 well. Avoid sudden changes in pH.

**Hardiness:** Cichlids do not tolerate nitrite at all. Even low levels of nitrite are fatal within a day or so. Do not use cichlids to cycle a tank. Perform regular partial water changes.

**Feeding:** Choose a high-quality flake food and baby cichlid pellets in both vegetable and carnivorous flavors. You may need to rotate their food periodically, for variety. Offer some romaine lettuce or fresh spinach as well as live mosquito larvae, and brine shrimp as supplements. Take care not to pollute the tank, feeding only what will be eaten.

**Compatible tankmates:** *M. johanni*, *M. auratus* and *M. chipokee*, tough customers from the Melanachromis family. Other large African cichlids from the Rift Lakes, synodontis catfish, Chinese algae eaters.

**Avoid these tankmates:** Small, gentle, tropical community fish, small African cichlids.

**Breeding:** These cichlids are mouthbrooders and usually quite easy to breed, if the male does not kill the female. The female lays eggs on the gravel or a rock, while the male swims with her in a tight circle. She then turns around to pick up the eggs with her mouth. "Egg spot" markings on the anal fin of the male look like eggs to the female and she tries to collect them in her mouth. In doing so, she collects a mouthful of sperm instead and this fertilizes the eggs. The female keeps the eggs in her mouth until they become free-swimming fry, which can take 21–50 days. During this time, the female does not usually feed and it is advisable to remove her (with the fry) to a separate maternity tank to develop in peace. Once the fry are released from the female's mouth, they are fully developed, like little replicas of their mother.

# ELECTRIC BLUE HAP AHLI

The electric blue hap ahli (*Sciaenochromis fry-eri/ahli*) is coveted for its color and relative hardiness. Only buy tank-bred specimens, if you can find them. (Best source is other aquarists). They reach 15cm (6in) in size, and are quite aggressive. However, multiple males will share a 500 liters (125 gallons) aquarium with several other species of mbuna. Provide plenty of rockwork and caves for cover, to help the fish feel secure. Rockwork should extend over most of the tank bottom, and be stacked up to about a third of the tank's height. Be sure the stacked rock is secure, and tuck the bases of plastic plants between rocks. Never add just one fish to an African cichlid tank. Rearrange the rockwork and add at least four at a time to reduce aggression, and possibly prevent deaths.

**Origin:** Lake Malawi, Africa.

**Temperature:** 27°C (80°F) is ideal, but they will tolerate temperatures from 23°C (74°F) to 28.3°C (83°F).

**GH:** 18°dGH, hard. Tolerates a range from 9°dGH to 19°dGH. Add a small amount of salt or marine salt to their tank to harden the water to this range.

**pH:** 8.0 is ideal, but will tolerate 7.8 to 8.3 well. Avoid sudden changes in pH.

**Hardiness:** Cichlids do not tolerate nitrite at all. Even low levels of nitrite are fatal within a day or so. Don't use cichlids to cycle a tank. Do regular partial water changes.

**Feeding:** Choose a high-quality flake food and baby cichlid pellets in both vegetable and carnivorous flavors. You may need to rotate their food periodically, for variety. Offer some romaine lettuce or fresh spinach as well as live mosquito larvae as supplements. Take care not to pollute the tank, feeding only what will be eaten.

**Compatible tankmates:** *M. johanni*, *M. auratus* and *M. chipokee*, zebra cichlids, the Malawi eye-biter. Other large African cichlids from the Rift Lakes, synodontis catfish, Chinese algae eaters.

**Avoid these tankmates:** Small, gentle, tropical community fish, small African cichlids, kennyi.

**Breeding:** These cichlids are mouthbrooders and usually quite easy to breed, if the male doesn't kill the female. Multiple females are recommended. The female lays eggs on the gravel or a rock, while the male swims with her in a tight circle. She then turns around to pick up the eggs with her mouth. "Egg spot" markings on the anal fin of the male look like eggs to the female and she tries to collect them in her mouth. In doing so, she collects a mouthful of sperm instead and this fertilizes the eggs. The female keeps the eggs in her mouth until they become free-swimming fry, which can take 21–50 days. During this time, the female does not usually feed and it is advisable to remove her (with the fry) to a separate maternity tank to develop in peace. Once the fry are released from the female's mouth, they are fully developed, like little replicas of their mother.

Lake Tanganyika cichlids are more varied in behavior, body shape, and breeding technique than those from Lake Malawi. Some are mouthbrooders, while others place their eggs on rocks and guard them even after they are free-swimming. Apart from these differences they require similar care and maintenance.

# FAIRY CICHLID

The fairy cichlid (*Neolamprologus brichardi*, formerly *Lamprologus brichardi*) is a shoaling species, forming pairs only at breeding. They may reach 10cm (4in) in length. Parents care for the youngest fry. Older fry help care for younger fry. It is difficult to distinguish between males and females. Provide plenty of rockwork and caves for cover, to help the fish feel secure. Rockwork should extend over most of the tank bottom, and be  stacked up to about a third of the tank's height. Be sure the stacked rock is secure, and tuck the bases of plastic plants between rocks. Never add just one fish to an African cichlid tank. Rearrange the rockwork and add at least four fish at a time to reduce aggression, and possibly prevent deaths.

**Origin:** Lake Tanganyika, Africa.

**Temperature:** 24°C (75°F) is ideal, but they will tolerate temperatures from 22°C (72°F) to 25°C (77°F).

**GH:** 15°dGH, hard. Tolerates a range from 10°dGH to 20°dGH. Add a small amount of salt or marine salt to their tank to harden the water to this range.

**pH:** 8.0 is ideal, but will tolerate 7.5 to 8.5 well. Avoid sudden changes in pH.

**Hardiness:** Cichlids do not tolerate nitrite at all. Even low levels of nitrite are fatal within a day or so. Do not use cichlids to cycle a tank. Perform regular partial water changes.

**Feeding:** Choose a high-quality flake food and baby cichlid pellets in both vegetable and carnivorous flavors. You may need to rotate their food periodically, for variety. Offer some romaine lettuce or fresh spinach as well as live mosquito larvae as supplements. Take care not to pollute the tank, feeding only what will be eaten.

**Compatible tankmates:** Other cichlids from Tanganyika, synodontis catfish, Chinese algae eaters.

**Avoid these tankmates:** Small, gentle, tropical community fish, larger African cichlids.

**Breeding:** These cichlids lay their eggs in a cave and carefully tend them. Raise the temperature to 28°C (82°F) to encourage spawning. The female guards the nest.

# FRONTOSA CICHLID

The frontosa cichlid (*Cyphotilapia frontosa*) is a prized species amount serious aquarists. Males can reach 35cm (14in) in length, females 30cm (12in). A large aquarium is recommended, 500 liters (125 gallons). Frontosas are relatively gentle African cichlids, breaking up squabbles just by swimming through them. Their size is enough to intimidate their tankmates. The young fry retreat to mother's mouth when frightened, until she decides they are large enough to care for themselves. The male has a forehead hump. Provide plenty of rockwork and large caves for

cover, to help the fish feel secure. Rockwork should extend over most of the tank bottom, and be stacked up to about a third of the tank's height. Be sure the stacked rock is secure, and tuck the bases of plastic plants between rocks. Never add just one fish to an African cichlid tank. Rearrange the rockwork and add at least four fish at a time to reduce aggression, and possibly prevent deaths.

**Origin:** Lake Tanganyika, Africa.

**Temperature:** 25°C (77°F) is ideal, but they will tolerate temperatures from 24°C (75°F) to 26°C (79°F).

**GH:** 10°dGH, moderately hard. Tolerates a range from 10°dGH to 20°dGH. Add a small amount of salt or marine salt to their tank to harden the water to this range.

**pH:** 8.0 is ideal, but will tolerate 7.5 to 8.5 well. Avoid sudden changes in pH.

**Hardiness:** Cichlids do not tolerate nitrite at all. Even low levels of nitrite are fatal within a day or so. Do not use cichlids to cycle a tank. Perform regular partial water changes.

**Feeding:** Live food is preferred, including small crustaceans and molluscs. Choose a high-quality flake food and baby cichlid pellets in both vegetable and carnivorous flavors when the fish are young, to ensure adequate food for growth. Fresh and frozen food should be offered, including black and bloodworms, adult brine shrimp, krill, bits of grocery store shrimp as they get larger. Offer some romaine lettuce or fresh spinach as well as live mosquito larvae, and freeze-dried tubifex worms. Take care not to pollute the tank, feeding only what will be eaten.

**Compatible tankmates:** Other cichlids from Tanganyika, synodontis catfish, Chinese algae eaters.

**Avoid these tankmates:** Small fish. Small, gentle, tropical community fish. kennyi.

**Breeding:** These cichlids are mouthbrooders and usually quite easy to breed, if the male doesn't kill the female. Multiple females are recommended. The female lays eggs on the gravel or a rock, while the male swims with her in a tight circle. She then turns around to pick up the eggs with her mouth. "Egg spot" markings on the anal fin of the male look like eggs to the female and she tries to collect them in her mouth. In doing so, she collects a mouthful of sperm instead and this fertilizes the eggs. The female keeps the eggs in her mouth until they become free-swimming fry, which can take 21–50 days. During this time, the female does not usually feed and it is advisable to remove her (with the fry) to a separate maternity tank to develop in peace. Once the fry are released from the female's mouth, they are fully developed, like little replicas of their mother.

# LEMON CICHLID

The lemon cichlid (*Neolamprologus leleupi*, formerly *Lamprologus leleupi*) comes from Lake Tanganyika, and can reach 10cm (4in). The male has a slight forehead hump. Lemon cichlids are possibly the most aggressive of the Tanganyika cichlids. They will fit in best with their cousins from Malawi, no matter how large. Provide plenty of rockwork and large caves for cover, to help the fish feel secure. Rockwork should extend over most of the tank bottom, and be stacked up to about a third of the tank's height. Be sure the stacked rock is secure, and tuck the bases of plastic plants between rocks. Never add just one fish to an African cichlid tank. Rearrange the rockwork and add at least four fish at a time to reduce aggression, and possibly prevent deaths.

**Origin:** Lake Tanganyika, Africa.

**Temperature:** 25°C (77°F) is ideal, but they will tolerate temperatures from 24°C (75°F) to 26°C (79°F).

**GH:** 15°dGH, hard. Tolerates a range from 10°dGH to 20°dGH. Add a small amount of salt or marine salt to their tank to harden the water to this range.

**pH:** 8.0 is ideal, but will tolerate 7.5 to 8.5 well. Avoid sudden changes in pH.

**Hardiness:** Cichlids do not tolerate nitrite at all. Even low levels of nitrite are fatal within a day or so. Do not use cichlids to cycle a tank. Perform regular partial water changes.

**Feeding:** Choose a high-quality flake food and baby cichlid pellets in both vegetable and carnivorous flavors. You may need to rotate their food periodically, for variety. Offer some romaine lettuce or fresh spinach as well as live mosquito larvae as supplements. Take care not to pollute the tank, feeding only what will be eaten.

**Compatible tankmates:** Malawi cichlids, no matter how large or how aggressive, synodontis catfish, Chinese algae eaters.

**Avoid these tankmates:** Other Tanganyika cichlids, kennyi. Small, gentle, tropical community fish.

**Breeding:** These cichlids lay their eggs in a cave and carefully tend them. Raise the temperature to 28°C (82°F) to encourage spawning. The female guards the nest. The male will guard the entire area.

# TROPHEUS

The Tropheus (*Tropheus duboisi*) come in two color morphs. The Maswa has a yellow band, while Kigoma has a white band. This is not a good species for beginners. Provide plenty of rockwork and large caves for cover, to help the fish feel secure. Rockwork should extend over most of the tank bottom, and be stacked up to about a third of the tank's height. Be sure the stacked rock is secure, and tuck the bases of plastic plants between rocks. Never add just one fish to an African cichlid tank. Rearrange the rockwork and add at least four fish at a time to reduce aggression, and possibly prevent deaths.

**Origin:** Lake Tanganyika, Africa.

**Temperature:** 27°C (81°F) is ideal, but they will tolerate temperatures from 25°C (77°F) to 29°C (83°F).

**GH:** 20°dGH, hard. Tolerates a range from 15°dGH to 25°dGH. Add a small amount of salt or marine salt to their tank to harden the water to this range.

**pH:** 8.0 is ideal, but will tolerate 7.5 to 8.5 well. Avoid sudden changes in pH.

**Hardiness:** Cichlids do not tolerate nitrite at all. Even low levels of nitrite are fatal within a day or so. Do not use cichlids to cycle a tank. Perform regular partial water changes.

**Feeding:** This fish is a vegetarian, but requires some protein. Choose a high-quality flake food and baby cichlid pellets in both vegetable and carnivorous flavors. You may need to rotate their food periodically, for variety. Offer some garden peas, romaine lettuce, or fresh spinach daily. Live mosquito larvae can be offered occasionally. Take care not to pollute the tank, feeding only what will be eaten.

**Compatible tankmates:** Frontosas, other Tanganyika cichlids, synodontis catfish, Chinese algae eaters.

**Avoid these tankmates:** Malawi cichlids. Small, gentle, tropical community fish. kennyi.

**Breeding:** This species may be a mouthbrooder.

Kribensis (*Pelvicachromis pulcher*) originate in West Africa. The conditions they require are similar to those of South American cichlids. Temperamentally, they vary. If there is not a female in the tank that is ready to breed, kribensis are wonderful community fish. Let a female develop a glowing pink abdomen, and the kribs will systematically murder the other species to prepare the home for their young. Provide plants and a couple of small, rocky caves.

**Origin:** West Africa. Most are now tank-bred.

**Temperature:** 25°C (77°F) is ideal, but they will tolerate temperatures from 24°C (74°F) to 28°C (82°F).

**GH:** 10°dGH, moderate. Tolerates a range from 4°dGH to perhaps 15°dGH. Do not add calcium or magnesium salts, or stones that might leach these minerals into your water.

**pH:** 6.5 is ideal, but will tolerate 6.5 to 7.3 well. Avoid sudden changes in pH.

**Hardiness:** Kribensis require excellent water quality, and should not be used to cycle a tank.

**Feeding:** They happily accept most foods. A high quality flake alternated with small live foods such as very small mosquito larvae or brine shrimp. Feed daily.

**Compatible tankmates:** Large tetras, dwarf or full-sized gouramis, corydoras catfish, loaches, bala sharks, and other gentle community fish that prefer soft water. Enjoys a densely planted aquarium with a variety of plants for cover.

**Avoid these tankmates:** Should not be kept with large mouthed South American cichlids.

**Breeding:** Kribensis are egg-layers. These cichlids lay their eggs in a cave and carefully tend them. Move them to a breeder tank or remove other community fish from the tank. Raise the temperature to 28°C (82°F) to encourage spawning. The female guards the nest. The male will guard the entire area.

South American cichlids require aquariums with little rockwork and a lot of plants. The water quality is much softer, with a lower pH than Africans from the Rift Lakes.

# BLUE RAM CICHLID

The very beautiful blue ram cichlid (*Papiliochromis ramirezi*) from South America is only about 5cm (2in) long. Rams are quite timid, but soon venture out if kept with other small, non-aggressive fish in a well-planted tank. They prefer soft water but will live in hard water, as long as it is clean and very warm, kept at 26°C (79°F). Buy fish that are full in the body and swimming actively. Rams eat most foods, but should have live food at least once a week. Provide plants and a couple of small, rocky caves.

**Origin:** South America. Most are now tank-bred.

**Temperature:** 27°C (81°F) is ideal, but they will tolerate temperatures from 25°C (77°F) to 28°C (82°F).

**GH:** 7°dGH, moderate. Tolerates a range from 4°dGH to perhaps 10°dGH. Don't add calcium or magnesium salts, or stones that might leach these minerals into your water.

**pH:** 6.8 is ideal, but will tolerate 6.5 to 7.4 well. Avoid sudden changes in pH.

**Hardiness:** Cichlids do not tolerate nitrite at all. Even low levels of nitrite are fatal within a day or so. Do not use cichlids to cycle a tank. Perform regular partial water changes.

**Feeding:** They happily accept most foods. A high quality flake alternated with small live foods such as very small mosquito larvae or brine shrimp. Feed daily.

**Compatible tankmates:** Large tetras, dwarf or full-sized gouramis, corydoras catfish, loaches, bala sharks, and other gentle community fish that prefer soft water. Enjoys a densely planted aquarium with a variety of plants for cover.

**Avoid these tankmates:** Rams should not be kept with large mouthed south American cichlids.

**Breeding:** When a pair is ready to spawn, both fish select a rock and peck it clean. An egg tube, or ovipositor, starts to protrude from the female's underside and eventually she lays her eggs on the rock and the male fertilizes them. They lay a total of 100–200 and once all the eggs are laid, the female takes up position fanning them with her fins and pecking them clean. Both parents guard the eggs from all other fish, attacking potential predators if they approach too closely. The eggs hatch after about three days and the parents take them to a hole that they have dug in the gravel. Here they are guarded for another week until they can swim for themselves. At this stage, the whole family go out and about together to find food, which you should supply in the form of newly hatched brine shrimp.

The keyhole cichlid (*Cleithracara maroni, Acara maroni*) from South America can reach 10cm (4in) in the wild, but rarely exceeds 7cm (2.5in) in an aquarium. Keyhole cichlids are excellent additions to a planted aquarium. Keyhole cichlids eat most foods, but should have a bit of algae or a frozen green bean occasionally to supplement their diet. Provide plants and a couple of small, rocky caves.

**Origin:** South America. Most are now tank-bred.

**Temperature:** 24°C (75°F) is ideal, but they will tolerate temperatures from 22°C (72°F) to 27°C (79°F).

**GH:** 7°dGH, moderate. Tolerates a range from 4°dGH to perhaps 10°dGH. Do not add calcium or magnesium salts, or stones that might leach these minerals into your water.

**pH:** 6.8 is ideal, but will tolerate 6.5 to 7.4 well. Avoid sudden changes in pH.

**Hardiness:** Cichlids do not tolerate nitrite at all. Even low levels of nitrite are fatal within a day or so. Do not use cichlids to cycle a tank. Perform regular partial water changes.

**Feeding:** They happily accept most foods. A high quality flake alternated with garden peas (peeled), and small live foods such as very small mosquito larvae or brine shrimp. Feed daily.

**Compatible tankmates:** Large tetras, dwarf or full-sized gouramis, corydoras catfish, loaches, bala sharks, and other gentle community fish that prefer soft water. Enjoys a densely planted aquarium with a variety of plants for cover.

**Avoid these tankmates:** Keyhole cichlids should not be kept with large mouthed South American cichlids.

**Breeding:** When a pair is ready to spawn, both fish select a rock and peck it clean. An egg tube, or ovipositor, starts to protrude from the female's underside and eventually she lays her eggs on the rock and the male fertilizes them. They lay a total of 100–200 and once all the eggs are laid, the female takes up position fanning them with her fins and pecking them clean. Both parents guard the eggs from all other fish, attacking potential predators if they approach too closely. The eggs hatch after about three days and the parents take them to a hole that they have dug in the gravel. Here they are guarded for another week until they can swim for themselves. At this stage, the whole family go out and about together to find food, which you should supply in the form of newly hatched brine shrimp.

Angelfish and discus aren't dwarf cichlids, but they have small mouths compared to the really large South American cichlids. Neither are beginner's fish, but they are not as difficult to keep as many people believe. Both require excellent filtration, soft, slightly acidic water, frequent water changes, and relatively calm tankmates. If your aquarium is large enough, at least 220 liters (55 gallons), a beautiful planted community can be established around two or three angels or discus.

# DISCUS

Most discus (*Symphysodon aequifasciata/discus*) now available in shops are tank-bred hybrids. All the discus fish have large eyes that range in color from orange to bright red. Usually, these fish are not sold at less than 5cm (2in) in diameter. With good care they can reach 15cm (6in) across and at this size command a high price and look really stunning. Whatever the species, all discus fish require the same care in the aquarium.

**Origin:** Central America. Most are now tank-bred.

**Temperature:** 26°C (79°F) is ideal, but they will tolerate temperatures from 24°C (76°F) to 29°C (83°F).

**GH:** 4°dGH, soft. Tolerates a range from 1°dGH to perhaps 10°dGH. Do not add calcium or magnesium salts, or stones that might leach these minerals into your water.

**pH:** 6.8 is considered ideal, but will tolerate 6.5 to 7.4 well. Some discus are being bred at a pH of 7.5 or higher. Ask your dealer to test the pH in their discus tank, so that you can match it. Avoid sudden changes in pH.

**Hardiness:** Cichlids do not tolerate nitrite at all. Even low levels of nitrite are fatal within a day or so. Do not use cichlids to cycle a tank. Perform regular partial water changes.

**Feeding:** Foods offered to them must be small enough to fit into their tiny mouths. They enjoy finely blended beef heart, bloodworm, daphnia and flake food, as well as freeze-dried tubifex. Never feed live tubifex worms to discus as they contain so much bacterial matter that they are potentially fatal.

**Compatible tankmates:** Adult small tetras such as neons or black neons, congo tetras, corydoras catfish, clown loaches, bala sharks, and otocinclus or a pleco to keep the algae tidied up. Live plants should be placed around the edges, leaving a large, open swim area. Dwarf gouramis can be kept with large discus, but the similarity in shape and coloring may cause dwarf gouramis to bully young discus.

**Avoid these tankmates:** Discus should not be kept with barbs, full sized gouramis, giant danios, or excessively nippy tetras, platies, or swordtails. (Not every live-bearer will attack a large fish, but some will try, and they can injure the discus.) Do not keep discus with oscars or jack dempseys.

**Breeding:** There are no visible differences between male and female discus fish, so to obtain a pair, buy half a dozen fish and let them pair off. Discus spawn in the typical cichlid method, females laying eggs on a rock or leaf to be fertilized by the male. Discus fish always choose a vertical spawning site, often favoring the uplift of the undergravel filter. The female fans and guards the eggs while the male guards the immediate territory. After three days, the eggs hatch and the adults move the young to another site, where they are stuck by little sticky filaments. The young live on a yolk sac for a few days and eventually become free swimming. At this stage, an amazing phenomenon takes place. The young rise up and start to feed from the skin of the adult fish, each of the adults taking their turn to feed the young. After about 10 days, the young need other food to supplement the mucus from the parents' skin, so offer them newly hatched brine shrimp.

# WILD ANGELFISH

The original wild angelfish (*Pterophyllum scalare/altum*) featured vertical striping that allowed them to hide in underwater grasses, while they foraged for insect larvae on the surface. Wild-caught altum angels require very soft water with a pH of 6.5. Through constant breeding, angelfish now rank among the hardier fish. With so many aquarium-bred fish available, it seems a shame to deplete the native environment of these beauties. Provide plants, lean a piece of slate on one end of the tank, and add a couple of small, rocky caves for bottom-feeders to hide in.

**Origin:** South America. Most are now tank-bred.

**Temperature:** 28°C (82°F) is ideal, but they will tolerate temperatures from 27°C (81°F) to 30°C (86°F).

**GH:** 2°dGH, soft. Tolerates a range from 1°dGH to perhaps 5°dGH. Do not add calcium or magnesium salts, or stones that might leach these minerals into your water.

**pH:** 6.0 is ideal, but will tolerate 5.8 to 6.2 well. Avoid sudden changes in pH.

**Hardiness:** Cichlids do not tolerate nitrite at all. Even low levels of nitrite are fatal within a day or so. Do not use cichlids to cycle a tank. Perform regular partial water changes.

**Feeding:** They happily accept most foods. A high quality flake alternated with small live foods such as mosquito larvae or brine shrimp. They will also beg and can overeat. Feed daily.

**Compatible tankmates:** Large tetras, dwarf or full-sized gouramis, silver dollars, corydoras catfish, loaches, bala sharks, a red-tailed shark, geophagus, and other gentle community fish that prefer soft water. Provide low caves or tubing for bottom-feeders to hide in. Enjoys a densely planted aquarium with a variety of plants for cover.

**Avoid these tankmates:** Angelfish should not be kept with barbs, giant danios, or excessively nippy tetras, platies, or swordtails. (Not every live-bearer will attack a large angel, but some will try, and they can injure the angel.) Do not keep angels with oscars or jack dempseys.

**Breeding:** To identify male from female with accuracy, Angels must be adults. Behaviorally, males are more aggressive and will battle until only one male is left alive. To identify an adult angel's gender, view the fish when it is facing the front of the tank. The opening just in front of the anal fin is round on a female, vertically elongated on a male. To prepare fish for breeding, feed ample live food such as mosquito larvae. Add a piece of slate near some tall plants. The angels will lay the eggs on the slate. Prepare a breeding tank, without gravel, just a sponge filter (with a live biological filter cultured in it), a pH of 6.5 and soft water. Move the slate into it. When the babies hatch, feed the fry infusoria, followed by brine shrimp, gradually moving up to very small flake food. If feeding only flake food, feed a small portion several times a day.

# TANK-BRED ANGELFISH

Tank bred angelfish (*Pterophyllum scalare*) are as diverse as they are hardy. Angelfish color varieties have evolved, including the marbled angelfish, which can be black and mottled, gold, white, and any mixture of these, as well as fish with very exaggerated fin development. Like the other varieties, this marbled angelfish is ideal for the average community. It is not overly aggressive unless new fish are added to the aquarium, or it is a male and there are other males. It will eat smaller fish. It enjoys the same temperatures as other tropicals—in the region of 26°C (79°F)—and eats flake, freeze-dried, and live foods. Provide plants and a couple of small, rocky caves. A tall piece of slate leaned against the end wall of the tank will provide a comfortable angel hiding place.

**Origin:** South America. Most angels are now tank-bred.

**Temperature:** 26°C (79°F) is ideal, but they will tolerate temperatures from 24°C (76°F) to 29°C (83°F).

**GH:** 4°dGH, soft. Tolerates a range from 1°dGH to perhaps 10°dGH. Do not add calcium or magnesium salts, or stones that might leach these minerals into your water.

**pH:** 6.8 is considered ideal, but will tolerate 6.5 to 7.4 well. Some angelfish are being bred at a pH of 8.0. Ask your dealer to test the pH in their angel tank, so that you can match it. Avoid sudden changes in pH.

**Hardiness:** Cichlids do not tolerate nitrite at all. Even low levels of nitrite are fatal within a day or so. Do not use cichlids to cycle a tank. Perform regular partial water changes.

**Feeding:** They happily accept most foods. A high quality flake alternated with small live foods such as mosquito larvae or brine shrimp. They will also beg and can overeat. Feed daily.

**Compatible tankmates:** Large tetras, dwarf or full-sized gouramis, silver dollars, corydoras catfish, loaches, bala sharks, a red-tailed shark, geophagus, and other gentle community fish that prefer soft water. Provide low caves or tubing for bottom-feeders to hide in. Enjoys a densely planted aquarium with a variety of plants for cover.

**Avoid these tankmates:** Barbs, giant danios, or excessively nippy tetras, platies, or swordtails. (Not every livebearer will attack a large angel, but some will try, and they can injure the angel. Observe the tank if you add these.) Do not keep angels with oscars or jack dempseys.

**Breeding:** To identify male from female with accuracy, Angels must be adults. Behaviorally, males are more aggressive and will battle until only one male is left alive. To identify an adult angel's gender, view the fish when it is facing the front of the tank. The opening just in front of the anal fin is round on a female, elongated on a male. To prepare fish for breeding, feed ample live food such as mosquito larvae. Add a piece of slate near some tall plants. The angels will lay the eggs on the slate. Prepare a breeding tank, without gravel, just a sponge filter (with a live biological filter cultured in it), a pH of 6.5, and soft water. Move the slate into it. When the babies hatch, feed the fry infusoria, followed by brine shrimp, gradually moving up to very small flake food. If feeding only flake food, feed a small portion several times a day.

The convicts (*Cichlasoma nigrofasciatum*) are slightly smaller neotropical cichlids, growing to about 18cm (7in), slightly less for females. The body color is a light gray with many vertical black bars. These fish can be very aggressive. Provide a tank measuring 75cm (30in) or more. They greedily accept all foods. Males tend to have longer pointed dorsal and anal fins and grow larger, whereas females usually (but not always) have a few bright orange scales on the belly and sides.

**Origin:** Central America. Most are now tank-bred.

**Temperature:** 24°C (76°F) is ideal, but they will tolerate temperatures from 22°C (72°F) to 29°C (83°F).

**GH:** 12°dGH, moderate. Tolerates a range from 5°dGH to perhaps 20°dGH.

**pH:** 7.3 is considered ideal, but will tolerate 6.5 to 8.3 well. Avoid sudden changes in pH.

**Hardiness:** Cichlids don't tolerate nitrite. Even low levels of nitrite are fatal within a day or so. Do not use cichlids to cycle a tank. Perform regular partial water changes.

**Feeding:** Pellet foods (both vegetarian and carnivorous), bugs, bits of fish, beef heart, bloodworm, and flake food, as well as freeze-dried tubifex.

**Compatible tankmates:** If you have a male and a female convict, there are no compatible tankmates. Once they start to court, every other fish in the tank is about to die, regardless of size. Can be kept with other cichlids and full-sized gouramis if only one sex is present.

**Avoid these tankmates:** Community fish, small or delicate fish.

**Breeding:** Once you have a pair of convicts, they are sure to breed. Remove other species or set up a breeding tank. They spawn on a large flat stone and the eggs hatch after only 48 hours. The young live on a large yolk sac on their belly for the first few days and can be fed on newly hatched brine shrimp as soon as they are free-swimming, four to five days after hatching.

# FIREMOUTH CICHLID

The firemouth cichlid (*Thorichthys meeki, Cichlasoma meeki*) has a very low, pointed snout with which it roots through the gravel for food. Its most attractive feature is the stunning red throat, especially of the male. It is one of the less aggressive cichlids; to frighten a competitor, it will blow out its gills, but this is nearly all bluff. These fish grow to a maximum of 15cm (6in). Provide a tank measuring 75cm (30in) or more. Plant with hardy plants protected by pots, and provide rocky hideouts and roots for cover. Males tend to have longer pointed dorsal and are more intensely colored.

**Origin:** Central America. Most are now tank-bred.

**Temperature:** 23°C (74°F) is ideal, but they will tolerate temperatures from 22°C (72°F) to 27°C (79°F).

**GH:** 10°dGH, moderate. Tolerates a range from 5°dGH to perhaps 20°dGH.

**pH:** 7.0 is considered ideal, but will tolerate 6.5 to 8.0 well. Avoid sudden changes in pH.

**Hardiness:** Cichlids don't tolerate nitrite. Even low levels of nitrite are fatal within a day or so. Do not use cichlids to cycle a tank. Perform regular partial water changes.

**Feeding:** Sinking tablets, a high-quality flake food, blood-worm, and freeze-dried tubifex.

**Compatible tankmates:** Other cichlids, three-spot gouramis, loaches, and catfish until breeding starts. When breeding behavior begins you may need another aquarium for either the parents or the community.

**Avoid these tankmates:** Small or delicate fish.

**Breeding:** When a pair is ready to spawn, both fish dig a pit and peck it clean. She lays her eggs in the pit and the male fertilizes them. They lay a total of 100–500. Once all the eggs are laid, both parents guard the eggs from all other fish, attacking potential predators if they approach too closely. The parents will protect the very young fry. Offer live baby brine shrimp, crumbled flake.

# GEOPHAGUS SURINAMENSIS

Earth-eater and devil-fish are nicknames for geophagus. The *Geophagus surinamensis* (shown) is far from the only species sold as *Geophagus jurupari*, *G. altifrons* and *G. brachybrancus* hybrids are common in fish shops. They all start small, can reach 30cm (12in) within a year, and charm their owners. An aquarium for a geophagus should be at least 120cm (48in) long. They are shy and timid in a new tank. When they discover that the tetras will fit in their mouths, the tetras will be gone in the morning.

When they notice that they are the largest fish in the tank, they tend to take over, ruling it from the carefully cleared cave they have chosen. They are the worst of the gravel moving cichlids, since in nature they sift the bottom of lakes or streams looking for worms and other treats. Plants should be in heavy pots, or artificial with a heavy base. Choose a heavy, rounded gravel mixed with a very fine gravel. Neither should have terribly sharp edges, or the geophagus will have an injured mouth.

**Origin:** South America. Most are now tank-bred.

**Temperature:** 23°C (74°F) is ideal, but they will tolerate temperatures from 22°C (72°F) to 27°C (79°F).

**GH:** 8°dGH, moderate. Tolerates a range from 5°dGH to 10°dGH.

**pH:** 7.0 is considered ideal, but will tolerate 6.5 to 7.6 well. Avoid sudden changes in pH.

**Hardiness:** Cichlids don't tolerate nitrite. Even low levels of nitrite are fatal within a day or so. Do not use cichlids to cycle a tank. Perform regular partial water changes.

**Feeding:** Sinking catfish tablets or pellets, small whole earthworms, a high-quality flake food, bloodworm, and freeze-dried tubifex.

**Compatible tankmates:** Most large fish such as angelfish, kribensis, South American cichlids, gouramis, silver dollars, clown loaches, and large mouthed catfish. A Chinese algae eater or pleco is fine for algae control. When breeding behavior begins you may need another aquarium some members of the community.

**Avoid these tankmates:** Unpotted live plants, small fish.

**Breeding:** These cichlids are mouthbrooders and usually quite easy to breed. The female lays eggs on the gravel or a rock, while the male swims with her in a tight circle, fertilizing them. She then turns around to pick up the eggs with her mouth. Both parents will hold and protect the young in their mouths, at night, and in times of danger.

# JACK DEMPSEY CICHLID

The jack dempsey cichlid (*Nandopsis octofasciatum*, formerly *Cichlasoma octofasciatum*) takes its common name from the legendary American heavyweight boxer. This is an aggressive fish that burrows and bites other fish. The body is quite long and slim, although it becomes bulkier with age. The body has eight vertical dark bars (hence the species name octofasciatum), but these do not often show up, as the whole body is covered in a profusion of metallic blue, green, and gold scales that intensify in color with age. Jack dempseys will reach about 20cm (8in) or perhaps more in a really large tank, but 15cm (6in) is more normal. As in most neotropical cichlids, males have longer, more pointed dorsal

and anal fins, whereas females usually remain smaller than their male counterparts. Provide floating plants, a large cave of rocks and roots, and adequate cover for any tankmates.

**Origin:** Central America. Most are now tank-bred.

**Temperature:** 23°C (74°F) is ideal, but they will tolerate temperatures from 22°C (72°F) to 27°C (79°F).

**GH:** 8°dGH, moderate. Tolerates a range from 5°dGH to 10°dGH.

**pH:** 7.0 is considered ideal, but will tolerate 6.5 to 7.6 well. Avoid sudden changes in pH.

**Hardiness:** Cichlids do not tolerate nitrite at all. Even low levels of nitrite are fatal within a day or so. Do not use cichlids to cycle a tank. Perform regular partial water changes.

**Feeding:** They require some vegetable matter in their diet to help prevent Hith disease. Offer a vegetarian cichlid pellet, romaine lettuce, peas, grean beans, or whatever they will accept. Then offer a meat dish. Jack dempseys will eat a wide range of foods; blended beef heart is a good staple food. Other ideal foods are earthworms, pellets, and any of the frozen foods with some substance, such as cockle or river shrimp.

**Compatible tankmates:** Other South American cichlids and large mouthed catfish. A large pleco is best for algae control, provide a shallow rock cave for the pleco. When the fish gets larger, you may need another aquarium for some members of the community.

**Avoid these tankmates:** Unpotted live plants, smaller or less aggressive fish.

**Breeding:** It is not difficult to persuade these fish to spawn. Raising the temperature slightly from the normal 25°C (77°F) to about 26°C (79°F) triggers spawning, but these fish are so accommodating that often the temperature need not be altered. The pair lay and fertilize several hundred little gray eggs, usually on a rock but sometimes on the gravel. The eggs are tended by both fish and hatch after two to three days. The young live on their yolk sacs for a few days and, once free-swimming, can feed on newly hatched brine shrimp. The parents care for the young until they are 1.25cm (0.5in) long or more, but at this point the male may start to bully the female with the intention of spawning again.

# OSCAR

The messy and aggressive oscar (*Astronotus ocellatus*) can grow to 30cm (12in) or more in a really large tank. A 90–20cm (36–48in) tank will suffice for a single oscar alone, but if oscars are kept in pairs or with other cichlids, they need at least a 150cm (60in) tank. The body is a mottled gray, black, olive, or beige, varying according to mood, and the mucus coating gives the fish a matt appearance; these characteristics account for its other common names "velvet" or "marble" cichlid. The red oscar, the long-finned oscar, and the albino oscar are aquarium-bred lines.

Provide floating plants, some artificial plants with heavy anchors (that won't break glass), and adequate rocks or roots to provide cover for any tankmates.

**Origin:** South America. Most are now tank-bred.

**Temperature:** 23°C (74°F) is ideal, but they will tolerate temperatures from 22°C (72°F) to 27°C (79°F).

**GH:** 8°dGH, moderate. Tolerates a range from 5°dGH to 10°dGH.

**pH:** 7.0 is considered ideal, but will tolerate 6.5 to 7.6 well. Avoid sudden changes in pH.

**Hardiness:** Cichlids do not tolerate nitrite at all. Even low levels of nitrite are fatal within a day or so. Do not use cichlids to cycle a tank. Perform regular partial water changes.

**Feeding:** They require some vegetable matter in their diet to help prevent Hlth disease. Offer a vegetarian cichlid pellet, romaine lettuce, peas, green beans, or whatever they will accept. Then offer a meat dish from the list that follows. These cichlids will eat a wide range of foods; blended beef heart is a good staple food. Other ideal foods are earthworms, pellets, and any of the frozen foods with some substance, for example the cockle or river shrimp.

**Compatible tankmates:** Other South American cichlids and large mouthed catfish. A large pleco is best for algae control (provide a shallow rock cave for the pleco). When the fish gets larger, you may need another aquarium for some members of the community.

**Avoid these tankmates:** Unpotted live plants, smaller or less aggressive fish.

**Breeding:** It is not difficult to persuade these fish to spawn. Raising the temperature slightly from the normal 25°C (77°F) to about 26°C (79°F) triggers spawning, but these fish are so accommodating that often the temperature need not be altered. The pair lay and fertilize 1,000 eggs, usually on a rock but sometimes on the gravel. The eggs are tended by both fish and hatch after two to three days. The fry may be kept in a pit, covered by the parents. The young live on their yolk sacs for a few days and, once free-swimming, can feed on cyclops or newly hatched brine shrimp. The parents care for the young.

# SEVERUM

The severum (*Heros severus*) is a majestic and long lived South American cichlid. It grows into a 20cm (8in) fish. The young fish sports vertical stripes that provide protective coloring. As an adult the stripes are replaced by small spots, with distinctive patches along the sides and a black band near the tail. Considering their size, they are a very gentle fish. They do not burrow, and will not harm live plants. They can be mixed with other relatively peaceful cichlids of a different size and coloration. Severum require a large tank 150cm (60in), clean water, and plenty of vegetable matter, such as garden peas, spinach, and broad beans.

**Origin:** South America. Most are now tank-bred.

**Temperature:** 24°C (75°F) is ideal, but they will tolerate temperatures from 23°C (73°F) to 25°C (77°F).

**GH:** 5°dGH, soft. Tolerates a range from 3°dGH to 10°dGH.

**pH:** 6.5 is considered ideal, but will tolerate 6.0 to 7.0 well. Avoid sudden changes in pH.

**Hardiness:** Cichlids don't tolerate nitrite. Even low levels of nitrite are fatal within a day or so. Do not use cichlids to cycle a tank. Perform regular partial water changes.

**Feeding:** Large cichlids require some vegetable matter in their diet to help prevent Hith disease. Offer a vegetarian cichlid pellet, romaine lettuce, peas, grean beans, or whatever they will accept. Then offer a meat dish from the list that follows. These cichlids will eat a wide range of foods; blended beef heart is a good staple food. Other ideal foods are earthworms, pellets, and any of the frozen foods with some substance, such as cockle or river shrimp. May take flake if accustomed to it.

**Compatible tankmates:** Other cichlids such as the firemouth cichlid, gouramis, silver dollars, and large mouthed catfish. A large pleco is best for algae control (provide a shallow rock cave for the pleco). When the fish gets larger, you may need another aquarium for some members of the community.

**Avoid these tankmates:** Nippy fish such as barbs, small fish that could be eaten.

**Breeding:** The fins of the male are more pointed, and there may be reddish brown spots on his head. The female has a dark marking on her dorsal fin. Severum are choosy about partners, and may choose not to breed until they are comfortable. Raise the temperature to 28°C (82°F) to encourage spawning, and see if they show interest in each other. These cichlids lay their eggs on a rock and carefully tend them. The female guards the nest. The male will guard the entire area. The young live on their yolk sacs for a few days and, once free-swimming, can feed on cyclops or newly hatched brine shrimp. The parents care for the young.

# BLOOD PARROT CICHLID

The blood parrot cichlid has aquarium hobbyists on battle lines. An accidental cross-breed between the quetzal or red head cichlid (*V. synspilum*) and the midas cichlid (*Amphilophus citrinellum*) produced an exotic looking fish with improbable body lines and a mouth that won't quite close. Despite these disadvantages, it has been sold in fish shops for over 10 years. Some of the fish are dyed bright colors, and do not live long. But the undyed fish live relatively well. The blood parrot has fans that have had a single specimen for 10 years, before finally losing their pet to old age. Like many of the large

South American cichlids, it is a pet fish, recognizing its owner, begging for food, and interacting well with humans. It competes successfully in an aquarium. Nature did not intend the mix, but I suspect that the blood parrot will be here as long as fish shops choose to sell them. And fishkeepers need to understand the needs of any fish they keep. Provide an open swimming area, with some protected plantings at the sides and back of the tank. They also need an overhang, and rocky caves. Considering their size and breeding, blood parrots are a fairly gentle fish. They occasionally burrow, so protect live plants with pots. They can be mixed with other community fish. Blood parrots are a heavy bodied fish, so choose a large tank, at least 120cm (48in) long. Provide plenty of vegetable matter, such as garden peas, spinach, and broad beans.

**Origin:** This is a hybrid. All are tank-bred.

**Temperature:** 28°C (83°F) is ideal, but they will tolerate temperatures from 25°C (77°F) to 29°C (85°F).

**GH:** 8°dGH, moderate. Tolerates a range from 5°dGH to 15°dGH.

**pH:** 7.0 is considered ideal, but will tolerate 6.0 to 7.0 well. Avoid sudden changes in pH.

**Hardiness:** Cichlids do not tolerate nitrite at all. Even low levels of nitrite are fatal within a day or so. Do not use cichlids to cycle a tank. Perform regular partial water changes.

**Feeding:** Large cichlids require some vegetable matter in their diet to help prevent Hith disease. Offer a vegetarian cichlid pellet, romaine lettuce, peas, grean beans, or whatever they will accept. Then offer sinking catfish or carnivore pellets, blended beef heart, or bloodworms. May accept flake if accustomed to it.

**Compatible tankmates:** Black ghost knifefish, diamond tetras, other large tetras, gouramis, silver dollars, loaches, and large mouthed catfish.

**Avoid these tankmates:** Nippy fish such as barbs, small fish that could be eaten.

**Breeding:** Not recommended.

# NEON BLUE DWARF RAINBOW

The neon blue dwarf rainbow (*Melanotaenia praecox*) is a charming addition to a planted community aquarium. Start with a school of at least six fish. Keep the temperature cool. They can just tolerate 28°C (83°F) when necessary for medical reasons, but not a degree higher. They are not fussy eaters, demolishing flake and sinking pellets with equal joy. Take care not to overfeed, or they may overeat and develop incurable bloat. They only grow to 6cm (2.3in) in length, but they are muscular jumpers. Keep the aquarium tightly covered. Provide an open swimming area with some protected plantings at the sides and back of the tank. They can be mixed with many community fish, and seem to limit aggression to their own species. The larger females appear to direct the shoal.

**Origin:** Australia and New Guinea.

**Temperature:** 24°C (75°F) is ideal, but they will tolerate temperatures from 22°C (72°F) to 28°C (83°F).

**GH:** 8°dGH, moderate. Tolerates a range from 5°dGH to 15°dGH.

**pH:** 7.0 is considered ideal, but will tolerate 6.0 to 7.0 well. Avoid sudden changes in pH.

**Hardiness:** Rainbowfish do not tolerate nitrite well. Do not use them to cycle a tank. Perform regular partial water changes.

**Feeding:** A high quality flake supplemented by the occasional sinking pellet. Offer romaine lettuce, peas, grean beans, or whatever they will accept as a vegetable.

**Compatible tankmates:** Live plants and most community fish. Tetras of all sizes, silver dollars, discus, corydoras catfish, loaches, a red-tailed shark.

**Avoid these tankmates:** All large-mouthed cichlids and catfish.

**Breeding:** Rainbow fish are egg-layers.

Each furcata rainbow (*Popondichthys furcatus* or *Pseudomugil furcatus*) is a miniature work of art, from its blue eyes to its delicate yellow forked tail. Add a dozen or so to shoal in a 40 liter (10 gallon) planted aquarium. Just be sure the tank has adequate oxygen, and stays cool. The furcata rainbow is hardy when kept in cool, well-oxygenated water. They only reach 5cm (2in) in length, but they are muscular jumpers. Keep the aquarium tightly covered. Provide an open swimming area with plantings at the sides and back of the tank. They can be mixed successfully with small-mouthed community fish.

**Origin:** New Guinea.

**Temperature:** 25°C (77°F) is ideal, but they will tolerate temperatures from 22°C (72°F) to 27°C (81°F).

**GH:** 14°dGH, moderate. Tolerates a range from 5°dGH to 12°dGH.

**pH:** 7.6 is considered ideal, but will tolerate 6.0 to 8.0 well. Avoid sudden changes in pH.

**Hardiness:** Rainbowfish do not tolerate nitrite well. Do not use them to cycle a tank. Perform regular partial water changes.

**Feeding:** A high quality flake supplemented by tiny live food such as freshly hatched brine shrimp. May nibble on the occasional sinking pellet. Keep with live plants and a bit of algae, or offer romaine lettuce, peas, grean beans, or whatever they will accept as a vegetable.

**Compatible tankmates:** Live plants and most small community fish. Small tetras such as neons, live-bearers, corydoras catfish, loaches.

**Avoid these tankmates:** Large-mouthed fish.

**Breeding:** Rainbow fish are egg-layers.

The Australian rainbow or western rainbow (*Melanotaenia splendida australis*) is a hardy, attractive, and active fish. They like to shoal, so add at least three, preferably six to a planted aquarium. They will add action. They may reach 10cm (4in) in the wild, but rarely exceed 8cm (3.3in) in an aquarium. They also like well oxygenated water and relatively cool temperatures, but are less vulnerable to environmental changes than the smaller species. They are muscular jumpers. Keep the aquarium tightly covered. Provide an open swimming area with plantings at the sides and back of the tank. They can be kept with most community fish.

**Origin:** Northwestern Australia.

**Temperature:** 25°C (77°F) is ideal, but they will tolerate temperatures from 22°C (72°F) to 28°C (83°F).

**GH:** 14°dGH, moderate. Tolerates a range from 5°dGH to 12°dGH.

**pH:** 7.6 is considered ideal, but will tolerate 6.5 to 8.0 well. Avoid sudden changes in pH.

**Hardiness:** Rainbowfish do not tolerate nitrite well. Do not use them to cycle a tank. Perform regular partial water changes.

**Feeding:** A high quality flake supplemented by live food such as live mosquito larvae. May nibble on the occasional sinking pellet. Keep with live plants and a bit of algae, or offer romaine lettuce, peas, grean beans, or whatever they will accept as a vegetable.

**Compatible tankmates:** Live plants and most community fish. Tetras of any size, gouramis, angelfish, silver dollars, live-bearers, corydoras catfish, loaches, a red-tailed shark.

**Avoid these tankmates:** Large-mouthed South American cichlids.

**Breeding:** Rainbow fish are egg-layers.

The yellow rainbow or Lake Tebera rainbowfish (*Melanotaenia herbertaxelrodi*) is another hardy, shoaling rainbow. Choose at least three, preferably six of this attractive species. They will add action and color. They may reach 9cm (3.75in) in the wild, but rarely exceed 8cm (3.3in) in an aquarium. They require well oxygenated water and relatively cool temperatures, but are less vulnerable to environmental changes than the smaller species. Rainbowfish are muscular jumpers. Keep the aquarium tightly covered. Provide an open swimming area with plantings at the sides and back of the tank. They can be kept with most community fish.

**Origin:** New Guinea.

**Temperature:** 23°C (73°F) is ideal, but they will tolerate temperatures from 20°C (68°F) to 26°C (79°F).

**GH:** 10°dGH, moderate. Tolerates a range from 5°dGH to 12°dGH.

**pH:** 7.6 is considered ideal, but will tolerate 7.0 to 8.0 well. Avoid sudden changes in pH.

**Hardiness:** Rainbowfish do not tolerate nitrite well. Do not use them to cycle a tank. Perform regular partial water changes.

**Feeding:** A high quality flake supplemented by live food such as live mosquito larvae. May nibble on the occasional sinking pellet. Keep with live plants and a bit of algae, or offer romaine lettuce, peas, grean beans, or whatever they will accept as a vegetable.

**Compatible tankmates:** Live plants and most community fish. Tetras of any size, gouramis, angelfish, silver dollars, live-bearers, corydoras catfish, loaches, a red-tailed shark.

**Avoid these tankmates:** Large-mouthed South American cichlids.

**Breeding:** Rainbowfish are egg-layers.

# NEW GUINEA "RED" RAINBOWFISH

The New Guinea "red" rainbowfish (*Glossolepis incisus*) is one of the more expensive rainbows, and it should be. Serious aquarists need to work on breeding this species soon. It is still being exported even though it is a threatened species. Can be kept as a single specimen with other varieties of rainbow, or most tropical fish. They will add action and brilliant, shimmering color.

They may reach 12cm (4.8in) in an aquarium. They require well-oxygenated water and relatively cool temperatures. Rainbowfish are muscular jumpers, so keep the aquarium tightly covered. Provide an open swimming area with plantings at the sides and back of the tank. They can be kept with most community fish.

**Origin:** Asia, Lake Sentani in Irian Jaya, Indonesia.

**Temperature:** 23°C (73°F) is ideal, but they will tolerate temperatures from 22°C (72°F) to 24°C (76°F).

**GH:** 10°dGH, moderate. Tolerates a range from 9°dGH to 19°dGH.

**pH:** 7.5 is considered ideal, but will tolerate 7.0 to 8.0 well. Avoid sudden changes in pH.

**Hardiness:** Rainbowfish do not tolerate nitrite well. Do not use them to cycle a tank. Perform regular partial water changes.

**Feeding:** A high quality flake supplemented by live food such as mosquito larvae, other insect larvae. May nibble on the occasional sinking pellet. Keep with live plants and a bit of algae, or offer romaine lettuce, peas, grean beans, or whatever they will accept as a vegetable.

**Compatible tankmates:** Live plants and most community fish. Tetras of any size, gouramis, angelfish, silver dollars, live-bearers, corydoras catfish, loaches, keyhole cichlids or rams, a red-tailed shark.

**Avoid these tankmates:** Large-mouthed South American cichlids, aggressive fish.

**Breeding:** Rainbowfish are egg-layers.

The green pufferfish, freshwater (*Tetraodon fluviatilis*) is not a fish for beginners. None of the pufferfish really are. Pufferfish are predators that require live food, large tanks, and brackish water. Proper brackish water for puffers means purchasing marine quality salt (not aquarium salt, not table salt), and mixing and testing until the tank is at the proper GH. With consistent care and the conditions listed above, they can live for a long time. They are attractive and endlessly on the move, searching for the next delicate, moving morsel they can eat. Keep the aquarium tightly covered, since puffers will jump, particularly if an insect flies across top of the tank. Provide a cave, or caves. Pufferfish will take bites out of much larger fish, so they do not belong in a community tank.

**Origin:** Asia, India, Bangladesh, Sri Lanka, Borneo.

**Temperature:** 26°C (79°F) is ideal, but they will tolerate temperatures from 24°C (76°F) to 28°C (83°F).

**GH:** 15°dGH, hard. Tolerates a range from 10°dGH to 25°dGH.

**pH:** 7.0 is considered ideal, but will tolerate 7.0 to 8.0 well. Avoid sudden changes in pH.

**Hardiness:** Pufferfish don't tolerate bad water conditions. Don't use them to cycle a tank. Do regular partial water changes with marine salt to harden the water.

**Feeding:** Live food. Ghost shrimp, insects, bloodworms, and pond snails.

**Compatible tankmates:** African cichlids and inexpensive mollies.

**Avoid these tankmates:** Most community fish, slow-moving aggressive fish, and invertebrates.

**Breeding:** Pufferfish have never been bred before in home aquariums.

# ALGAE EATING SHRIMP

The Algae eating shrimp (*Caradina japonica*) is a shrimp just slightly larger than a ghost shrimp, measuring about 3cm (1.2in). It has a brown streak visible running the length of its body. Its claim to fame is its longevity, and a taste for hair or thread algae. When it runs out of algae, the shrimp will scavenge for flake food on the bottom. This shrimp can live for two years, as long as it doesn't jump out of the aquarium. Keep the tank tightly covered. It can survive in most community aquariums without being eaten, and where it lives thread algae disappears. It will attempt to eat red brush algae, but doesn't seem to be as successful with it. Malachite green will kill this shrimp (and many other things), but the shrimp survives most other medications used in aquaria.

**Origin:** Asia

**Temperature:** 26°C (79°F) is ideal, but they will tolerate temperatures from 21°C (70°F) to 28°C (83°F).

**GH:** 8°dGH, moderate. Tolerates a range from 4°dGH to 12°dGH.

**pH:** 7.0 is considered ideal, but will tolerate 6.5 to 8.0 well. Avoid sudden changes in pH.

**Hardiness:** Algae eating shrimp do not tolerate nitrite

Do not use them to cycle a tank. Perform regular partial water changes.

**Feeding:** Algae, all varieties, flake food that falls to the bottom of the tank.

**Compatible tankmates:** Community fish.

**Avoid these tankmates:** African cichlids, large-mouthed South American cichlids.

**Breeding:** Algae eating shrimp have not been bred in home aquariums.

# MARINE FISH FOR YOUR AQUARIUM

In simple terms, there are two sorts of fish; those that live in freshwater and those that live in saltwater. The species described and discussed in this final section of the book are all tropical marine fish, and nearly all are found on or around the world's tropical reefs—in the Indian Ocean, in the Pacific, or in and around the Caribbean.

Many fishkeepers have happily kept tropical freshwater fish for many years before deciding one day to move on to marines. Perhaps it is the sight of a clownfish darting among the tentacles of an anemone that sparks their interest, perhaps it is the brilliance of the colors and patterns of marine fish, or maybe it is the challenge of keeping these beautiful species in a carefully monitored environment that makes the prospect so exciting. Whatever the reason, marine fishkeeping has increased enormously in popularity. On the following pages you will find examples of many of the commonly available species, along with some more unusual varieties and some to avoid.

Fish density is critical in a marine aquarium as marine fish are much more territorial than freshwater fish. Add fish after, or during, re-arranging the aquarium. Providing additional cover, such as rockwork, live rock, or even artificial "silk" marine plants can help preserve your new fishes' lives. Allow a minimum of 40 liters (10 gallons) of water volume for each large fish and minimum of 20 liters (5 gallons) water volume for each small fish. Compatible tankmates are not suggested, since every marine aquarium and every individual marine fish is different. Particularly good combinations are suggested under "special requirements," and particularly bad ones are noted in "avoid these tankmates."

# DAMSELFISH—
# BOLD AND ENERGETIC

Damsels are found worldwide around the tropical reefs, living in shallow waters and rarely exceeding 7.5cm (3in) in length. Scientists call them filter-feeders, but in an aquarium they readily take solids, including flaked foods. They have many advantages for the home aquarist in that they are among the cheapest available fish, exceedingly hardy and disease-resistant, nitrite-tolerant, and very easy to feed. Many are boldly colored, and they do not grow too large for any but the smallest aquarium. They can be housed safely with many types of fish and most invertebrates, and they can be bought singly or in small shoals.

However, there is a catch; damsels are related to freshwater cichlids and tend to share that family's aggressive behavior. As damsels are so robust and adventurous themselves, they seem to expect other fish to share the same instincts, and many more shy and sensitive fish lose out in the competition for food and space.

## Hints and tips on damselfish

Do not keep the larger species of damselfish with butterflyfish and cowfish or any fish with trailing appendages likely to be nipped. The damselfish family is hermaphrodite by nature, i.e. each fish can become either sex. Put ten of these fish together in a tank, and you will identify one dominant male and nine females. Remove the male and soon one of the females will take over the male role and coloring!

# BLUE-GREEN DAMSELFISH OR CHROMIS

The untypically shy blue-green damselfish or chromis (*Chromis viridis*) is a small gentle species with subtle rather than bold coloring. It is perfect for an invertebrate set-up, but always keep it in a shoal of its own species.

**Origin:** Indo-Pacific

**Temperature:** 26°C (79°F) is ideal, but will tolerate temperatures from 25°C (77°F) to 27°C (81°F).

**SG:** 1.018-1.023

**pH:** 8.3

**Special requirements:** Unhappy alone, chromis are hardiest when kept in a shoal. These fish are comfortable in a reef environment.

**Feeding:** Feed every other day, alternating foods. Frozen marine blend, fresh shrimp pieces, freeze-dried plankton, and quality marine flake are recommended.

**Avoid these tankmates:** Groupers, lionfish.

**Breeding:** Chromis have not been successfully bred in home aquariums.

# DOMINO DAMSEL

The popular domino damsel (*Dascyllus trimaculatus*) is usually 2.5cm (1in) long when you buy it and grows to about 5cm (2in) in the tank. Juveniles sometimes have an identity problem, behaving like cleaner wrasse at one moment and "cleaning" other fish, and then frightening their owners by diving into anemones with the clownfish. Dominos are not as aggressive as some other species of damsels.

**Origin:** Indo-West Pacific

**Temperature:** 26°C (79°F) is ideal, but will tolerate temperatures from 25°C (77°F) to 27°C (81°F).

**SG:** 1.018-1.023

**pH:** 8.3

**Special requirements:** Comfortable in a reef environment, juveniles often rest in coral heads or anemones.

**Feeding:** Feed every other day, alternating foods. Frozen marine blend, fresh shrimp pieces, freeze-dried plankton, and quality marine flake are recommended.

**Avoid these tankmates:** Groupers, lionfish.

**Breeding:** These fish have not been successfully bred in home aquariums.

The electric blue damsel or sapphire devil (*Chrysiptera cyanae*) is usually 3cm (1.3in) long when you buy it and grows to about 8cm (3in) in the tank. The fish will patiently clear a gravel pit beneath the edge of its chosen rock, and occupy it. It is sturdy enough to cycle the aquarium. Either return it to the pet store or be sure to rearrange and move its chosen rock when you add more fish. Electric blue damsels are very territorial, but their color is truly brilliant.

**Origin:** Indo-West Pacific

**Temperature:** 26°C (79°F) is ideal, but will tolerate temperatures from 25°C (77°F) to 27°C (81°F).

**SG:** 1.018-1.023

**pH:** 8.3

**Special requirements:** These fish are best kept one to a tank. They are very comfortable in a reef environment.

**Feeding:** Feed every other day, alternating foods. Frozen marine blend, fresh shrimp pieces, freeze-dried plankton, quality marine flake.

**Avoid these tankmates:** Groupers, lionfish.

**Breeding:** Have not been successfully bred in home aquariums.

# THREE-STRIPE DAMSEL

The three-stripe damsel (*Dascyllus aruanus*) is usually 2.5cm (1in) long when you buy it and grows to 8cm (3in) or larger in the tank. They are very attractive fish, and can be kept in a shoal. Do not keep them in a reef aquarium with gorgonian corals as they are notorious coral nippers. They are hardy and can be used to cycle a tank.

**Origin:** Indo-West Pacific

**Temperature:** 26°C (79°F) is ideal, but will tolerate temperatures from 25°C (77°F) to 27°C (81°F).

**SG:** 1.018-1.023

**pH:** 8.3

**Special requirements:** These fish will shoal if all are added at the same time. They enjoy reef tanks, and will not disturb anemones. However, they will nip at gorgonians and possibly other corals.

**Feeding:** Feed every other day, alternating foods. Frozen marine blend, fresh shrimp pieces, freeze-dried plankton, quality marine flake.

**Avoid these tankmates:** Gorgonian corals, groupers, lionfish.

**Breeding:** Has been reared in captivity, but this would be a very difficult task in a home aquarium.

# CLOWNFISH—
# COMPANIONS TO ANEMONES

Clownfish, or anemonefish, are not as widespread as damsels. The 30 or so species are distributed throughout the Pacific Basin, but none are native to the Caribbean area. Without exception, clownfish are good-natured toward other species, and make ideal companions in fish and in mixed fish and invertebrate systems. Unfortunately, they are not so tolerant of each other and it sometimes proves difficult to keep two members of the same or different species together. Clowns are easy to feed, accepting any of the proprietary foods, and are reasonably hardy and disease-resistant, though they are not nitrite-tolerant. All clownfish enjoy what is called a symbiotic relationship with certain species of anemones. Anemones have stinging cells in their tentacles with which they stun their food—and most fish are included as potential meals. Somehow, however, clownfish are immune to the stings and use the anemones for shelter and, at least to human eyes, for comfort.

## Hints and tips for clownfish

Most clownfish do seem to survive perfectly adequately without anemones and it seems reasonably certain that it is not cruel to keep them apart. However, there is no doubt that if you deny yourself the opportunity of observing this fascinating relationship then you are missing one of the major joys of marine fishkeeping. Keeping an anemone alive for your clownfish will involve substantially more light than standard aquarium fixtures offer. Feed the anemone a bite of shrimp at least weekly, when the light first comes on.

# SEBAE OR YELLOWTAIL CLOWNFISH

Sebae or yellowtail clownfish (*Amphiprion clarkii*) are great fans of the sebae anemone. If the anemone dies, or there is no anemone, the fish adapts by feeding its rock. It will literally choose a rock in the aquarium as its own, and faithfully drop food on it at every feeding, and even sleep near it at night. If an anenome is present, the fish will feed it, then take the food away, rearrange it, swim around with it, drop it on the tank floor, and forget all about it. Feeding the anemone a bit of shrimp can involve netting the clownfish and confining it for 20 minutes or so. At least the clownfish faithfully sleeps in his anemone.

**Origin:** Indo-West Pacific

**Temperature:** 26°C (79°F) is ideal, but will tolerate temperatures from 25°C (77°F) to 27°C (81°F).

**SG:** 1.018-1.023

**pH:** 8.3

**Special requirements:** A pair of these clowns added at the same time might share the aquarium peacefully. They enjoy reef tanks, and are very fond of anemones.

**Feeding:** Feed every other day, alternating foods. Frozen marine blend, fresh shrimp pieces, freeze-dried plankton, quality marine flake.

**Avoid these tankmates:** Groupers, lionfish.

**Breeding:** Has been reared in captivity, but this would be difficult to achieve in a home aquarium.

A tomato clownfish (*Amphiprion frenatus*) will not want to share its tank, or anemone, with another clown of any color. Other bright red clowns include *A. ephippium* and *A. rubrocinctus*. All these species have different markings as juveniles and all have regional variations. Most "tomato" clowns have a white vertical stripe just behind their eyes, and many also have a dark blotch on their flanks. Tomato clowns are one of the few truly red marine fish available, and so are popular just for the sake of variety. They all grow to a length of about 8cm (3in) in captivity and are a little more boisterous than most other clownfish. If you can buy a matched pair, at the same time, they will often live together in harmony for many years.

**Origin:** Indo-West Pacific

**Temperature:** 26°C (79°F) is ideal, but will tolerate temperatures from 25°C (77°F) to 27°C (81°F).

**SG:** 1.018-1.023

**pH:** 8.3

**Special requirements:** A pair of these clowns added at the same time might share the aquarium peacefully. They enjoy reef tanks, and are very fond of anemones.

**Feeding:** Feed every other day, alternating foods. Frozen marine blend, fresh shrimp pieces, freeze-dried plankton, quality marine flake.

**Avoid these tankmates:** Groupers, lionfish.

**Breeding:** Has been reared in captivity, but it would be difficult in a home aquarium.

# ANGELFISH—
# SPECTACULAR AND MAJESTIC

With their spectacular markings and regal bearing, angelfish remain the undisputed "kings" of the home aquarium. However, they are a little more demanding than damsels and clownfish, so if you are a novice aquarist you should gain a few months experience before attempting to keep this group.

Angels are reasonably hardy and robust and generally easy to feed, but they do demand very high water quality. Regular water changes are essential, as angels react adversely to positive nitrate readings and a pH level that is too low (i.e. too acidic). Angels are omnivores and their diet must include vegetable matter. Since they are natural grazers and nibblers, it is important to house angels in tanks containing a sufficient layer of natural algae. In practice, this means that angels should only be housed in aquariums with lighting sufficiently powerful to create the necessary growth of algae. Most angels are also suitable to some extent in invertebrate tanks. Other than sponges and anemones, there are very few invertebrates that angels would directly harm, so it is only their size that could cause a problem in an invertebrate tank.

## Hints and tips for angelfish

Angelfish make very obvious show fish in virtually any type of marine aquarium, but only keep them if you are committed to high water quality. Dwarf angels are perfect cohabitants with any invertebrates except anemones or sponges. In spacious invertebrate aquariums it is quite in order to introduce some juvenile specimens of the larger angels.

The flame angel (*Centropyge loriculus*) is one of the most striking of dwarf angelfish. This beautiful fish reaches only 10cm (4in) in length and thrives in reef or invertebrate environments.

**Origin:** Pacific Ocean, from Australia and Papua New Guinea to Hawaii.

**Temperature:** 26°C (79°F) is ideal, but will tolerate temperatures from 25°C (77°F) to 27°C (81°F).

**SG:** 1.018-1.023

**pH:** 8.3

**Special requirements:** The flame angel needs very high water quality with frequent water changes and does not tolerate nitrates well. It thrives best in a reef or invertebrate aquarium, where it nibbles algae from the living rock. It will not harm corals, but should not share a tank with an anemone as angels consider anemone tips a gourmet treat.

**Feeding:** Feed every other day, alternating foods. Frozen marine blend, fresh shrimp pieces, freeze-dried plankton, quality marine flake.

**Avoid these tankmates:** Anemones, groupers, lionfish.

**Breeding:** Has been reared in captivity, but it would be very difficult in a home aquarium.

# CORAL BEAUTY, OR PURPLE ANGEL

The coral beauty, or purple angel, (*Centropyge bispinosus*) is probably the best-known dwarf angel, and it also seems to be the hardiest. It does not exceed 7.5cm (3in) in length, but supplies are plentiful. The rusty angel (*C. ferrugatus*) and the russet angel (*C. potteri*) are similar in appearance and make very useful additions to any set-up. All three dwarf angels are beautiful, but bearing compatibility in mind, it is not a good idea to house any two of them together.

**Origin:** Indo-Pacific, from East Africa to the Tuamoto islands, throughout Micronesia.

**Temperature:** 26°C (79°F) is ideal, but will tolerate temperatures from 25°C (77°F) to 27°C (81°F).

**SG:** 1.018-1.023

**pH:** 8.3

**Special Requirements:** These fish demand very high water quality with frequent water changes and do not tolerate nitrates well. The purple angel thrives best in a reef or invertebrate aquarium, where it nibbles algae from the living rock. It will not harm corals, but should not share a tank with an anemone.

**Feeding:** Feed every other day, alternating foods. Frozen marine blend, fresh shrimp pieces, freeze-dried plankton, quality marine flake.

**Avoid these tankmates:** Anemones, groupers, lionfish.

**Breeding:** Has not been reared in captivity.

The koran angel (*Pomacanthus semicirculatus*) is a large, majestic loner. It can reach 40cm (16in) in the wild, and frequently reaches 15cm (6in) in an aquarium. It also thrives in reef or invertebrate environments.

**Origin:** Indo-West Pacific

**Temperature:** 26°C (79°F) is ideal, but will tolerate temperatures from 25°C (77°F) to 27°C (81°F).

**SG:** 1.018-1.023

**pH:** 8.3

**Special requirements:** The koran angel will need very high water quality with frequent water changes. It does not tolerate nitrates well. It will live happily in a fish-only aquarium, but enjoys an invertebrate environment, where it nibbles algae from the living rock. It will not harm corals, but should not share a tank with an anemone.

**Feeding:** Feed every other day, alternating foods. Frozen marine blend, fresh shrimp pieces, freeze-dried plankton, quality marine flake.

**Avoid these tankmates:** Anemones, groupers, lionfish.

**Breeding:** Has not been reared in captivity.

# EMPEROR ANGEL

The most popular of the angels is the emperor angel (*Pomacanthus imperator*), a magnificent creature that can reach about 25cm (10in) in captivity. It can become very tame and will live for many years. Take a little care when buying juvenile angels as it is easy to confuse a juvenile emperor with a juvenile koran, which has very similar markings. Usually the latter is much less expensive.

**Origin:** Indo-Pacific Red Sea and East Africa to Hawaii, U.S.A. Japan to the Great Barrier Reef.

**Temperature:** 26°C (79°F) is ideal, but will tolerate temperatures from 25°C (77°F) to 27°C (81°F).

**SG:** 1.018- 1.023

**pH:** 8.3

**Special requirements:** Very high water quality with frequent water changes. Does not tolerate nitrates well. The emperor angel thrives best in a reef or invertebrate aquarium, where it nibbles from the living rock, eating algae, sponges and encrusting microscopic creatures. It will not harm corals, but should not share a tank with an anemone. Angels consider anemone tips a gourmet treat.

**Feeding:** Feed every other day, alternating foods. Frozen marine blend, fresh shrimp pieces, freeze-dried plankton, quality marine flake.

**Avoid these tankmates:** Anemones, groupers, lionfish.

**Breeding:** Has not been reared in captivity.

# BUTTERFLYFISH—
# BEAUTIFUL BUT SHY

Marine butterflyfish are closely related to marine angels, but are quite different in both appearance and in habits. Butterflies are very widespread throughout the world's tropical seas wherever there are coral reefs. They rely heavily on the reefs for food, as well as for protection, and would not normally stray even a few meters away from their natural home.

Butterflies have a small mouth and need to peck at food constantly; consequently they are slow growers, rarely exceeding 15cm (6in) long. Butterflyfish are not fast swimmers and have no natural protection against predators other than camouflage. Therefore, not surprisingly, they are shy and rather sensitive fish. Never put butterflyfish with boisterous fish, such as damsels and triggers, as they cannot compete with either for territory or for food.

Translating a butterflyfish's natural lifestyle into a captive environment requires careful consideration. Firstly, with only two exceptions, butterflyfish are unsuitable for invertebrate systems, since they readily attack and eat coral heads, anemones, tubeworms, cucumbers, etc. Since they cannot consume much food at one meal, the only chance of keeping them alive for a reasonable time is to provide frequent snacks. To compound the problem, many butterflyfish will not touch flaked food, so frozen or preserved mysis shrimps or brine shrimp (*Anemia sauna*) are essential.

Many serious aquarists prepare food for their marine fish by purchasing small quantities of white fish, shrimp, clams, or other seafood in a grocery store. Clean, rinse thoroughly, and chop and divide it into single servings suitable for your aquarium. Package it in plastic wrap, and freeze it. Be sure to rotate the type of food you are feeding to offer your fish a variety of nutrients as well as flavors.

The sunburst butterflyfish (*Chaetodon kleinii*) is the easiest of the butterflyfish species to keep in the marine aquarium. Once settled in, it is hardy, happily accepts flake food supplemented with small bits of fresh or frozen shrimp, and never seems to become involved in territorial disputes with tankmates. It grows to about 10cm (4in) long.

**Origin:** Indo-Pacific, from the Red Sea and East Africa to Hawaii and Australia.

**Temperature:** 26°C (79°F) is ideal, but will tolerate temperatures from 25°C (77°F) to 27°C (81°F).

**SG:** 1.018- 1.023

**pH:** 8.3

**Special requirements:** Very high water quality with frequent water changes. Does not tolerate nitrates well. Best suited to a fish only environment, since they eat corals. Butterflyfish consider anemone tips a gourmet treat. Sometimes the anemone kills the butterflyfish.

**Feeding:** Feed every other day, alternating foods. Frozen marine blend, fresh shrimp pieces, freeze-dried plankton, quality marine flake.

**Avoid these tankmates:** All invertebrates, especially anemones, groupers, lionfish.

**Breeding:** Has not been reared in captivity.

# THREADFIN BUTTERFLYFISH

The threadfin butterflyfish (*Chaetodon auriga*) is found widely throughout the Indo-Pacific. It grows to 23cm (9in) in the wild but only half this size in a tank. It makes a good, hardy aquarium subject and enjoys a varied diet but, unfortunately, it will not accept flake food.

**Origin:** Indo-Pacific: Red Sea and East Africa to Hawaii, Japan, Micronesia.

**Temperature:** 26°C (79°F) is ideal, but will tolerate temperatures from 25°C (77°F) to 27°C (81°F).

**SG:** 1.018- 1.023

**pH:** 8.3

**Special requirements:** Very high water quality with frequent water changes. Does not tolerate nitrates well. Best suited to a fish-only environment, since they eat corals. Butterflyfish consider anemone tips a gourmet treat. Sometimes the anemone kills the butterflyfish.

**Feeding:** Feed every other day, alternating foods. Frozen marine blend, fresh shrimp pieces, freeze-dried plankton, quality marine flake.

**Avoid these tankmates:** All invertebrates, especially anemones, groupers, lionfish.

**Breeding:** Has not been reared in captivity.

# FOUR-EYED BUTTERFLYFISH

The four-eyed butterflyfish (*Chaetodon capistratus*) is the most common butterflyfish in the West Indies. It is relatively hardy but will not accept flake food in its diet.

**Origin:** Indo-Pacific: Red Sea and East Africa to Hawaii, Japan, Micronesia.

**Temperature:** 26°C (79°F) is ideal, but will tolerate temperatures from 25°C (77°F) to 27°C (81°F).

**SG:** 1.018- 1.023

**pH:** 8.3

**Special requirements:** Very high water quality with frequent water changes. Does not tolerate nitrates well. Best suited to a fish only environment, since they eat corals. Butterflyfish consider anemone tips a gourmet treat. Sometimes the anemone kills the butterflyfish.

**Feeding:** Feed every other day, alternating foods. Frozen marine blend, fresh shrimp pieces, freeze-dried plankton, quality marine flake.

**Avoid these tankmates:** All invertebrates, especially anemones, groupers, lionfish.

**Breeding:** Has not been reared in captivity.

The copperbanded butterflyfish (*Chelmon rostratus*) is one of the most attractive butterflyfish. It may eat flake, but only one day a week. Provide a diet that includes seafood, whether from the fish shop or bits that you have prepared, and serve it every other day. Fish can reach 20cm (8in) in the wild, but only half that size in an aquarium. Like other butterflyfish, it should not be kept in a reef.

**Origin:** Indo-West Pacific: Andaman Sea to Ryukyu Islands, south to Australia

**Temperature:** 26°C (79°F) is ideal, but will tolerate temperatures from 25°C (77°F) to 27°C (81°F).

**SG:** 1.018- 1.023

**pH:** 8.3

**Special requirements:** Very high water quality with frequent water changes. Does not tolerate nitrates well. Best suited to a fish-only environment, since they eat corals. Butterflyfish consider anemone tips a gourmet treat. Sometimes the anemone kills the butterflyfish.

**Feeding:** Feed every other day, alternating foods. Frozen marine blend, fresh shrimp pieces, freeze-dried plankton, quality marine flake.

**Avoid these tankmates:** All invertebrates, especially anemones, groupers, lionfish.

**Breeding:** Has not been reared in captivity.

# WIMPLEFISH

Large shoals of the spectacularly shaped wimplefish (*Heniochus acuminatus*) are often seen in wildlife films, but they adapt well to aquarium life and are relatively easy feeders. They grow to about 15cm (6in) in the aquarium, and live longer than many butterflies. This is another fish that often acts as a parasite cleaner for other fish when it is young.

**Origin:** Indo-West Pacific: East Africa and the Persian Gulf to Japan, Micronesia.

**Temperature:** 26°C (79°F) is ideal, but will tolerate temperatures from 25°C (77°F) to 27°C (81°F).

**SG:** 1.018- 1.023

**pH:** 8.3

**Special requirements:** Very high water quality with frequent water changes. Does not tolerate nitrates well. Best suited to a fish-only environment, since they may start to nip corals.

**Feeding:** Feed every other day, alternating foods. Frozen marine blend, fresh shrimp pieces, freeze-dried plankton, quality marine flake.

**Avoid these tankmates:** Need to observe carefully around selected hardy invertebrates. Avoid anemones, groupers, lionfish.

**Breeding:** Has not been reared in captivity.

# TANGS AND SURGEONS

What is the difference between a surgeonfish and a tang? Well, there is no difference; some of the fish in the group are invariably known as tangs, such as the regal tang, while others are known as surgeons, such as the clown surgeon, and a few are known by both names, e.g. the achilles tang or achilles surgeon. Here, we use both names, with no biological difference intended.

Surgeons are so-called because of their "scalpels," the two sharp bony points on either side of the body at the base of the tailfin. The scalpels can give a nasty cut to a clumsy human, but are rarely used on other fish. Perhaps wise to the dangers, other fish are not stupid enough to tangle with the surgeons or the tangs, which also have these weapons.

Tangs and surgeons are magnificent fish, sporting the boldest and brightest markings. They are a good size, grow steadily, are relatively hardy, cause very few problems with other fish, and are easy to feed. They are safe with tiny and large fish alike, and they are ideal inhabitants for an invertebrate tank.

Tangs present only two problems. Firstly, it is absolutely essential that they be given plenty of green matter in their diet. Therefore, they should only be housed in an aquarium with plenty of light and a guaranteed supply of green algae covering the rocks on which they can nibble. They will also quickly consume any and all macro algae, such as caulerpa. Secondly, tangs and surgeons can fight among themselves. As a rule, you should not keep two of the same type together.

# REGAL BLUE TANG

The regal blue tang or palette surgeonfish (*Paracanthurus hepatus*) is one of the least demanding of the tangs. But this fish has bad habits in reef tanks. In addition to eating the algae, they've been known to eat the coral tips. A single regal tang remains an excellent choice for a very large 400 liter (100gallon) fish only aquarium, although it needs very high quality water with frequent water changes.

**Origin:** Indo Pacific: East Africa to the Line Islands to Japan, Micronesia, the Great Barrier Reef, Samoa

**Temperature:** 26°C (79°F) is ideal, but will tolerate temperatures from 25°C (77°F) to 27°C (81°F).

**SG:** 1.018- 1.023

**pH:** 8.3

**Special requirements:** Very high water quality with frequent water changes. Does not tolerate nitrates well. Best suited to a fish-only environment, since they often start to nip corals.

**Feeding:** Offer romaine lettuce on a clip weekly unless algae is obviously overgrown. Feed every other day, alternating foods from this group: Frozen marine blend, fresh shrimp pieces, freeze-dried plankton, quality marine flake.

**Avoid these tankmates:** Corals, groupers.

**Breeding:** Has not been reared in captivity.

Of the sailfin tangs, the yellow sailfin (*Zebrasoma flavescens*) is the one most often seen. Because of its bright single color, and its efficiency at clearing rocks of algae, the yellow sailfin tang is one of the most popular marine fish. A regal tang and a yellow sailfin tang together in an aquarium provide a startling contrast. Sailfin tangs need green food even more than other tangs and surgeons; even a few days without algae can cause them to become thin and emaciated. Sailfins are small and rarely exceed 10cm (4in) and make an ideal community fish.

**Origin:** Pacific: Ryukyu, Mariana, Marshall, Marcus, Wake, and Hawaiian islands.

**Temperature:** 26°C (79°F) is ideal, but will tolerate temperatures from 25°C (77°F) to 27°C (81°F).

**SG:** 1.018- 1.023

**pH:** 8.3

**Special requirements:** Very high water quality with frequent water changes. Does not tolerate nitrates well. Can be kept in a reef. Will not harm corals or anemones. Needs to have algae regularly.

**Feeding:** Offer romaine lettuce on a clip weekly or twice-weekly unless algae is obviously overgrown. Feed every other day, alternating foods from this group: Frozen marine blend, fresh shrimp pieces, freeze-dried plankton, quality marine flake.

**Avoid these tankmates:** Groupers.

**Breeding:** Has not been reared in captivity.

# JAPANESE TANG

The Japanese tang or orangespine unicornfish (*Naso lituratus*)—an affable fish—is also known as the lipstick tang because its orange or red-rimmed lips look like they have been freshly outlined in bright lipstick. With a chief diet of leafy brown algae, this fish can be difficult to feed in an aquarium.

**Origin:** Pacific: Indo-Pacific, Red Sea and East Africa, Hawaiian islands, Japan, Great Barrier Reef, Micronesia.

**Temperature:** 26°C (79°F) is ideal, but will tolerate temperatures from 25°C (77°F) to 27°C (81°F).

**SG:** 1.018- 1.023

**pH:** 8.3

**Special requirements:** Very high water quality with frequent water changes. Does not tolerate nitrates well. May do best in a reef, but dietary problems are likely as needs to be fed on mainly leafy brown algae.

**Feeding:** Offer romaine lettuce on a clip weekly or twice-weekly unless algae is obviously overgrown. Feed every other day, alternating foods from this group: Frozen marine blend, fresh shrimp pieces, freeze-dried plankton, quality marine flake.

**Avoid these tankmates:** Groupers.

**Breeding:** Has not been reared in captivity.

An Achilles tang (*Acanthurus achilles*) is a truly stunning specimen. If it is near adult size, it will be the "leader of the tank" bullying other large fish into their corners or into submission. It must be kept with a yellow tang or it will die. The waste of the yellow tang provides a trace element necessary to the achilles survival. It also needs plenty of algae or romaine lettuce as a supplement. Often bought at 7.5–10cm (3–4in), it rarely grows to more than about 15–18cm(6–7in) in captivity.

**Origin:** Pacific Plate, W. Caroline, Hawaiian, Marshall Islands, Micronesia, Baja California, Mexico.

**Temperature:** 26°C (79°F) is ideal, but will tolerate temperatures from 25°C (77°F) to 27°C (81°F).

**SG:** 1.018- 1.023

**pH:** 8.3

**Special requirements:** Must be kept with a yellow tang. Very high water quality with frequent water changes. Does not tolerate nitrates well. Can be kept in a reef. Will not harm corals or anemones. Spine in caudal peduncle may be venomous, but injuries to humans from a fish in captivity are rare or none.

**Feeding:** Offer romaine lettuce on a clip weekly or twice-weekly unless algae is obviously overgrown. Feed every other day, alternating foods from this group: Frozen marine blend, fresh shrimp pieces, freeze-dried plankton, quality marine flake.

**Avoid these tankmates:** Groupers. May harass other dominant fish in the tank.

**Breeding:** Has not been reared in captivity.

# WRASSES AND HOGFISH

The wrasse family is far more difficult to encompass in a general paragraph than other families. Some of the wrasses grow to only 5–7.5cm (2–3in), some grow to 60cm (24in). Some are ideal in an invertebrate system, others would destroy the same setup. Some need to bury at nights, some need a cave, others require neither. So really the only way to examine the wrasses in a balanced way is to describe examples of each of the most popular groups. Hogfish are closely related to the wrasses. There are half a dozen or so of this subspecies, and two or three of them are quite commonly seen.

*Below: Neon cleaner wrasse (Labroides dimidiatus)*

The Cuban hogfish or spotfin hogfish (*Bodianus pulchellus*) is imported either at about 5cm (2in) in its juvenile polka dot markings or, more often, as a 15cm (6in) adult. It is usually quite inexpensive. Although hogfish are suitable companions for virtually any other fish, they will soon mess up an invertebrate system. In the wild they can reach 28.5cm (11in).

**Origin:** Atlantic, South Carolina, Bermuda, Honduras, South America.

**Temperature:** 26°C (79°F) is ideal, but will tolerate temperatures from 25°C (77°F) to 27°C (81°F).

**SG:** 1.018- 1.023

**pH:** 8.3

**Special requirements:** Very high water quality with frequent water changes. Does not tolerate nitrates well.

**Feeding:** Feed every other day, alternating foods from this group: Frozen marine blend, fresh crab, fresh shrimp pieces, freeze-dried plankton, quality marine flake.

**Avoid these tankmates:** Groupers. May harass other dominant fish in the tank.

**Breeding:** Has not been reared in captivity.

# GREEN BIRDMOUTH WRASSE

Another marine favorite is the green birdmouth wrasse (*Gomphosus caeruleus*). While the female is a brown, drab 10cm (4in) fish with a small snout, the male is a 15–18cm (6–7in) bottle green, dolphin-shaped beauty—the star character in any large tank. But the truly amazing feature of these fish is that they are hermaphrodite, just like the damsel fish, and it is quite possible to observe the drab, uninteresting females transform themselves in a few days.

**Origin:** Indian Ocean, East Africa to South Africa, and the Andaman Sea.

**Temperature:** 26°C (79°F) is ideal, but will tolerate temperatures from 25°C (77°F) to 27°C (81°F).

**SG:** 1.018- 1.023

**pH:** 8.3

**Special requirements:** Very high water quality with frequent water changes. Does not tolerate nitrates well.

Should have some living rock in the aquarium, even if no other invertebrates are present. It feeds on small invertebrates from the living rock, and these may be necessary for its long-term health.

**Feeding:** Feed every other day, alternating foods from this group: Frozen marine blend, fresh crab, fresh shrimp pieces, freeze-dried plankton, quality marine flake.

**Avoid these tankmates:** Other wrasses, groupers.

**Breeding:** Has not been reared in captivity.

The African clown wrasse or queen coris (*Coris frerei*, *C. formosa*) is bright red as a juvenile, and grows to a considerable size—30cm (12in) or more—during which their coloration changes completely. Growing them from juveniles to adults gives you the chance to observe the spectacular color changes as they develop. Their diet in the wild consists mainly of molluscs and sea urchins, in the shell, so this fish may be difficult to feed.

**Origin:** Western Indian Ocean, Red Sea to Natal, South Africa, and east to Sri Lanka.

**Temperature:** 26°C (79°F) is ideal, but will tolerate temperatures from 25°C (77°F) to 27°C (81°F).

**SG:** 1.018- 1.023

**pH:** 8.3

**Special requirements:** (*See* Feeding below.) Requires high water quality with frequent water changes. Does not tolerate nitrates well.

**Feeding:** Feed every other day, alternating foods from shelled molluscs and frozen marine blend, to fresh crab and shrimp pieces, freeze-dried plankton, marine flake.

**Avoid these tankmates:** Other wrasses, groupers.

**Breeding:** Has not been reared in captivity.

# BANANA WRASSE

The banana wrasse is the juvenile version of the bluefin wrasse (*Thalassoma bifasciatum*), usually seen at 10–13 cm (4–5in). It is an interesting specimen that feeds mainly on small zooplankton and tiny invertebrates from living rock. It is best purchased young and kept in an invertebrate setup, where it can feed itself while possibly learning to accept food. The color changes that take place as it matures are striking.

**Origin:** Western Atlantic, Gulf of Mexico, the Caribbean.

**Temperature:** 26°C (79°F) is ideal, but will tolerate temperatures from 25°C (77°F) to 27°C (81°F).

**SG:** 1.018- 1.023

**pH:** 8.3

**Special requirements:** Requires high water quality with frequent water changes. Does not tolerate nitrates well.

**Feeding:** Keep in an aquarium with living rock. Feed every other day, alternating foods from this group: frozen marine blend, fresh crab, fresh shrimp pieces, freeze-dried plankton, quality marine flake.

**Avoid these tankmates:** Other wrasses, groupers.

**Breeding:** Has not been reared in captivity.

# CHRISTMAS WRASSE

The Christmas wrasse (*Halichoeres ornatissimus*) is as ornamental as his name. It can reach 18cm (7in) in the wild. When you are sure this wrasse has died, and is lost in your aquarium, wait until the next feeding time before giving up. He requires gravel to bury himself in. He dives in and covers himself, sometimes for more than a day. He resurrects at his chosen moment, suddenly shooting out of the gravel.

**Origin:** Indo-Pacific, Cocos and Christmas islands, eastern Indian ocean, Japan, Hawaiian islands.

**Temperature:** 26°C (79°F) is ideal, but will tolerate temperatures from 25°C (77°F) to 27°C (81°F).

**SG:** 1.018- 1.023

**pH:** 8.3

**Special requirements:** Requires high water quality with frequent water changes. Does not tolerate nitrates well.

**Feeding:** Keep in an aquarium with living rock. Feed every other day, alternating foods from this group: molluscs, frozen marine blend, fresh crab, fresh shrimp pieces, freeze-dried plankton, quality marine flake.

**Avoid these tankmates:** Other wrasses, groupers.

**Breeding:** Has not been reared in captivity.

# LYRETAIL OR MOON WRASSE

The lyretail or moon wrasse (*Thalossoma lunare*) is similar to the bluefin wrasse, but maybe not so well marked. However, it is cheap, very hardy, and, like most wrasses, easy to feed in the aquarium. It can get very large 25cm (10in) and can become quite aggressive over time.

**Origin:** Indo-Pacific, Red Sea and East Africa to Japan, northern New Zealand

**Temperature:** 26°C (79°F) is ideal, but will tolerate temperatures from 25°C (77°F) to 27°C (81°F).

**SG:** 1.018- 1.023

**pH:** 8.3

**Special requirements:** Requires high water quality with frequent water changes. Does not tolerate nitrates well. Might do well in an invertebrate aquarium.

**Feeding:** Feed every other day, alternating foods from this group: frozen marine blend, fresh crab, fresh shrimp pieces, freeze-dried plankton, quality marine flake.

**Avoid these tankmates:** Other wrasses, groupers.

**Breeding:** Has not been reared in captivity.

# LIONFISH, TRIGGERFISH, AND FILEFISH

Lionfish are both dangerous and very poisonous to humans and must not be handled at all. The spines of the dorsal fin carry a poison that can be lethal. However, lionfish are hardy and nitrite tolerant, long-lived, slow moving, and good aquarium fish. Do not put lionfish with mobile invertebrates or small fish. They can be difficult to feed in captivity. In the wild they hang under ledges, and are happier if given similar protection in an aquarium.

The triggerfish family is fairly small but quite widespread. Triggers can be bought at any size from 2.5–23cm (1–10in) and their hardiness and nitrite tolerance make them suitable fish for beginners. All the triggers grow to a large size and can be quite aggressive. In the wild, triggers eat crustaceans, sea urchins, etc., so never put them in an invertebrate tank. Feeding them in captivity is easy, as they will eat anything with their strong, sharp teeth. More peaceful triggerfish include the blue trigger (*Odonus niger*), the pink-tailed trigger (*Melichthys vidua*), and the white-tailed trigger (*Sufflumen chrysoptera*).

The filefish are closely related to triggers but they are quite different. Filefish are not hardy, they are not nitrite tolerant, they grow very slowly in captivity, they are shy and retiring, and not very easy to feed. In that they are peaceful, they make good aquarium fish, but feeding them may be difficult.

# PTEROIS VOLITANS

The best-known lionfish is *Pterois volitans*, usually seen at 10–15cm (4–6in). Its finnage is longer than that of other lionfish. *Pterois antennata* and *P. sphex*, are often referred to as the spotfin lionfish. The regal lionfish, *P. radiata*, is also popular. There are two types of dwarf lionfish that rarely grow to more than 7.5–10cm (3–4in) in captivity, *Dendrochirus zebra* and *D. brachypterus*.

**Origin:** Indo-Pacific, Australia, Malaysia, Japan, Micronesia.

**Temperature:** 26°C (79°F) is ideal, but will tolerate temperatures from 25°C (77°F) to 27°C (81°F).

**SG:** 1.018- 1.023

**pH:** 8.3

**Special requirements:** The *Pterois volitanus* is venomous so wear gloves when working in the tank. Requires high water quality with frequent water changes. Does not tolerate nitrates well.

**Feeding:** Feed every other day, alternating foods from frozen marine blend, white fish or lancefish, fresh crab and shrimp pieces, freeze-dried plankton, quality marine flake.

**Avoid these tankmates:** Mobile invertebrates, small fish.

**Breeding:** Has not been reared in captivity.

The spectacular picasso trigger, or blackbar trigger, (*Rhinecanthus aculeatus*), is full of personality and far cheaper than most other triggers. Tiny specimens are not easily caught and the fish are usually seen at 13–15cm (5–6in). He should be kept with other large fish, because he will eat invertebrates and smaller fish.

**Origin:** Indo-Pacific, Red Sea, South Africa, Hawaii, Japan, Micronesia.

**Temperature:** 26°C (79°F) is ideal, but will tolerate temperatures from 25°C (77°F) to 27°C (81°F).

**SG:** 1.018- 1.023

**pH:** 8.3

**Special requirements:** Requires high water quality with frequent water changes. Doesn't tolerate nitrates.

**Feeding:** Feed every other day, alternating foods from this group: frozen marine blend, white fish or lancefish, fresh crab, fresh shrimp pieces, freeze-dried plankton, quality marine flake.

**Avoid these tankmates:** Invertebrates, small fish.

**Breeding:** Has not been reared in captivity.

# EMERALD FILEFISH

The emerald filefish or harlequin filefish (*Oxymonocanthus longirostris*) feeds exclusively on acropora polyps. This makes it an unsuitable aquarium specimen, but it is a beautiful fish.

**Origin:** Indo-Pacific, East Africa, Great Barrier Reef, Micronesia.

**Temperature:** 26°C (79°F) is ideal, but will tolerate temperatures from 25°C (77°F) to 27°C (81°F).

**SG:** 1.018–1.023

**pH:** 8.3

**Special Requirements:** Feeds exclusively on acropora polyps. Due to dietary difficulties, this is not a recommended species for your aquarium. Also, requires high water quality with frequent water changes. Does not tolerate nitrates well.

**Feeding:** Feeds exclusively on acropora polyps. Not recommended, but you could try offering alternating foods from this group: frozen marine blend, white fish or lancefish, fresh crab, fresh shrimp pieces, freeze-dried plankton, quality marine flake.

**Avoid these tankmates:** Acropora, unless you are raising it to feed the fish.

**Breeding:** Has not been reared in captivity.

# GROUPERS, SWEETLIPS, AND PARROTFISH

Groupers are hardy, nitrite-tolerant, easy to feed, and disease resistant. The grouper likes to lurk at the cave entrance, just darting out occasionally to warn off intruders or to grab a passing meal, any fish will do. Provide a cave, and feed it solid chunks of food, such as mussel meat and lancefish. Groupers need a very large aquarium of 400 liters (100 gallons). Only triggers, lionfish, and perhaps very large tangs are suitable tankmates. Groupers will attack and kill angelfish three times their size. Groupers grow quite rapidly.

Related to the groupers are the snappers, another very large food fish. They are hardy, nitrite-tolerant, and easy to feed. Snappers can double their size in a few weeks. They are too large for most home aquariums. Avoid buying juvenile emperor snappers (*Lutjanus sebae*), because they soon outgrow their tank.

The sweetlips family is closely related to the snappers, but is different in many ways. They are slow to adapt to captivity. Their natural diet consists of huge amounts of tiny crustaceans, so they are difficult to feed. Parrotfish are wrasse-like fish that grow many meters long in the wild. Their natural diet consists of coral heads, so they are only suitable for fish only aquariums. They mix well with wrasses and groupers.

# PANTHERFISH, POLKADOT, OR HUMPBACK GROUPER

The pantherfish, polkadot, or humpback grouper (*Chromileptis altivelis*) is suitable for an aquarium containing triggers and lionfish. It is a little less solitary than other groupers. They may be headed for endangered species status in Australia, but attempting breeding in captivity will require a huge area.

**Origin:** Western Pacific, Japan, Australia, the Indian Ocean

**Temperature:** 26°C (79°F) is ideal, but will tolerate temperatures from 25°C (77°F) to 27°C (81°F).

**SG:** 1.018- 1.023

**pH:** 8.3

**Special requirements:** Requires high water quality with frequent water changes. Does not tolerate nitrates well.

**Feeding:** Feed every other day, alternating foods from this group: frozen marine blend, white fish or lancefish, fresh crab, fresh shrimp pieces, freeze-dried plankton, quality marine flake.

**Avoid these tankmates:** Groupers, large triggers, lionfish.

**Breeding:** Has not been reared in captivity.

Another untypical grouper is the marine betta or comet (*Calloplesiops altivelis*), a beautifully marked, slow-growing midwater swimmer. The marine betta may reach 15cm (6in) in the wild, but rarely exceeds 10cm (4in) in captivity. He does well in reef aquariums, and will not disturb corals, mushroom polyps, or anemones. He will eat crustaceans and tubeworms, however. He uses the false eye on his tail to convince his prey that it is safe to swim past his head.

**Origin:** Indo-Pacific, Red Sea, and East Africa.

**Temperature:** 26°C (79°F) is ideal, but will tolerate temperatures from 25°C (77°F) to 27°C (81°F).

**SG:** 1.018- 1.023

**pH:** 8.3

**Special requirements:** Requires high water quality with frequent water changes. Does not tolerate nitrates well.

**Feeding:** Feed every other day. Requires some live food such as feeder guppies or ghost shrimp, alternated with items from this list: frozen marine blend, white fish or lancefish, fresh crab, fresh shrimp pieces, freeze-dried plankton, quality marine flake.

**Avoid these tankmates:** Crustaceans such as peppermint shrimp are snack food. Also avoid large groupers, large triggers, lionfish. This timid fish can be bullied into a corner by an Achilles tang or a hawkfish.

**Breeding:** Has been reared in captivity but would be very difficult in a home aquarium.

# ROYAL GRAMMA

The basslets, or "dwarf groupers," include the well-known royal gramma (*Gramma loreto*) shown here. It must be kept singly, but its small size allows it to be put with almost any other types of fish, and with most invertebrates. The royal gramma rarely exceeds 7.5cm (3in) long, as does the dotty-back (*Pseudochromis paccagnellae*), a similarly marked fish. Do not put two members of this family in the same aquarium, or murder will occur.

**Origin:** West central Atlantic, Bahamas, central America, South America.

**Temperature:** 26°C (79°F) is ideal, but will tolerate temperatures from 25°C (77°F) to 27°C (81°F).

**SG:** 1.018- 1.023

**pH:** 8.3

**Special requirements:** Requires high water quality with frequent water changes. Doesn't tolerate nitrates. Thrives in a reef environment and does not harm anemones or corals. Shares a tank with the marine betta harmoniously.

**Feeding:** Feed every other day. Live guppies or ghost shrimp are an excellent treat. Regular feeding can alternate between items from this group: frozen marine blend, white fish or lancefish, fresh crab, fresh shrimp pieces, freeze-dried plankton, quality marine flake.

**Avoid these tankmates:** Groupers, large triggers, lionfish.

**Breeding:** Has been reared in captivity but would be very difficult in a home aquarium.

Easily the most popular of the sweetlips is the polka-dot, or harlequin, sweetlips (*Gaterin chaetodonoides* formerly called *Plectorhynchus chaetodonoides*). This fish has gorgeous clownlike markings, and is an almost irresistible buy when offered for sale. Unfortunately, these fish often do not survive in captivity, probably due to their need for live food.

**Origin:** Western Pacific, Sumatra to Fiji, Micronesia; Indian Ocean, Maldives, and Cocos islands.

**Temperature:** 26°C (79°F) is ideal, but will tolerate temperatures from 25°C (77°F) to 27°C (81°F).

**SG:** 1.018- 1.023

**pH:** 8.3

**Special requirements:** Requires high water quality with frequent water changes. Does not tolerate nitrates well. Requires some live food, such as guppies, ghost shrimp, or other small crustaceans weekly.

**Feeding:** Feed every other day. Regular feeding can alternate between items from this group: frozen marine blend, white fish or lancefish, fresh crab, fresh shrimp pieces, freeze-dried plankton, quality marine flake.

**Avoid these tankmates:** Small fish and crustaceans.

**Breeding:** Has not been reared in captivity.

# RED-AND-WHITE CLOWN PARROTFISH

The attractive red-and-white clown parrotfish or bicolor parrotfish (*Bolbometopon bicolor*) fits into any largish fish only set up. This is a marine fish in which the adult markings are totally different to those of the juveniles.

It can reach 90cm (36in) in the wild. Juvenile species are available for aquariums, but a very large tank is recommended for these.

**Origin:** Indo-Pacific, Red Sea to the Tuamotus, Izu islands to Great Barrier Reef, throughout Micronesia.

**Temperature:** 26°C (79°F) is ideal, but will tolerate temperatures from 25°C (77°F) to 27°C (81°F).

**SG:** 1.018- 1.023

**pH:** 8.3

**Special requirements:** Requires high water quality with frequent water changes. Does not tolerate nitrates well.

**Feeding:** Requires algae to graze on. Supplement with romaine lettuce offered on a clip at least weekly. Feed every other day. Regular feeding can alternate between items from this group: frozen marine blend, white fish or lancefish, fresh crab, fresh shrimp pieces, freeze-dried plankton, quality marine flake.

**Avoid these tankmates:** Large groupers.

**Breeding:** Has not been reared in captivity.

# BOXFISH, PUFFERFISH, AND HAWKFISH

Boxfish are cube or cuboid in shape, and have a hard exterior. The hardened skin is only softer around the eyes, mouth, and fins. They are slow swimmers, do well in an aquarium, and thrive if hand-fed. Smaller species fit well into invertebrate systems. A word of caution—many boxfish species give off a poison if severely threatened. This does not occur often, but in an aquarium the result is a total wipe out, so choose their companions carefully. It may be best to introduce the boxfish to the aquarium first.

Pufferfish, like boxfish, have an awkward shape and use their fins, rather than their bodies, for forward motion. Puffers have soft and pliable skin, which allows the fish to inflate itself in times of danger. Puffers do not give off a poison, but have poisonous flesh if eaten. Puffers are hardy, have strong personalities and are disease-resistant. They rarely cause problems with other fish and eat almost anything. The puffers' natural diet includes small crustaceans, molluscs and urchins, so they are not suitable subjects for a mixed invertebrate aquarium, although they would not harm corals or anemones.

Hawkfish are smallish predators that readily adapt to aquarium life. Most species do not exceed 7.5–10cm (3–4in) in length. Hawkfish spend most of their time perched on rocks and ledges watching the world go by. When something takes their interest, whether it be food or a threat, they dart off the rock in a hawk-like fashion in order to investigate. The tank should be tightly covered, or they will investigate the floor in a flying leap. They never cause problems with other fish unless there is a long, full tail to nip. If they are regularly fed and the aquarium is tightly covered they can live for many years in captivity.

# WHITE-SPOTTED BOXFISH

The white-spotted boxfish (*Ostracion meleagris*), is one of the few sexable species. Both sexes have a dark body with white spots, but the male's patterns are more vivid, with additional tints of blue on the fins. This species should not be kept in a reef aquarium, since it eats most of its occupants.

**Origin:** Indo Pacific, East Africa to the Americas, Japan to Hawaii, throughout Micronesia.

**Temperature:** 26°C (79°F) is ideal, but will tolerate temperatures from 25°C (77°F) to 27°C (81°F).

**SG:** 1.018- 1.023

**pH:** 8.3

**Special requirements:** This fish is venomous. Consider gloves before working on the tank. Requires high water quality with frequent water changes. Does not tolerate nitrates well.

**Feeding:** Feed daily or every other day. Regular feeding can alternate between items from this group: frozen marine blend, white fish or lancefish, fresh crab, fresh shrimp pieces, freeze-dried plankton, quality marine flake.

**Avoid these tankmates:** Small fish, crustaceans, invertebrates of all types.

**Breeding:** Has not been reared in captivity.

The cube boxfish or yellow boxfish (*Ostracion cubicus*) starts out as small as 1cm (0.15in) and very pale yellow with black dots. As it grows, the body elongates and the patterning turns dark mustard with blue spots. This species should not be kept in a reef aquarium, since he eats most of its occupants.

**Origin:** Indo Pacific, Red Sea, East Africa to the Americas, Japan to Hawaii, throughout Micronesia. South Atlantic, south coast of South Africa.

**Temperature:** 26°C (79°F) is ideal, but will tolerate temperatures from 25°C (77°F) to 27°C (81°F).

**SG:** 1.018–1.023

**pH:** 8.3

**Special requirements:** Requires high water quality with frequent water changes. Does not tolerate nitrates well.

**Feeding:** Feed daily or every other day. Regular feeding can alternate between items from this group: frozen marine blend, white fish or lancefish, fresh crab, fresh shrimp pieces, freeze-dried plankton, quality marine flake.

**Avoid these tankmates:** Small fish, crustaceans, invertebrates of all types.

**Breeding:** Has not been reared in captivity.

The porcupinefish or spotfin porcupinefish (*Diodon hystrix*) is covered with sharp spines but is suitable for most set-ups. They can become very affectionate to their owners, coming to the top of the tank to beg for food and accepting it from a hand. They are poisonous to eat, but not to handle. The spines could inflict injury, protecting them from predators.

**Origin:** Eastern Pacific, from southern California to Chile, Galapagos islands; Bermuda, northern Gulf of Mexico to Brazil.

**Temperature:** 26°C (79°F) is ideal, but will tolerate temperatures from 25°C (77°F) to 27°C (81°F).

**SG:** 1.018–1.023

**pH:** 8.3

**Special requirements:** Requires high water quality with frequent water changes.

**Feeding:** Feed daily or every other day. Regular feeding can alternate between items from this group: frozen marine blend, white fish or lancefish, fresh crab, fresh shrimp pieces, freeze-dried plankton, quality marine flake.

**Avoid these tankmates:** Small fish, crustaceans, invertebrates of all types.

**Breeding:** Has not been reared in captivity.

# LONGNOSED HAWK FISH

The most spectacular hawkfish is the longnosed hawk fish (*Oxycirrhites typus*), which can be housed safely with almost anything except shrimps and marine bettas. It is quite expensive, but makes an attractive addition to any aquarium with enough rockwork for him to find a home. He should not be kept in a bare, fish only tank with large fish.

**Origin:** Indo Pacific, Red Sea to Hawaii, Japan, Micronesia, eastern Pacific, from southern California to Colombia, Galapagos islands.

**Temperature:** 26°C (79°F) is ideal, but will tolerate temperatures from 25°C (77°F) to 27°C (81°F).

**SG:** 1.018- 1.023

**pH:** 8.3

**Special requirements:** Requires high water quality with frequent water changes.

**Feeding:** Feed daily or every other day. Regular feeding can alternate between items from this group: frozen marine blend, white fish or lancefish, fresh crab, fresh shrimp pieces, freeze-dried plankton, quality marine flake.

**Avoid these tankmates:** Marine bettas, triggers, groupers, possibly lionfish can snack on the hawkfish.

**Breeding:** Has not been reared in captivity.

# GOBIES, BLENNIES, AND BATFISHES

A goby is a small, tube-shaped fish, perhaps about 5–10cm (2–4in) long. It spends most of its life scurrying along the sand. Many gobies live in small caves or among coral branches. Since most gobies are very hardy and disease resistant and never cause compatibility problems they make excellent aquarium inhabitants. Some species are easy to feed. Others must feed themselves from living rock. These fascinating little fishes are widely available at dealers and not expensive.

The blenny family is similar to the gobies. Blennies are also smallish, bottom-dwelling fish, and some species do not obviously fit into either family. Blennies are as hardy and varied as the gobies.

Cardinal fish require a quiet, reef environment, or they will pine away in captivity. Like the gobies, they feed on the small micro-organisms that inhabit live rock. A healthy cardinalfish will also accept some food from human sources, but they rarely accept flake.

The batfish, often acquired at 2.5–7.5cm (1–3in) long, soon reaches 25–30cm (10–12in) in size, being tall rather than long. It outgrows its immediate environment, and many aquarists are faced with the problem of either buying another tank or exchanging their rapidly expanding fish. Batfish like to rule a tank by swimming unhindered in the open spaces, and as long as other fish do not challenge this right of way, batfish are normally content to live with any other fish, from small gobies up to larger groupers and triggers. A young batfish could not live with a large grouper, so a large tank with only a small batfish might be best to start. Batfish will eat virtually anything, including most invertebrates, even anemones.

# WHITE FIREFISH

The very popular white firefish (*Nemateleotris magnifica*) is a burrowing fish imported in large numbers. It needs to live in a reef aquarium at slightly cooler temperatures than most reef fish.

**Origin:** Indo Pacific, east Africa to Hawaii, Micronesia.

**Temperature:** 22°C (72°F) is ideal, but will tolerate temperatures from 21°C (70°F) to 26°C (79°F).

**SG:** 1.018–1.023

**pH:** 8.3

**Special requirements:** Requires living rock, a reef environment, and high water quality with many water changes.

**Feeding:** Will feed itself with micro-organisms from living rock. Feed every other day. Regular feeding can alternate between items from this group: frozen marine blend, tiny bits of white fish or lancefish, fresh crab, fresh shrimp pieces, freeze-dried plankton, quality marine flake.

**Avoid these tankmates:** Triggers, groupers, lionfish.

**Breeding:** Has not been reared in captivity.

# BICOLOR BLENNIE

The bicolor blennie (*Ecsenius pulcher*) is a very slimy, slithery fish, 5–7.5cm(2–3in) in length. It chooses to live in a small hole in the rocks, constantly darting out inquisitively and returning with equal speed. It can reach 11cm (4in) in the wild, somewhat less in an aquarium. It needs to live in a reef aquarium and will feed itself by eating tiny micro-organisms that inhabit the living rock.

**Origin:** Persian Gulf, Gulf of Oman, northwestern coast of India to the Gulf of Kutch.

**Temperature:** 26°C (79°F) is ideal, but will tolerate temperatures from 25°C (77°F) to 27°C (81°F).

**SG:** 1.018–1.023

**pH:** 8.3

**Special requirements:** The blennie requires living rock, a reef environment, and high water quality with frequent water changes.

**Feeding:** Will feed itself with micro-organisms from living rock. Offer food to the entire aquarium every other day, perhaps some of it will be accepted. Regular feeding can alternate between items from this group: frozen marine blend, tiny bits of white fish or lancefish, fresh crab, fresh shrimp pieces, freeze-dried plankton, quality marine flake.

**Avoid these tankmates:** Triggers, groupers, and also possibly lionfish.

**Breeding:** Has not been reared in captivity.

The scooter goby, scooter blennie, or ocellated drag-onet (*Neosynchiropus ocellatus*) has excellent protective coloration. Its rocky pattern grows darker on a dark stone, lighter on white gravel. It wanders the reef aquarium in search of tiny, invisible snacks. It can reach 11cm (4in) in the wild, somewhat less in an aquarium. It needs to live in a reef aquarium and will feed itself by eating tiny micro-organisms that inhabit the living rock.

**Origin:** Western Pacific, southern Japan to the Marquesan Islands.

**Temperature:** 25°C (77°F) is ideal, but will tolerate temperatures from 24°C (75°F) to 26°C (79°F).

**SG:** 1.018–1.023

**pH:** 8.3

**Special Requirements:** The scooter goby requires liv-ing rock, a reef environment, and high water quality with frequent water changes.

**Feeding:** Will feed itself with micro-organisms from living rock. Offer food to the entire aquarium every other day, perhaps some of it will be accepted. Regular feeding can alternate between items from this group: frozen marine blend, tiny bits of white fish or lancefish, fresh crab, fresh shrimp pieces, freeze-dried plankton, quality marine flake.

**Avoid these tankmates:** Triggers, groupers, and also possibly lionfish.

**Breeding:** Has not been reared in captivity.

# MANDARIN GOBY

The mandarin goby, green mandarin, or mandarinfish (*Neosynchiropus ocellatus*) has the coloring of an exotic butterfly, delicate and distinct. It has the deep blue wings of a butterfly, and the face of a delicate tree frog, right down to its pale neck. They must live in a reef aquarium with plenty of living rock, but their beauty has drawn many fishkeepers into reef keeping. It can reach 11cm (4in) in the wild, somewhat less in an aquarium. Put only one mandarin in an aquarium. They will not peacefully share a tank with their own species.

**Origin:** Western Pacific, Ryukyu Islands to Australia.

**Temperature:** 25°C (77°F) is ideal, but will tolerate temperatures from 24°C (75°F) to 26°C (79°F).

**SG:** 1.018–1.023

**pH:** 8.3

**Special requirements:** Requires high water quality with frequent water changes. It needs to live in a reef aquarium and will feed himself by eating tiny micro-organisms that inhabit the living rock.

**Feeding:** Will feed itself with micro-organisms from living rock. Offer food to the entire aquarium every other day, perhaps some of it will be accepted. Regular feeding can alternate between items from this group: frozen marine blend, tiny bits of white fish or lancefish, fresh crab, fresh shrimp pieces, freeze-dried plankton, quality marine flake.

**Avoid these tankmates:** Triggers, groupers, and also possibly lionfish.

**Breeding:** Has been reared in captivity, but would be very difficult in a home aquarium.

The most interesting of the cardinal fish, the red spotted or pajama cardinal (*Sphaeramia nematoptera*), could easily be mistaken for a freshwater variety—its colors are unusual but not dramatic. It only grows to 5cm (2in) long, is a slow, peaceful swimmer, and exceedingly hardy and ideal for a beginner, except that it will not eat flake foods.

**Origin:** Western Pacific, Java to New Guinea, Ryukyu Islands to Micronesia.

**Temperature:** 25°C (77°F) is ideal, but will tolerate temperatures from 24°C (75°F) to 26°C (79°F).

**SG:** 1.018–1.023

**pH:** 8.3

**Special requirements:** Requires high water quality with frequent water changes. Needs to live in a reef aquarium.

**Feeding:** Will feed itself with micro-organisms that inhabit living rock. Offer food to the entire aquarium every other day, perhaps some of it will be accepted. Regular feeding can alternate between items from this group: frozen marine blend, tiny bits of white fish or lancefish, fresh crab, fresh shrimp pieces, freeze-dried plankton, quality marine flake.

**Avoid these tankmates:** Triggers, groupers, possibly lionfish. One tang is acceptable, but should not be kept with multiple, squabbling, tangs.

**Breeding:** Has been reared in captivity, but would be very difficult in a home aquarium.

# BANNER CARDINAL

The most elegant of the cardinal fish is the banner or banggai cardinal (*Pterapogon kauderni*). It is much more delicate than the pajama, and much choosier about tankmates. It belongs in a very quiet reef with mainly invertebrates. If fast-swimming fish make it nervous, it refuses food and simply fades away. It can grow to 8cm (3in) in the wild, but rarely reaches that size in an aquarium. It will not eat flake foods, and is threatened with extinction. Serious aquarists might induce it to breed. It is not a beginner's fish.

**Origin:** Banggai islands, Indonesia.

**Temperature:** 25°C (77°F) is ideal, but will tolerate temperatures from 24°C (75°F) to 26°C (79°F).

**SG:** 1.018–1.023

**pH:** 8.3

**Special requirements:** Requires high water quality with frequent water changes. It needs to live in a reef aquarium and must eat some tiny micro-organisms that inhabit the living rock.

**Feeding:** Primarily feeds at night, so offer food shortly before turning out the light. Requires micro-organisms from living rock. Offer food to the entire aquarium every other day, perhaps some of it will be accepted. Regular feeding can alternate between items from this group: frozen marine blend, tiny bits of white fish or lancefish, fresh crab, fresh shrimp pieces, freeze-dried plankton.

**Avoid these tankmates:** Fast-swimming territorial fish such as damsels. Triggers, groupers, possibly lionfish. One tang is acceptable, but should not be kept with multiple, squabbling tangs.

**Breeding:** Has been reared in captivity, but would be very difficult in a home aquarium.

The roundfin batfish (*Platax orbicularis*) starts off like a leaf in the fall drifting in the current. A few months later, it is the size of a plate. Providing cover to protect it when young, and space that will accommodate it at its adult size, will be a challenge. In the wild they can reach 50cm (20in).

**Origin:** Indo Pacific, Red Sea and East Africa, Tuamotu islands, Japan, Australia.

**Temperature:** 25°C (77°F) is ideal, but will tolerate temperatures from 24°C (75°F) to 26°C (79°F).

**SG:** 1.018–1.023

**pH:** 8.3

**Special requirements:** Needs high water quality with frequent water changes. The batfish eats invertebrates.

**Feeding:** Feed daily, alternating between items from this group: frozen marine blend, tiny bits of white fish or lancefish, fresh crab, fresh shrimp pieces, freeze-dried plankton, quality marine flake. Offer live guppies or ghost shrimp as a treat.

**Avoid these tankmates:** Small fish and invertebrates.

**Breeding:** Has not been reared in captivity.

# OTHER VARIETIES FOR THE AQUARIUM

Most of the fish described so far fit into neat categories and it would be fairly simple for the reader with, for example, a trigger species not mentioned in the text to determine the likely characteristics of the fish in question. But nature does not like neat packages and you will encounter many types of fish that are, say, in a family of their own or the only member of a larger family suitable for the aquarium. Here we take a brief look at some of the other species occasionally offered for sale that make interesting aquarium occupants, including the hardiest of all species suitable for a marine tank—the brackish species—and some of the most awkward and delicate subjects—the seahorses.

The freshwater aquarist will be familiar with quite a few so-called brackish fish, i.e. fish that normally inhabit river estuaries and can adapt to both freshwater and saltwater, but are probably happiest in conditions that lie somewhere in between. Brackish water fish include the rare, more difficult *Monodactylus sebae*, which will not tolerate completely freshwater, the scat (*Scatophagus argus*) and the targetfish (*Therapon jarbua*).

# MALAYAN ANGEL

The Malayan angel (*Monodactylus argenteus*) is an incredibly hardy species, often used as a starter fish. It is usually bought at about 2.5–5cm (1–2in) long and slowly grows to 13–15cm(5–6in). Its brilliant silver markings make a fine display as an adult in salt water, although pale against the brighter colors of true marine fish. This fish can live in freshwater but should have some marine salt added for trace elements.

**Origin:** Indo Pacific, Red Sea, and East Africa Yaeyamas to Australia.

**Temperature:** 25°C (77°F) is ideal, but will tolerate temperatures from 24°C (75°F) to 28°C (83°F).

**SG:** 1.010–1.015

**pH:** 7.6 to 8.0

**Special requirements:** Requires high water quality with frequent water changes and a fish-only aquarium.

**Feeding:** Feed daily, offering romaine lettuce on a clip weekly. Plankton and algae form much of their diet in the wild. Other foods: frozen marine blend, tiny bits of white fish or lancefish, fresh crab, fresh shrimp pieces, freeze-dried plankton, quality marine flake.

**Avoid these tankmates:** Either have a single specimen or a large shoal. These fish are very territorial, so provide adequate cover.

**Breeding:** Has not been reared in captivity.

# FOXFACE RABBITFISH

The foxface rabbitfish (*Siganus vulpinus*) is a nicely marked, rather innocuous fish that is not very common. It should not be handled, as its spines contain a stinging venom. It can be kept in an invertebrate community system, but has been known to nip certain varieties of coral (such as gorgonian sp.) as well as eating algae.

**Origin:** Western Pacific: Philippines, New Guinea, Great Barrier Reef, Caroline Islands, Marshall Islands, New Caledonia.

**Temperature:** 26°C (79°F) is ideal, but will tolerate temperatures from 26°C (79°F) to 28°C (83°F).

**SG:** 1.018–1.023

**pH:** 8.3

**Special requirements:** Requires high water quality with frequent water changes. Keep in an aquarium with plenty of algae or supplement with Romaine lettuce. Observe around corals, will clean algae, but also nips small polyps.

**Feeding:** Offer romaine lettuce on a clip weekly. Feed every other day, alternating between items from this group: frozen marine blend, tiny bits of white fish or lancefish, fresh crab, fresh shrimp pieces, freeze-dried plankton, quality marine flake.

**Avoid these tankmates:** Gorgonian and other non-stinging, small polyp corals.

**Breeding:** Has not been bred in captivity.

Seahorses have great appeal but, sadly, few survive in captivity. They not only seem very reluctant to feed in an aquarium, they also seem accident prone, blundering into anemones, succumbing to the clutches of a hermit crab or the suction force of a power filter inlet. So, if you wish to keep seahorses, provide a tank with no dangers, virtually no competition as far as feeding is concerned and remember they need live foods every day.

**Origin:** Spain, Hong Kong.

**Temperature:** 25°C (77°F) is ideal, but will tolerate temperatures from 24°C (75°F) to 26°C (79°F).

**SG:** 1.018- 1.023

**pH:** 8.3

**Special requirements:** Requires live brine shrimp and tender algae and macro-algae. Maintain high water quality with frequent water changes.

**Feeding:** Offer live brine shrimp in small quantities regularly. Keep with living rock in adequate light to promote macro-algae growth.

**Avoid these tankmates:** Anemones, stinging corals such as bubble corals, all fish. Seahorses cannot compete with fish for food, they will starve. They do not swim fast enough to avoid being nipped by fish. They will anchor themselves to anemones or corals and be stung to death.

**Breeding:** Have been bred in captivity. Provide ideal conditions and start with a group of four adults.

# WEBSITES AND USEFUL INFORMATION

The Internet has greatly improved the quantity and quality of information available to aquarium hobbyists. Information on new species, diseases, and treatments, aquarium-building techniques, tips for designing your own filter system, and much more are now only a click away.

The following websites are very helpful. There are many more. Most of these sites have links to other helpful sites. Serious hobbyists, authors, universities, aquarium clubs, aquatic stores, and product testing firms set up these websites. Free information comes from many sources.

## Freshwater Only:

| | | |
|---|---|---|
| Great interactive site | Age of Aquariums | http://www.aquahobby.com/ |
| Cichlids | The Sydney Cichlid Page | http://www.sydneycichlid.com |
| Angelfish | Breeding the Angelfish | http://members.aol.com/angelbook/angel0.htm |
| Great hobbyist site | Cathy's | http://www.geocities.com/Heartland/Plains/3515/photos.htm |
| Up & coming | Mud Minnow | http://www.networksplus.net/maxmush/mudminnow.html |
| The author's site | Everything Fishy | http://www.everythingfishy.com |
| A Snail Control Article | | http://www.geocities.com/CapeCanaveral/4742/snail_faq.html |
| Enteric Septicemia | SRA | http://agpublications.tamu.edu/pubs/efish/477fs.pdf |
| Enteric Septicemia | University of Florida | http://edis.ifas.ufl.edu/BODY_FA029 |

## Saltwater Only:

| | | |
|---|---|---|
| Saltwater specialists | Aquasite | http://www.aquasite.com/ |
| Salt How-to, modern | Simplified Reefkeeping | http://www.simplifiedreefkeeping.com/ |
| Breeding Banggai | | http://www.breeders-registry.gen.ca.us/Articles/v4_i4_marini/marini.htm |

## Fresh and Saltwater:

| | | |
|---|---|---|
| Great hobbyist forums | Just Aquaria WebSite | http://fishgeeks.com/ |
| Best site search | Fish Information Service | http://www.actwin.com/fish/index.php |
| A favorite | The Krib | http://www.networksplus.net/maxmush/mudminnow.html |
| Very Large Site | Aquaria Central | http://aquariacentral.com |
| Technical Info | BioFilter.com | http://www.biofilter.com/ |
| Technical Info | The Shop FAMA | http://www.mag-web.com/fama/theshop.html |
| Species Identification | Fishbase | http://www.fishbase.org/search.cfm |

## Bibliography

Riehl, Dr. Rudiger, and Baensch, Hans A, *Aquarium Atlas*. Hans A Baensch, 1987
A collaborative effort: FishBase Website— www.fishbase.org  Many dedicated people, 1992–2002
Avila, Marcos A, and volunteers: Age of Aquariums website—www.aquahobby.com  Avila, 1999–2002

# INDEX